THE COMMON AGRICULTURAL POLICY
BEYOND THE MACSHARRY REFORM

CONTRIBUTIONS
TO
ECONOMIC ANALYSIS

230

Honorary Editor:
J. TINBERGEN†

Editors:
D. W. JORGENSON
J. -J. LAFFONT
T. PERSSON
H. K. VAN DIJK

ELSEVIER
Amsterdam – Lausanne – New York – Oxford – Shannon – Tokyo

THE COMMON AGRICULTURAL POLICY BEYOND THE MACSHARRY REFORM

C. FOLMER
Central Planning Bureau (CPB)
The Hague, The Netherlands

M.A. KEYZER
M.D. MERBIS
Centre for World Food Studies, SOW-VU
Amsterdam, The Netherlands

H.J.J. STOLWIJK
Central Planning Bureau (CPB)
The Hague, The Netherlands

P.J.J. VEENENDAAL
Agricultural Economics Research Institute, LEI-DLO
The Hague, The Netherlands

1995

ELSEVIER
Amsterdam – Lausanne – New York – Oxford – Shannon – Tokyo

ELSEVIER SCIENCE B.V.
Sara Burgerhartstraat 25
P.O. Box 211, 1000 AE Amsterdam, The Netherlands

Library of Congress Cataloging-in-Publication Data

The common agricultural policy beyond the MacSharry reform / C. Folmer
  ... [et al.].
       p.   cm. -- (Contributions to economic analysis ; 230)
    Includes bibliographical references and index.
    ISBN 0-444-81972-X
    1. Agriculture and state--European Union countries. 2. Produce
  trade--Government policy--European Union countries. 3. Tariff on
  farm produce--European Union countries. 4. Uruguay Round (1987-)
  I. Folmer, C. II. Series.
  HD1920.5.Z8C6223   1995
  338.1'84--dc20
                                                           95-5647
                                                              CIP

ISBN: 0 444 81972 X

 This book is printed on acid-free paper.

PRINTED IN THE NETHERLANDS

INTRODUCTION TO THE SERIES

This series consists of a number of hitherto unpublished studies, which are introduced by the editors in the belief that they represent fresh contributions to economic science.

The term "economic analysis" as used in the title of the series has been adopted because it covers both the activities of the theoretical economist and the research worker.

Although the analytical methods used by the various contributors are not the same, they are nevertheless conditioned by the common origin of their studies, namely theoretical problems encountered in practical research. Since for this reason, business cycle research and national accounting, research work on behalf of economic policy, and problems of planning are the main sources of the subjects dealt with, they necessarily determine the manner of approach adopted by the authors. Their methods tend to be "practical" in the sense of not being too far remote from application to actual economic conditions. In additon they are quantitative.

It is the hope of the editors that the publication of these studies will help to stimulate the exchange of scientific information and to reinforce international cooperation in the field of economics.

The Editors

Contents

Chapter 1

Introduction

1.1 Scope of the study

The implementation of a Common Agricultural Policy (CAP) was, certainly from an administrative point of view, an important step in the process of European unification. The integration of six national agricultural policies that initially were organised in very different ways into a common system provided a unique opportunity for gaining experience in decision making at the European level. Yet the CAP was contentious from the very beginning. Foreign countries denounced the protectionism of the scheme while farmers frequently complained that agricultural prices were too low.

To those not directly involved, the CAP was seen as a mystery wrapped in an enigma: a matter for technocrats meeting in Brussels at regular intervals to reach agreement on premia for sheep, on wine prices or on export subsidies for butter and dairy. Once in a while there were conflicts that reached the press and ended with an unfathomable settlement only to be understood by insiders who debated about presumed winners and losers.

However, since the early eighties, when the EU turned into a net exporter of an increasing range of agricultural products, more parties became effectively involved. Ministers of Finance started to complain about export subsidies and storage costs, whereas foreign countries, the US and Australia in particular, increasingly made use of the public media to attack the EU's protectionist policies. As the sector's yields improved, also the worries intensified about negative side-effects for the environment. Many expressed their doubts regarding the rationality of a policy that caused butter and grain mountains to pile up, while hunger and malnutrition persisted in other parts of the world. Finally, while nutritionists maintained their longstanding claim of margarine (from imported oilseeds) being more healthy than (EU produced) dairy products, newspapers reported about hormones and other pharmaceutical residuals detected in various types of meat.

The CAP had come under siege. To cope with the criticism, various ad hoc measures were taken to curb the surpluses. Farmers suffered from severe price reductions, but - except for milk, where production quotas had been introduced - surpluses did not diminish and budgetary costs kept on rising. This strengthened the conviction that only a radical change of policy could avoid budgetary disaster and alleviate mounting trade conflicts. This awareness was reinforced in the second half of the eighties, when it became clear that the CAP was a major stumbling block in the Uruguay Round of negotiations under the GATT. As a reaction, the CAP underwent an important reform in 1992, the MacSharry reform, named after the Commissioner for Agriculture who initiated it. This reform made it possible for the EU to reach agreement with the US in the so-called Blair House accord, which, finally, made it possible to conclude the Uruguay Round in April 1994. Thus, after introduction of the MacSharry reform and its modification in the final phase of the Uruguay Round negotiations, the CAP is now entering a new policy regime.

The MacSharry reform and the associated new regulations were again quite complicated and for that reason it took some time before finance ministries, farmers, consumer organizations and other interest groups could pronounce themselves clearly. From the beginning it was obvious, however, that parties disagreed on the implications of the reforms. The European Commission claimed that European farmers would hardly suffer any income losses in the wake of the MacSharry reform; subsequently it was claimed that the GATT agreement was perfectly compatible with the earlier reform and required no further change in the CAP. Yet farmers were not convinced, especially because the validity of the Commission's claim depends on what will happen in the future e.g. with respect to world prices and technical progress.

In this book we take a closer view at these issues and investigate likely developments under the new policy regime, both in the medium term until 2005 and in the long term until 2020. In spite of the assurances given by the EU Commission we do not take it for granted that the agreements reached so far mark the beginning of a sustained transition towards more liberal conditions. First, the budgetary costs of the direct payments, that are currently given to farmers as compensation for reduced price support, could become unsustainable politically and lead to revisions. Secondly, the United States, Japan and France, among others, have expressed the view that trade is an instrument of national policy and should be managed actively. Finally, environmental concerns increasingly call for interventions through taxes and quantitative restrictions which affect agriculture, particularly the intensive livestock sector.

In contrast to much of the recent literature on EU agriculture which tends to focus on the effects of liberalization, we will also look at its opposite: more interventionism. In short, the purpose of the present study is:

(i) To investigate the consequences of the agreed reforms of the CAP (the MacSharry reform and the GATT agreement) and to situate these on the axis free trade - interventionism.

(ii) To analyze policy alternatives along this axis.

This requires the study of the official regulations as well as the statistical evidence concerning EU agriculture, but that is not sufficient. Since many of the new regulations will only become effective in a more distant future, many of their effects can only be analyzed on the basis of projections, which in turn requires a simulation model. In this book we present the EC Agricultural Model (ECAM) and use it to perform this task. Results of the analysis were used in the formulation of the report 'Agriculture towards the 21st century', that was recently published by the European Commission (CEC (1994)).

1.2 Structure of the book

The book is structured as follows. Chapter 2 contains an overview of the history of the CAP and the impact it has had on European agriculture, from the CAP's creation in 1962 until the present day. This overview introduces the main problems which the CAP and EU agriculture were facing until recently as well as those which they will have to address in the near future. We classify the various cures to these problems which are being proposed into three categories, which we call 'perspectives'. We distinguish a free trade perspective, that seeks to eliminate all interventions, an interventionist perspective, that opts for quantity regulation combined with high internal prices and, finally, a bureaucratic perspective, that weaves a fine tissue of quantity and price regulations around EU agriculture and tries above all to keep transitions smooth.

In Chapter 3 we analyze these perspectives from a welfare-theoretical angle. We start with a discussion of the classical propositions which advocate free trade and perfect competition. To many economists outside agriculture, these propositions settle the debate on the CAP. To them, the CAP is not a fine tissue of regulations that support rural development in Europe, but a spider's web to be removed at the earliest opportunity by a thorough cleaning operation. However, even the most radical free trader must admit that the process of transition to free trade is not so simple, particularly for an agricultural sector that consists largely of farmers over 45 years of age. To the interventionist, the CAP should not be abandoned but should be changed fundamentally away from regulation through prices to regulation through quantity restrictions. Interventionists basically challenge the notion that it is possible to decentralize a welfare optimum through competitive markets, particularly in agriculture. We shall discuss the theoretical basis for this point of view, trying to find out whether the special conditions of European agriculture can justify the regulations implemented in the CAP or those proposed by interventionists. We shall come to the conclusion that, while welfare theoretical investigation can clarify many issues, it is not sufficient if one wants to compare specific reform proposals and has to be supplemented with model simulations.

This naturally leads us, in Chapter 4, to a description of ECAM, the applied general equilibrium model that has been developed for this purpose. Although applied general equilibrium modelling has become a widely used tool, the representation of the CAP calls for extensions of the basic framework, for example to account for buffer stocks and production quotas and to incorporate supply and demand for green fodders. The chapter will focus on these extensions.

We are then ready for a discussion of alternative proposals for reforming the CAP. In Chapter 5 we discuss the medium term implications (1992-2005) of the regulations already adopted: the MacSharry reform and the GATT agreement, comparing these with a no-reform scenario which assumes that the pre-MacSharry version of the CAP continues with only minor modifications.

In Chapter 6 we modify the regulations of the MacSharry reform to account for criticism, first from free traders and then from interventionists. We find that more free trade indeed creates welfare gains but that the welfare losses caused by a more interventionist approach are not unbearable. In this chapter we also study the consequences of a possible financial renationalization of the CAP, with every member state carrying the financial cost of its agricultural policy but with the principle of a common market maintained.

In Chapter 7, we study the long run consequences of the policies, extending the time horizon until the year 2020. We try to sketch a picture of what EU agriculture could look like after the shocks of the reform process, focusing on the implications of a sustained labour outflow from agriculture (largely due to demographic causes), the use of land for non-agricultural purposes (urbanization, natural parks, forestry) and technical progress (increases in yields). We assess the production potential and confront it with the expected demand on international markets. It is our contention that, in view of its natural conditions (soil fertility, fresh water), its well-developed infrastructure and food processing industry, its stagnant population and its satiated consumer demand, the EU may have a future in export-oriented commercial farming. Chapter 8 concludes.

1.3 Limitations of the study

The study develops in four 'dimensions': the history and regulations of the CAP, the statistics on EU agriculture, economic theory and scenario simulation. Of the four, scenario simulation is the most controversial mainly because outcomes may critically depend on technical assumptions, the implications of which are not always perfectly clear to the modeller himself, let alone to the reader.

We are well aware of this limitation but there is in our opinion little alternative. It is not possible to analyze future implications of practical reform proposals without a simulation model. All we can do is to avoid pitfalls. For this we proceed as follows. First, we only make use of model simulations when a problem cannot be investigated by simpler means. We use straight calculations and theoretical arguments if these are sufficient to make the point. Secondly, we keep the specification of our simulation model close to the three other dimensions, i.e. incorporating economic theory, statistics, historical evidence and institutional detail within its specification. Thirdly, we report on its validation (Annexes 4A and 4B) and finally, in many instances we also report on the sensitivity of the findings to particular assumptions.

Another limitation of the study is that it focuses on the EU-9, excluding Greece, Portugal and Spain. This is due to statistical limitations and to the fact that the three southern member states have only recently left a special regime of transition with respect to the implementation of the CAP. The value of our study is also limited by the exclusion of the former German Democratic Republic, the EFTA countries that have joined in 1995 and the Central European countries that will probably enter into closer association by the end of this century. However, we shall in several instances consider implications of reforms with respect to these countries.

1.4 Project organisation and acknowledgements

This book is the final report of the ECAM project, a joint venture of three institutes in The Netherlands: the Agricultural Economics Research Institute (Dutch acronym LEI-DLO), the Central Planning Bureau (CPB) and the Centre for World Food Studies of the Free University of Amsterdam (Dutch acronym SOW-VU). The tasks and responsibilities of the team that produced this report were as follows:

Kees Folmer (CPB): empirical elaboration of migration, investment and feed modules, preparation of data on non-agriculture and EU budget.

Michiel Keyzer (SOW-VU): project leader, formal model specification, programming and simulation, final editor.

Max Merbis (SOW-VU): empirical elaboration of supply module (crop and livestock allocation), preparation and maintenance of model data files, scenario formulation and evaluation, editing.

Herman Stolwijk (CPB): empirical elaboration of supply module (data on feed and net revenues), scenario formulation and evaluation, drafts of several chapters.

Paul Veenendaal (LEI-DLO): processing of supply utilization accounts, estimation feed module, coefficients of MacSharry scenario.

Ms. A. de Graaf has translated parts of the text and Ms. L. Jacobs-Sie has processed several tables. Over the years many others have contributed to the project, we list them in alphabetical order. Jacques Loyat made several suggestions for scenario simulations and evaluated various scenario outcomes. His participation was funded by the French Ministry of Agriculture. Jerzy Michalek from the University of Kiel was responsible for the development, data collection and econometric estimation of the consumer demand system. His three-year research was funded under a grant by the German Ministry of Agriculture. Euan Phimister contributed to the social accounting matrix of the model. He also made many useful suggestions for revision of the manuscript. His two-year participation was funded under a grant from the UK by the Milk Marketing Board. Henny Schweren, previously at SOW-VU, contributed to the social accounting matrix and the collection of feed data.

The authors gratefully acknowledge the suggestions for revision of the manuscript made by Gerrit Meester, Arie Oskam and Wouter Tims, and thank them for their patient interest in and guidance to the project over the years. Thanks for their patience and support are also due to David Colman, Jean-Marc Boussard, Henk Don, Françoise Gérard, Jaap Post, Jerrie de Hoogh, Wilhelm Henrichsmeyer, Louis Mahé, Knud Munk, Jan de Veer†, Gerrit Zalm, Aart de Zeeuw and Dick de Zeeuw.

Chapter 2[1]

The CAP: its history, operation and proposals for its reform

It is primarily through the Common Agricultural Policy that the agricultural sectors of EU member states are bound together, both economically and institutionally. Therefore, it is useful to start our investigation with a discussion on the origins, objectives and principles of the CAP (Section 2.1), and its operation (Section 2.2). Since it is not our intention to duplicate the many studies already covering these topics (e.g. Harris et al. (1983), Meester and Strijker (1985), OECD (1987), Tracy (1989) or Kjeldahl and Tracy (1994)), we will be brief. The main purposes here are to provide the basic background information, to introduce terminology that will be used in the other chapters, and to supplement the existing literature with a short update on recent developments. In Section 2.3 the evolution of the EU agricultural sector over the last two decades will be discussed on the basis of statistical evidence. It will be shown that the EU agricultural sector was in many respects fairly dynamic during the seventies and eighties. Section 2.4 contains a list of the most common criticism on the CAP. This gives us the opportunity (in Section 2.5) to describe, in more detail than in Chapter 1, the various perspectives on reform (bureaucratic, free trade, interventionist). Section 2.6 summarizes the implications of the discussion for model specification.

2.1 The CAP: origins, objectives and principles

2.1.1 Origins

During the 1950s, when the establishment of a common European market was being considered, the agricultural sector within all prospective member states was characterized by strong government intervention. Although the particular

---

[1] This chapter has benefited from comments by Cees van Bruchem.

ways in which this intervention took place differed from country to country (see Louwes (1970) or Tracy (1989)), they did have one property in common: each country tried to support farm incomes by keeping the internal prices of primary farm products above the price level on the world market. Their intervention was mainly driven by concerns with the backward position of the sector and the inelastic demand for its products. It was generally believed that without support average producer prices and farm incomes would be too low, while exposure to the vagaries of the world markets would cause them to fluctuate heavily. In the aftermath of World War II this was found unacceptable. By providing a minimum price guarantee, it was hoped that the income in the sector would improve and that farmers would be protected against excessive fluctuations of world prices. Besides this distributional motive, there was also a food security motive. It was felt that, without decent and stable incomes for the farmers, the sector would be unable to survive and long term national food supplies would be deficient.

Minimum prices well above and independent of the average world market levels can only be guaranteed if wedges are driven between price levels on the national markets and the world market. Prior to the CAP the instruments used to create these wedges varied by country. For example, in West Germany,[2] at the time a large net importer of agricultural products, policy instruments mainly consisted of import quota restraints and levies. Prices were stabilized through public procurement on the internal market. In France and The Netherlands, both net exporters of agricultural products, a more comprehensive set of policy instruments was used. The grain market in France was fully regulated. The Netherlands (and Luxembourg) paid guaranteed prices for dairy and grain (deficiency payments). In order to dispose of its surpluses, France and The Netherlands provided subsidies on exports. Production quota regulations and minimum prices lay at the heart of agricultural policy in Belgium and Italy, although only a relatively small part of total production had guaranteed prices in these countries.

---

[2] Unless specified otherwise all data will refer to the Federal Republic of Germany prior to German unification. We shall also refer to the Federal Republic as West Germany, and occasionally as Germany for short, thus disregarding the fact that West Berlin was not part of West Germany.

Table 2.1 gives an impression of the extent to which agricultural production was supported on the eve of the establishment of the European Community and the CAP. Although governments also intervened in other economic sectors exposed to international competition, in agriculture protection was definitely important.

Table 2.1   Total agricultural production with guaranteed prices, 1957, percentage

Belgium	39
France	72
Italy	27
Luxembourg	75
The Netherlands	79
Germany, Fed. Rep.	75

Source: Louwes (1970, p. 94).

The six prospective member countries were convinced that the integration process of their national economies could only succeed if the special position of the agricultural sector was taken into account. It was thought that a gradual harmonization of existing barriers to external trade, as envisaged for all products under the regime of the customs union, would not be sufficient to integrate the six agricultural economies: in order to reconcile the disparate national agricultural interests and differences in market organization schemes, a *Common Agricultural Policy* was needed.

2.1.2   Objectives of the CAP

In the Treaty of Rome, which laid the foundation of the EU and came into force on 1 January 1958, the 'special position' of agriculture was recognized in a separate section (Articles 38-47). The need for a common agricultural policy is explicitly stated in Article 38. Article 39 describes the objectives of such a common agricultural policy as follows:

-        to increase agricultural productivity by promoting technical progress and by ensuring the rational development of agricultural production and the optimal utilization of the factors of production, in particular labour;

- thus to ensure a fair standard of living for the agricultural community, in particular by increasing the individual earnings of persons engaged in agriculture;
- to stabilize markets;
- to assure the stability of supplies;
- to ensure that supplies reach consumers at reasonable prices.

It is remarkable that no reference is made to relations with third countries. Although this relation is referred to in Article 110, it is only in very general terms: 'the establishment of a customs union between member states should contribute to the harmonious development of world trade, the progressive abolition of restrictions on international trade and the lowering of customs barriers'.

The general nature of these objectives leaves ample room for interpretation. The same is true of Articles 43 and 46, which describe the instruments to be used in achieving the objectives. Instead of a set of clear guidelines, the articles list a wide variety of agricultural policy instruments. Apprehension about whether national parliaments would approve the Treaty was probably the main reason for the vague and general nature of the wording.

The steps from the very general formulations in the Treaty of Rome to detailed operational proposals were taken in the late fifties and early sixties. In July 1958 the signatories of the Treaty met at a conference in Stresa, Italy. During this conference the objectives, problems, principles and instruments of a common agricultural policy were further discussed. The final resolution of the conference stated that 'the structures of European agriculture were to be reformed to become more competitive, without any threat to family farms; as production costs were higher in the Community than in the other main producing countries, the common prices must provide adequate earnings and must be established at levels above those of world prices, without this becoming an incentive to over-production; the common agricultural policy could not be autarkic, but must protect the internal market against distortion by outside competition' (CEC (1958)).

It was the task of the Commission to work out the ideas of the Stresa Conference into concrete policy proposals. The primary challenge was to find a balance between the interests of net exporting countries such as France and The Netherlands, which wanted to enlarge their markets, and net importing countries, such as West Germany, which did not want to give up their heavily protected agricultural sector. In June 1960 detailed operational proposals were submitted by the Commission. And in December 1960 the Council of Ministers decided on the foundations of a 'Green Europe'.

2.1.3   Principles of the CAP

The CAP is based on three principles: market unity, Community preference and common financial responsibility.

Market unity means that products can freely circulate in all member states. Trade among member states may not be hindered by customs duties or other protective measures. Eliminating protectionism among member states would, under perfectly competitive conditions and if one disregards transportation margins, result in a single farm-gate price for the same product throughout the Community. Section 2.2.4 will explain why even today market unity has not been achieved completely.

Community preference means that on the internal market, products from member states are given priority over products from non-member countries. In practical terms this is achieved by levying a variable tariff on imports from non-member countries that is sufficiently high to become prohibitive.

Common financial responsibility has two implications. First, expenses incurred as a result of the CAP are financed by the Community. Secondly, all tax revenue generated by the CAP is regarded as revenue of the Community. The common financial responsibility found its expression in the foundation of the European Agriculture Guidance and Guarantee Fund, known by its French acronym, FEOGA. The FEOGA is not a fund in the technical sense, as it cannot build up any reserves of its own. It should rather be viewed as the Commission's budget for agriculture.

2.2 Instruments of the CAP: market organization schemes and structural measures

There are two types of policy instruments by which the EU is trying to achieve its objectives. These are, first, measures directed at the organization of markets for various products, and secondly, the so-called structural measures. The first category is by far the most important. In the early nineties market organization schemes covered more than ninety per cent of the value of agricultural output. The schemes are not the same for all products and regulations have over the years often been subject to change. Significant changes occurred in 1984, when the quota system was introduced in the dairy sector, and in 1993, when the MacSharry reform first came into effect.[3] Therefore, in our discussion of the market organization schemes we distinguish three periods: 1968-84, 1985-92 and 1993-present.

2.2.1   Market organization schemes between 1968 and 1984

Although the Council of Ministers had agreed on the principles of the CAP in 1960, it was not until 1968 that the principle of market unity had been implemented for practically all agricultural products.[4] At that time four types of support mechanisms were in place:[5]

(i)   Minimum producer prices were guaranteed for cereals, sugar, milk, beef, pork, a number of types of fruit and vegetables and, later, table wine, through a combination of sales at floor prices to a buffer stock agency (this is 'intervention' in the CAP sense) and measures taken at the border.

---

[3] The completion of the Uruguay Round of multilateral trade negotiations conducted under the auspices of the General Agreement on Tariffs and Trade (GATT) marks a new period for EU agriculture.

[4] Wine and tobacco were main exceptions. Market support arrangements for table wine and tobacco were agreed to in 1970.

[5] Here we only describe the main principles. A detailed description of the market organization schemes can be found in Harris et al. (1983) and OECD (1987).

Through a system of variable levies,[6] imports from third countries were only allowed to enter the Community at prices well above these minimum prices. Surpluses could either be exported with a variable subsidy to bridge the gap between the internal price and world market price, or be submitted to the intervention office at the minimum price. It must be stressed that products whose markets were arranged in this manner, did not all receive the same degree of support. Support for cereals, milk, beef and table wine was much stronger than for sugar, pork, fruit and vegetables. For example, the intervention system for grains functioned throughout the year and applied to unlimited quantities. Import levies and export subsidies kept the EU grain prices well above the world market level. For sugar, however, the full price guarantee only applied to certain basic quotas. The intervention system for pork was only effective in periods of excess supply and the levies and export subsidies mainly served to compensate for the negative consequences on feeding costs of the high internal grain price.

(ii) For a second group of products, including poultry, eggs, various types of fruit and vegetables, flowers and wines (other than table wines), it was agreed not to intervene on the internal markets, and to limit support to external protection via border measures (tariffs and levies).

(iii) For durum wheat, olive oil, cotton, tobacco, oilseeds and sheep it was decided to effectuate the support primarily through producer subsidies (deficiency payments). This enabled the food industry (e.g. bread from durum wheat, margarine from oilseeds) and the producers of animal feeds (e.g. protein feeds from oilseeds) to benefit from lower input costs. For durum wheat and olive oil this payment was in addition to minimum price guarantees. For cotton, tobacco and oilseeds, the producer subsidies were meant to 'compensate' for the lack of border protection.

(iv) Finally, a flat-rate producer subsidy based on area harvested or on production quantity was introduced for some products, including durum wheat, cottonseed, flaxseed, hops and silkworms.

---

[6] Table wine imports were subject to customs duties.

2.2.2   Market organization schemes during the 1984-93 period

The 1968-84 period witnessed a growth in agricultural production that exceeded the growth in demand. This led to significant reductions in net imports, which often turned into exports, and, consequently, also to important increases in budgetary outlays. In response to these developments, efforts were made to adjust the policies. In the seventies and early eighties steps were taken to narrow the gap between Community prices and world market prices and to let producers bear a larger share of the costs. This resulted in three adjustments: the price policy became 'restrictive'; co-responsibility levies were introduced, which effectively functioned as excise duties on production; and 'guarantee thresholds', which charged producers for part of the costs when production exceeded a predesignated amount. However, these adjustments had only limited effects.

Hence, the need was felt to introduce new policy instruments and the system of milk quotas introduced in 1984 falls within this category. Nonetheless, the FEOGA expenditures continued to rise, systematically exceeding budgetary guidelines. As a result, there was growing resistance to all proposals involving an increased Community budget, because the agricultural market support could always run away with it. In 1988 this culminated in an agreement on a more watertight 'financial guideline'. Between 1988 and 1992 real FEOGA guarantee expenditures were not allowed to rise by more than 74 per cent of the annual growth rate of the Community gross national product. This financial guideline was backed up by so-called 'stabilizers' for all major commodities: any increase in production above a prespecified threshhold would result in a price decrease, so that, on balance, production increases would not entail additional FEOGA expenditures. Another key element of the stabilizer package was the 'set-aside scheme' for land. Producers wanting to participate had to withdraw at least twenty per cent of their arable land for at least five years. They would then be compensated by payment of a fixed amount per hectare.[7] The need for such new instruments grew so strong in the late eighties because the rate of inflation had dropped dramatically, especially in Germany. Under such conditions it is

---

[7] For a more detailed description of the CAP adjustments during this period, see: CEC, *Green Europe*, various issues, or Tracy (1989).

only possible to curb production growth either through nominal price cuts, which tend to evoke strong political resistance, or through rationing schemes.

2.2.3   Market organization schemes and the MacSharry reform

Whatever the effects of the milk quotas, set-aside scheme and stabilizers, they were already considered insufficient after a few years. As a result the EU Commission, through its commissioner for agriculture, Mr Ray MacSharry, launched in 1991 a plan aimed at fundamental reform of the CAP. After some minor adjustments, the plan was accepted in 1992 (CEC (1991a-b)). It is to be implemented during the 1993-95 period.[8]

In the *MacSharry reform*, existing market regulations for cereals, oilseeds, tobacco, milk, beef and lamb are modified to a significant degree. There is no doubt that the reform is most radical with regard to cereals. Minimum prices are due to decrease by some thirty per cent.[9] In order to compensate cereal-growers for income losses, co-responsibility levies are abolished and replaced by subsidies in fixed amounts per hectare. The reform distinguishes between small-scale and large-scale farmers.[10] Large-scale farmers are only eligible to hectare compensations if they set aside at least fifteen per cent of their so-called *basic area*, which is defined as the average acreage allocated to cereals, oilseeds, fodder maize and protein crops during the 1989-91 period. This set-aside condition also applies to growers of oilseeds, fodder maize and protein crops. For tobacco, the reform introduces production quotas for individual producers.

The reform measures are less drastic for animal products. The intervention prices for butter and dairy products are reduced by 9 and 7.5 per cent, respectively; intervention prices for beef are lowered by fifteen per cent. From 1996 onwards farmers may apply for premiums for bulls and suckler cows.[11]

---

[8] See CEC, *Green Europe*, 1993/1, for a detailed description of the market organization schemes following the MacSharry reform.

[9] The intervention price for cereals is brought to 100 green ecu per metric ton in 1996.

[10] Small scale farmers are defined as those who produce less than 92 metric tons of grain equivalents.

[11] The premia are subject to limitations of two kinds: there is a limit of 90 heads per holding and the livestock density should remain below two livestock units per hectare of fodder area. Farmers with 15 livestock units or less are exempt from the density requirement. The scheme also defines regional reference herd sizes, which, if exceeded, reduce the number of eligible animals per producer.

Moreover, if the livestock density does not exceed 1.4 livestock units per hectare, the farmer receives an additional extensification premium. The reform also introduces a measure aimed at curbing the rapid increase in spending on sheep by putting a ceiling on the maximum amount of subsidy individual producers are able to receive.

There are 'accompanying measures' to stimulate the adjustment of the agricultural structure. These aim at more extensive modes of production, forestry, conservation of natural resources and using land for public leisure (the FEOGA budget bears one half of the total cost). Moreover, the reform provides for early retirement schemes which include annual payments and lump sum payments for farmers and farm workers of over 55 years of age.

It should be stressed that because the system of variable levies at the Community border remains unchanged, prohibitive import tariffs (the Community preference) can be maintained. This makes it possible to maintain a wedge between internal and world market prices. Under the agreement reached in the Uruguay Round of the General Agreement on Tariffs and Trade (GATT), the fixed internal price is replaced by tariffs that over time are to be reduced, so that eventually the link between intra-EU and world market prices will be restored. This issue will be taken up in Chapter 5.

2.2.4   Monetary Compensatory Amounts

Market unity, one of the three principles on which the CAP was founded, can be achieved by abolishing customs duties and other protective measures which impede the free circulation of goods within the Community. In the absence of such border measures, differences in farm-gate prices within the Community should, under perfectly competitive conditions, be limited to the differences in trade and transport costs from or to market places. This theoretical 'ideal' has rarely been achieved. For many products the trade flow among member countries has, up to 1993, been subject to border taxes or subsidies, the so-called *monetary compensatory amounts* (MCAs). Price differences within the Community have consequently been much larger than can reasonably be explained by differences in trade and transport costs. Figure 2.1 illustrates this point; it compares prices of soft wheat in West Germany with those in France.

Depending on the year, i.e. on the extent of the MCAs, there are price differences of 16 to nearly 30 per cent. Such large differences have a distorting effect on the allocation of production factors within the Community.

Figure 2.1 Farm-gate prices of soft wheat

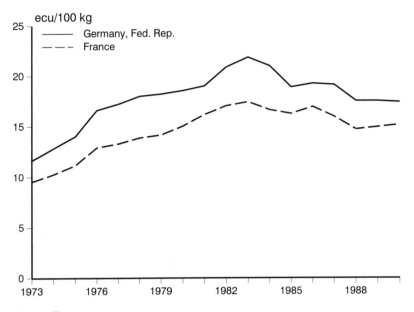

Source: Eurostat.

To explain why it took so long to accomplish market unity in agriculture, one must review the historical process of integrating the markets. At the beginning of the CAP it was decided to use an artificial currency, the so-called Unit of Account (UA) to express agricultural support prices, rather than using one of the EU's national currencies. The value of one UA was put on a par with the gold parity of one US dollar. The step from UA prices to national currency prices, i.e. to prices at which the actual transactions took place, was made by multiplying the UA price by an exchange rate with respect to the UA. Hence, for commodity k and country c one has:

$$p_{kc} = \pi_c \cdot p_k \qquad\qquad\qquad\qquad (2.1)$$

where

p_k = support price of commodity k in UA,

p_{kc} = support price of commodity k in currency of country c.

π_c = the exchange rate UA vs. the currency of country c (e.g. franc per UA).

As long as the exchange rates remain constant, such a procedure is consistent with the principle of 'equal prices throughout the Community'. However, in 1969, i.e. less than two years after the introduction of common prices, the exchange rates for the French franc and the Deutschmark began fluctuating. In August 1969 the French franc was devalued; and in October 1969 this was followed by a revaluation of the Deutschmark. Support prices p_k were obviously left unchanged, since the UA was tied to the US dollar, but the exchange rates π_c were changed.

In terms of equation (2.1), a devaluation (or revaluation) will result in a proportional change of the support prices p_{kc} expressed in the national currency of the devaluating (revaluating) country. Thus, the devaluation of the French franc by 12.5 per cent with respect to the UA implied that agricultural support prices expressed in French francs would increase by the same percentage. On the other hand, the revaluation of the Deutschmark by 8.5 per cent would mean that support prices expressed in the Deutschmark would decrease by 9.3 per cent. However, both the French and German government found it difficult to accept such a change in domestic agricultural prices. In the aftermath of the 1968 disturbances, the French government was afraid of further social unrest should food prices be raised, and the German government did not want to confront its farmers with a reduction in support prices in local currency. Therefore, both France and West Germany insisted on a transition period before realigning with the 'real' level of CAP support. As a result special arrangements were agreed upon. France was allowed a two-year period before returning fully to the CAP pricing system. A so-called 'green conversion' (exchange) rate was introduced to convert UA prices to French franc prices. For Germany the arrangements were even more complicated. In addition to a green conversion rate, the German government was also allowed to compensate its farmers in other ways (see Harris et al. (1983)).

Figure 2.2 Intervention price-level in autumn 1969

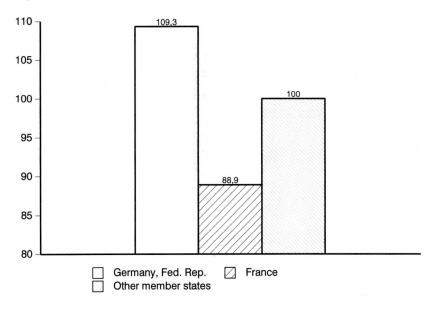

Source: Harris et al. (1983).

When exchange-rate changes are not followed by proportional changes in internal prices, the principle of 'equal prices throughout the Community' is in fact abandoned and border measures have to be introduced in order to maintain price wedges between countries. Figure 2.2 shows the situation in the autumn of 1969. Clearly, if no additional measures would have been taken, the effective internal price level within the Community would have become equal to the German level, since the price level there was higher than in the other member states. In order to maintain the original price levels in Belgium-Luxembourg, The Netherlands and Italy, as well as the 'exchange rate-adjusted' new price level in France, customs duties were imposed in trade among member states. German exports to other member countries became subject to export subsidies and German imports were taxed. The opposite occurred in France, where exports were taxed and imports were subsidized.

These border taxes and subsidies in intra-EU trade are known as MCAs. Variable levies and export refunds on trade at the external border had to be adjusted accordingly. One speaks of a positive MCA when the country has revalued, so that there is a subsidy on exports and a tax on the imports. When the country has devalued the MCA is said to be negative.

At the time of their introduction, green conversion rates and MCAs were seen as short term, temporary phenomena. In retrospect, this view was too optimistic. The monetary uncertainties in the 1970s led to sharp exchange-rate fluctuations. As a result the MCA system had to be amended and refined many times. In 1973 the system underwent a major modification when the definition of the Unit of Account was changed. Instead of being linked to the US dollar, the UA became linked to the so-called 'joint float', a group of mainly EU currencies with mutual exchange rates only allowed to fluctuate within narrow margins. This change from the US dollar to 'joint float' meant that a value change of the US dollar no longer affected the level of the UAs directly. In 1979 the 'joint float' was replaced by the European Monetary System (EMS) and the UA by the European Currency Unit (ecu). The ecu is a so-called 'basket unit' consisting of specified amounts of the member states' currencies. The value of the ecu is equal to the weighted value of the currencies in the basket.

Transition to the ecu meant that, since 1979, support prices have been expressed in ecu. Prices in national currencies are obtained after multiplication with the relevant *green conversion rates*. MCAs were, in principle, equal to the differences in intervention prices between member states. When intervention was not an important support mechanism for a product, MCAs were only applied if the cost of production was strongly 'related' to a product for which intervention was important. For example, pork was included in the MCA system because of its close price links with the price of cereals (feed).

From the outset it was agreed to reduce MCAs gradually. The ultimate aim was complete abolition, although there was no definite regulation about the rate at which reductions would take place. In terms of equation (2.1), the exchange rate π_c, had become 'green' and, hence, a policy variable without any direct link to the market rate. Consequently, the levels of the green rates became part of CAP negotiations between member states.

In 1984 the decision was reached to move to a system of negative MCAs only ('switch-over system'), so that realignments would only give rise to price increases. This was done by linking the green conversion rates to the strongest currency, i.e. the Deutschmark. Hence, the national intervention price for commodity k in country c became:

$$ p_{kc} = \pi_c/\pi_0 \cdot f \cdot p_k \tag{2.2} $$

where p_k was now the support price in ecu and $f = \overline{\pi_0}$ the central rate, initially set equal to the German rate (in Deutschmark per ecu). The central rate was only adjusted after major realignments of currencies. The ratio π_c/π_0, the green exchange rate in national currency per Deutschmark was to be adjusted at regular intervals, so as to move it towards the market rate. However, due to exchange rate fluctuations and for political reasons this adjustment has been slow.

In 1987 an agreement was reached to complete the market unification by 1992, implying the complete abolition of MCAs. Due to developments in the monetary domain during the second half of 1992, when Italy and the United Kingdom left the European Monetary System in 1992 it was decided to keep the central rate frozen (the variable f in (2.2)) and to let the green rate follow the market rate 'closely' (i.e. with a few days or weeks delay). Internal prices would, therefore, become almost, but not completely, equal between member states. Whereas the elimination of borders inside the Community makes it impossible to have MCAs effectuated through border taxes and subsidies, the smoothing procedure on the exchange rate can make it profitable for a country with a weak currency to engage in arbitrage by selling to the intervention stock in a country with a strong currency, and such activities have indeed been observed.

2.2.5   Structural measures

The market organization schemes constitute the heart of the CAP, both from a budgetary and an economic point of view. Nonetheless, the CAP consists of more. In order to improve economic conditions in agriculture more fundamentally, the market organization schemes were supplemented by a so-called 'structural policy'.[12] In practical terms it is not always easy to make a distinction between a structural and a non-structural measure, but administratively everything is clear: structural measures are those that are recognized as such, i.e. those that are (partly) financed by the guidance section of the FEOGA. From an economic perspective, the distinctive characteristic of a structural measure is that it impacts primarily on the factors of production, such as land or labour.

Until the early seventies the structural policy of the Community consisted mainly of coordinating national structural policies. A major initial step towards a 'separate' structural policy was made in 1972 when the Council of Ministers adopted three basic directives on agricultural reform. The prime objective of these directives was to create modern farms capable of providing a fair income and satisfactory working conditions for those persons involved in agriculture. To this end selective aids were granted for the modernization and cessation of farms, and for vocational training of farmers.

However, these structural measures did not work out as hoped or expected. Modernization schemes seemed beyond the reach of the main body of European farms. In practice only those farms which were already modern and productive benefited from the measures. Most of these farms are located in the northern part of the Community, where physical and infrastructural conditions for farming are generally more favourable than in the southern part. This is why the structural policy was reformulated in 1975 and a special support scheme was instituted for less-favoured agricultural areas. These included mountainous areas needing to be farmed in order to conserve the countryside or meet leisure requirements, as well as other areas with natural physical handicaps to farming. Support measures aimed at the encouragement of farming and improvement of farmers' incomes in less-favoured areas consisted of annual subsidies for hill

---

[12] For a detailed description of the structural measures, see CEC, *Green Europe*, various issues.

cattle and sheep, a modernization programme, and support to farms not involved in a modernization programme. Within the scheme, the member states provided the annual subsidy, while the FEOGA reimbursed a part of the costs.

A further step was taken in 1977 through the introduction of the so-called 'Mediterranean Package'. This programme was primarily directed at regions in Italy and southern France with typically Mediterranean agriculture. The measures included special investment programmes for irrigation, forestry and rural infrastructure, as well as a programme for the development of rural information services. In subsequent years the regional approach was developed further. In 1979 the concept of 'integrated development programmes' was put forward. Its aim was to integrate agricultural development measures with the development of other activities important to the rural economy, e.g. food processing, and craft and leisure activities. In view of the growing environmental awareness and the over-production in many agricultural sectors, the mid-eighties saw a further shift in emphasis with regard to structural policy. Measures became more directed at improving the quality of production, preserving the environment and converting production from surplus products to products in which the EU was not self-sufficient.

In 1988, coinciding with the introduction of the stabilization measures, a new set of structural measures was also introduced. New elements included a land set-aside programme (see Section 2.2.2), and an income support programme aimed at encouraging farmers aged 55 or over to abandon farming. This early-retirement scheme is both extended and refined under the structural measures of the MacSharry reform (see Section 2.2.3), which also includes a reafforestation programme and measures that promote an environmentally friendly way of farming.

2.3 The dynamics of the agricultural sector of the EU during the 1973-90 period

Through the system of variable levies at the external border, which applied in the pre-MacSharry period to the bulk of the agricultural products, internal market prices could be kept at predesignated levels for both farmers and consumers. Potential price effects resulting from fluctuations in internal demand and supply could be passed on to the world market, while price fluctuations on the world market could be stopped at the EU border. For the small minority of products to which the system of deficiency payments applied, the price fluctuations on the world market were transmitted to the consumers, the food industry (oils and fats) and the producers of animal feeds (protein feeds from oilseeds). However, internal producer prices could be kept within a predesignated range, through a countercyclical adjustment of the deficiency payments.

This section describes how the EU agricultural sector has evolved under these policies. Figures on production, input, labour productivity, income, trade, etc. are presented and briefly commented on. With some exceptions, data are presented for three benchmark years: for 1973, when Denmark, Ireland and the United Kingdom became members of the Community; for 1982, the year for which ECAM's base year social accounting matrix has been constructed; and for 1990, the most recent year for which, at the time of writing, sufficient data were available. Because ECAM excludes Greece, Portugal and Spain, and because these countries had not yet fully joined the CAP by 1990, (most) figures refer to the EU-9 only.

2.3.1   Production and value added

Table 2.2 shows growth figures for the volume of total agricultural production, intermediate demand and gross value added during the 1973-1990 period. A comparison is made with overall GNP growth. The figures have been broken down into the subperiods 1973-1982 and 1982-1990.

The figures in the table are, of course, affected by the particular choice of years and method of deflation. Nonetheless, it is possible to glean certain important trends from them. It is striking that growth in volume of agricultural production has been rather modest since 1973. Average gross production increased by 1.5 per cent per year only during the 1973-90 period. Moreover, as will be shown below, production growth on the whole certainly did not concentrate on products heavily supported by the CAP. The figures suggest that the EU's agricultural surplus problems are not so much related to rapid

Table 2.2   Total production, intermediate demand and gross value added of agriculture and
GNP, EU-9, annual growth rate

	Agriculture			GNP
	Production	Intermediate demand	Gross value added	
1973-90	1.5	1.3	1.7	2.3
1973-82	2.1	1.6	2.5	1.8
1982-90	0.8	0.9	0.7	2.8

Sources: CEC, *The Agricultural Situation of the Community*, various issues; CPB (1993).
Notes:
(a) Growth figures for the volume of total agricultural production and intermediate demand in
period t relative to period t-1 have been calculated using $(\Sigma p_t\ q_t)/(\Sigma p_{t-1}\ q_t)$, where p and q
refer to prices and quantities, respectively.
(b) In calculating the growth figures for gross value added, the growth in volume of total
production is defined as the weighted sum of the growth in volume of intermediate demand
and gross value added. Value shares were used as weights.

production growth, as to sluggish internal demand. A second remarkable point
is that in the course of time, growth in agricultural production has decreased
rather drastically. Between 1973 and 1982 growth in total production was more
than 2.5 times as much as during the subsequent eight-year period. Therefore,
EU measures aimed at curbing production growth must have had some effect,
to say the least.

The aggregate figures conceal fairly large differences in developments
among individual member countries. To illustrate this, growth figures for volume
of gross value added have been broken down on a country-by-country basis in
Figure 2.3. Average yearly growth in volume during the 1973-90 period varied
from less than one per cent in Belgium-Luxembourg to more than three per cent
in The Netherlands. It is remarkable that, except for The Netherlands, growth
rates for the six 'old' member countries are all below the EU-9 average, whereas
the 'newcomers', Ireland and the United Kingdom experienced above average
growth. This does not mean that these countries have benefited more from the
CAP. For example, a breakdown of growth figures for Dutch agriculture reveals
that the products for which CAP-protection was almost non-existent (e.g.
horticultural products) are responsible for the greater part of expansion in the
agricultural sector (see Stolwijk (1992)).

Figure 2.3 Volume of gross agricultural value added, 1973=100

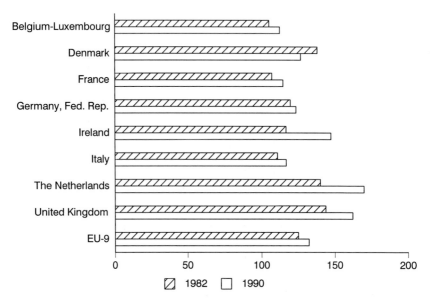

Source: CEC, *The Agricultural Situation in the Community.*

2.3.2   Output of primary crops and livestock products

Table 2.3[13] gives an impression of the diversity within the agricultural sector and the economic significance of individual products in the EU-9. In value terms the most important single product is milk. Cattle and pigs are second and third, respectively. The category 'other vegetable crops' contains a wide range of products, including cut flowers and ornamental plants. In all years the value of livestock products exceeded the value of crop products but since demand for intermediate products is greater in the livestock sector than in the crop sector, this does not necessarily mean that the livestock sector is more important in terms of value added. In the eighties the opposite was true. According to our calculations for 1982, the value added was slightly higher in the crop sector than in the livestock sector (see Folmer et al. (1988)). Because the crop sector grew

---

[13] The computations based upon FAO's Agrostat Supply Utilization Accounts are documented in Merbis (1995a).

faster than the livestock sector in subsequent years, this is still the case at present.

The last two columns of the table show widely diverging growth figures for individual products (or product groups). Very high figures can be noted for oilseeds. The upsurge in oilseed production can largely be attributed to the CAP. In order to alleviate its cereal surplus, the EU encouraged farmers to switch over to oilseeds during the eighties. This was done by raising the price of oilseeds, relative to the price of cereals. For example, the basic intervention price for soft wheat rose by 37 per cent during the 1973-90 period while, in the same period, the basic intervention price for rape seed rose by 66 per cent.[14] This substitution policy was successful and led to a reduction in the cereals acreage, because oilseeds and cereals can be grown on the same soil in many regions. The growth in cereals production that subsequently took place nonetheless, is entirely attributable to increases in per hectare yields.

Another point to be noted is the slow down in production growth of the animal sector. Except for sheep, growth rates for all animal products decreased during the second subperiod, compared with the first. The quota regulations for milk caused the relative stagnation for milk and beef. In the pig, poultry and egg sectors, it was a matter of market satiation more than anything else. Since EU farmers could not really compete on the world market and the prices of these products were supported to a limited extent only, stagnating internal demand resulted in price decreases and in lower growth rates.

2.3.3   Inputs

Production growth during the 1973-90 period was attributable not so much to increases in the usage of traditional farm inputs such as land and labour, as to technical progress and increases in inputs such as fertilizer and feed.

Table 2.4 summarizes certain relevant data on land input. Due to problems of measurement and other statistical imperfections, the figures in the table are rough approximations only. Nonetheless, the trend is quite clear: the amount of agricultural land in the EU-9 decreased during the last decennia. This decline

---

[14] Source: CEC, *The Agricultural Situation in the Community*, various issues.

Table 2.3   Total production value and growth in production quantity, EU-9

	Share in produc-tion value 1990	Production, annual growth rate	
		1973-82	1982-90
Crop production	48.9		
Wheat	6.9	3.6	3.2
Coarse grains	4.3	0.8	-1.6
Rice	0.3	-0.6	3.9
Sugar beet	2.5	3.7	0.4
Oilseeds	2.4	11.0	14.4
Potatoes	2.0	-1.9	-0.2
Vegetables	8.2	1.3	2.3
Temperate fruit	4.5	0.5	-2.4
Nontemperate fruit	1.3	-0.6	2.5
Olives	0.3	-2.6	-8.8
Grapes	6.6	-0.3	-4.2
Industrial crops	0.5	2.6	2.8
Other vegetable products	9.1	n.a.	n.a.
Livestock production	51.1		
Milk	18.5	1.2	-0.7
Eggs	2.5	1.2	-0.8
Cattle	13.6	1.0	0.6
Sheep and goats	1.3	2.6	3.0
Pigs	10.6	2.2	1.7
Poultry	4.6	3.5	1.2
Total	100.0		
Total production value	164,022 mln ecu		

Sources: CEC, *The Agricultural Situation in the Community*, various issues, and own computations using FAO's Agrostat Supply Utilization Accounts.

was caused by losses due to urbanization and land uses for other non-agricultural purposes which was not offset by an expansion of the land base due to reclamation (mainly in The Netherlands).

In addition to the aggregate trend, the table shows a shift in land use within agriculture. The areas of grassland and land with permanent crops decreased, whereas the area of arable land hardly changed at all, as losses were compensated for by converting grassland into land planted with fodder maize. As shown earlier, the shrinking land base did not result in lower output. Even the production of such typically land-tied crops, like wheat, oilseeds or sugar beet increased (see Table 2.3). Technological progress thus ensured that the

Table 2.4   Agricultural land use, EU-9

Land use category	Land use, mln ha	Annual growth rate 1973-90
Arable land	45.8	-0.0
Permanent crops	4.8	-0.5
Rangeland	39.4	-0.7
Total agricultural area	90.0	-0.3

Source: Calculated from CEC, *The Agricultural Situation in the Community*, various issues and FAO, *Production Yearbook*, various issues.

land's productive capacity could be increasingly exploited. As a result, yields per hectare increased steadily. Average yields for wheat, coarse grains, oilseeds and sugar beet increased by 2.5, 1.6, 1.4 and 1.2 per cent per year, respectively. These four crops covered more than 65 per cent of the total arable land area of the EU-9 in 1990.

A variety of factors contributes to the abstract phenomenon commonly referred to as 'technological progress', including improved farming methods, the availability of more productive seeds, an increase in fertilizer consumption, improvements in water control, etc. With the exception of fertilizer, it is very difficult to compile a direct quantitative measure for most of these factors. The literature on the subject therefore devotes much attention to indirect measures, that involve shifts in the coefficients of some production function. Here we limit attention to fertilizer use.

Table 2.5   Fertilizer use, EU-9

Fertilizer	Use in 1990, kg/ha arable land	Annual growth rate 1973-90
Nitrogen (N)	173	2.8
Phosphate (P_2O_5)	77	-1.4
Potash (K_2O)	92	0.2
Total	344	1.0

Source: Computations based on FAO, *Fertilizer Yearbook*.
Note: It is assumed that all fertilizer applications occurred on arable land.

Table 2.5 shows the pattern of fertilizer consumption over time within the EU-9. It appears that fertilizer use per hectare of arable land has increased since 1973, albeit by a mere 1 per cent per year. The figures seems to corroborate the agronomic 'law' which states that an improvement of 'other conditions' will also raise the efficiency of fertilizer use (see e.g. De Wit (1992)).

Table 2.6 Livestock numbers, EU-9

	Number of heads in 1990 (mln)	Annual growth rate	
		1973-82	1982-90
Dairy cows	20.8	-0.1	-2.3
Non-dairy cattle	49.6	0.3	-0.3
Sheep and goats	64.8	-0.2	2.9
Pigs	81.5	1.2	0.8
Laying hens	257.9	-0.8	-0.9
Poultry	607.8	1.6	1.5

Source: Computed from FAO's Agrostat Supply Utilization Accounts.

In the livestock sector it is the number of animals, rather than the land area, that provides a natural starting point for a discussion on input use. Table 2.6 shows the average annual growth rates of primary animal types within the Community. Since 1973 the number of dairy cattle and laying hens has decreased, the number of non-dairy cattle has stabilized, and the number of sheep and goats, pigs and poultry has increased. These diverging patterns are partly the result of the CAP. The quota regulation in the dairy sector, which was introduced in 1984, led to a decrease in the number of dairy cattle, whereas the introduction of the ewe premium stimulated growth in the sheep sector.

From Tables 2.3 and 2.6 it follows that production per animal has increased in the EU-9. Depending on the particular type, annual production growth per animal varied from 0.8 per cent to 1.5 per cent during the 1973-90 period. Of course, the quality of data and the high level of aggregation mean that these percentages only give rough indications. Nonetheless, the trend is unmistakable: over the course of time production per animal has increased systematically. As in the crop sector, here too technical progress was the driving force. The ways in which this has become evident include the steady improvement in feed conversion rates and an increase in feed use per animal (for further details, see Merbis et al. (1994) and Folmer et al. (1990)).

Table 2.7 Aggregate feed intake, EU-9, metabolisable energy in 10^{15} Joules

	1973	1982	1990	Annual growth rate 1973-90
A. Total marketable feed of which:	1366	1560	1551	0.7
cereals	829	776	713	-0.9
cereal substitutes	368	539	608	3.0
other feed intakes	169	245	230	1.8
B. Total nonmarketable feed (mainly grass)	1968	1956	2012	0.1
C. Total feed	3334	3516	3563	0.4

Source: Merbis et al. (1994) for 1973 and 1982 and model outcomes for 1990.

Table 2.7 summarizes data on aggregate feed intake. In terms of energy, annual feed intake rose by an average of about 0.4 per cent during the 1973-90 period. The table shows two interesting developments. First, the importance of marketable feed evidently increased at the expense of non-marketable feed (mainly grass). This shift reflects the change in composition of the livestock population as well as higher dietary requirements. The second development is the relative decline of cereals within the category marketable feed. The shift in favour of so-called 'grain substitutes' was a direct consequence of the CAP, which kept cereal prices artificially high, but at the same time allowed grain substitutes (mainly tapioca, corn-gluten feed and protein feeds) into the EU without any import tariff.

Labour and capital goods

Inputs such as land, animals, fertilizer and feed have in common that they directly influence the (potential) production of the agricultural sector. Their point of impact is above all *biological*, either via the amount of productive capacity (land area and number of animals), or via the (potential) yield per unit of capacity (fertilizer and feed). The character of labour and capital goods (buildings and equipment) is different. Application of these inputs is primarily directed at the *organization* of the production process.

Table 2.8   Agricultural labour, EU-9

| | 1973 | 1982 | 1990 | Annual growth rate | |
				1973-82	1982-90
Labour in agriculture (1000)	9,409.0	7,109.0	5,407.0		
Share in overall labour force, percentage	9.2	6.7	4.9		
Average annual outflow, percentage				3.1	3.4

Source: Calculated from CEC, *The Agricultural Situation in the Community.*

Tables 2.8 and 2.9 present information on the use of labour and equipment during the 1973-1990 period. Table 2.8 shows that the size of the labour force has decreased significantly. The 1973-1990 period saw an average annual outflow of labour of more than three per cent (3.1 per cent in the period 1973-82 and 3.4 per cent for the years 1982-90). An index of labour productivity can be computed from the data underlying Table 2.2. The result shows that labour productivity in the agricultural sector of the EU-9 has, on average, increased by some 5 per cent annually. This is extremely high, especially when compared with a rise in labour productivity of a mere 1.9 per cent annually during the same period for the overall economy of the EU-9.

Table 2.9   Tractors, combine harvesters and milking machines, EU-9

	1973 (1000 units)	1990 (1000 units)	Annual growth rate 1973-90
Tractors	4,425.0	5,452.0	1.2
Combine harvesters	474.0	443.0	-0.4
Milking machines	1,320.0	1,015.0	-1.5

Source: Calculated from FAO, *Production Yearbook.*

Labour and capital can, to a large extent, be considered substitutes of one another. Therefore, one would expect that the combination of labour outflow and production growth would have also meant a substantial increase in capital inputs. Though data on capital inputs are scarce, incomplete and not very reliable, they do not point to any such increase. From Table 2.9 it follows that in terms of numbers, the input of such important labour saving machines as combine harvesters and milking machines actually decreased. However, since the capacity of individual machines is not taken into account, the figures presented in the table may be somewhat misleading. An alternative estimate of the volume of machine input which accounts indirectly, (i.e via an estimated shift in the technical coefficient) for changes in capacity, results in an annual input growth for capital of 3.0 per cent for the 1973-1980 period, and a drop of 0.3 per cent per year for the 1980-1985 period (see Folmer (1989, 1991)). A justifiable conclusion would be that the impressive growth in labour productivity was, more than anything else, the result of changes in the quality of capital goods (rather than, say in the tractor power that was available), improvements in infrastructure, the introduction of better seeds and effective pesticides, and other forms of technical progress within the input-producing industries.[15]

2.3.4   Size and number of farms

---

[15] See also Dosi, Pavitt and Soete (1990, p. 125) for a general discussion on the effects of developments in the input-producing sectors on labour productivity and capital-output ratios.

An annual outflow of labour of more than three per cent, combined with an annual increase in volume of value added by 1.7 per cent, will naturally have a large impact on the structure of a sector. So it was for the EU agricultural sector. In the 1970-1987 period, (1970 and 1987 being years for which data are available on farm sizes) the number of farms decreased from 5.7 million to 4.3 million, or at a rate of 1.7 per cent per year (CEC, *The Agricultural Situation in the Community*, various issues). Since the decrease was concentrated among smaller and medium-sized farms, the average farm size has increased. As the number of farms did not decrease at the same speed as the agricultural labour force, the average number of labourers per farm declined, from 1.8 in 1970 to 1.4 in 1987.

Table 2.10   Size distribution of farms, EU-9

| Farm size in ha | Share in total number of farms (%) | | Area distribution in 1987 | |
	1970	1987	1000 ha	Percentage
1- 5	43	42	4,311	5.2
5-10	⎫	16	4,760	5.7
10-20	⎬ 37	16	9,546	11.5
20-50	15	18	24,188	29.2
≥50	5	8	40,152	48.4
Total	100	100	82,957	100.0

Source: Calculated from CEC, *The Agricultural Situation in the Community*.
Note: The agricultural area of farms in the size class ≤ 1 hectare is omitted from this table.
         Therefore, the figure for total land area deviates from the figure in Table 2.4.

Table 2.10 shows the distribution of farms in the EU-9 according to size. In relative terms, there was, during the 1980-87 period, an increase in the number of farms belonging to the two upper classes but in absolute terms, only the number of farms of 50 hectares or more has increased. Nonetheless, the bulk of the farms still belongs to the category of 1-5 hectares, which means that within the EU-9, farming continues to be a small-scale operation. The last two columns of the table indicate quite an uneven distribution of land among farms. The smallest 42 per cent of the farms cultivate slightly more than five per cent of the total area; while the largest eight per cent cultivate nearly fifty per cent.

The distribution of farms according to size class contains a certain regional dimension (Table 2.11). At one extreme of the scale, in Italy, 68 per cent of the farms cultivate between 1 and 5 hectares. At the other extreme, in the United Kingdom, most farms fall into the category of 50 or more hectares. A skewed distribution often indicates structural problems. Because an optimum application of available technologies usually requires a minimum size of a farm far above the EU average, it follows as a matter of course that many small farms are in a technologically backward position.[16]

Table 2.11   Size distribution of farms, 1987

	Share belonging to size class (%, size class in hectares):					Average farm size in hectares
	1-5	5-10	10-20	20-50	≥50	
Belgium-Luxembourg	28	18	25	24	6	17.3
Denmark	2	16	25	39	17	32.5
France	18	12	19	33	18	30.7
Germany, Fed. Rep.	29	18	22	25	6	17.6
Ireland	16	15	29	31	9	22.7
Italy	68	17	9	5	2	7.7
The Netherlands	25	18	25	27	4	17.2
United Kingdom	14	12	15	25	33	68.9
EU-9	42	16	16	18	8	19.3

Source: CEC, *The Agricultural Situation in the Community.*
Note: See note to Table 2.10.

2.3.5   Terms of trade with respect to the non-agricultural sector

The sharp drop in the number of workers, a process which occurred together with continuing growth in the volume of gross value added, is perhaps the clearest indication that there was a great deal of activity in European agriculture during the seventies and eighties. The growth rate of labour productivity in

---

[16] Although average farm size and distribution of farms according to size do provide interesting parameters with respect to the structure of an agricultural sector, one should be careful in attaching too much significance to them. The diverse nature of agriculture means that the size of a farm, as such, can be a very misleading indicator of technological potential. For example, the agricultural sector in The Netherlands is increasingly characterized by very efficient and technologically modern horticultural farms, nearly all of which fall into the 1-5 hectare category.

agriculture was more than double the rate outside agriculture. This raises the question of who has reaped the benefits of this huge productivity growth. Is it the farmer, as owner of most of the labour, land and capital, or the consumer, via lower (real) prices?

Table 2.12   Real price indices of gross production, intermediate demand and gross value added in the agricultural sector of the EU, 1973=100

Real price index	Gross production	Intermediate demand	Gross value added
1973	100	100	100
1982	75	88	58
1990	53	62	44
Annual growth rate, percentage			
1973-90	-3.7	-2.8	-4.7
1973-82	-3.1	-1.4	-5.9
1982-90	-4.2	-4.3	-3.4

Source: Calculated from CEC, *The Agricultural Situation in the Community*.
Note: Price indices used in the calculations for the years 1973-84 refer to the EU-10, and for the years thereafter to the EU-12.

Table 2.12 summarizes certain price indices that are useful in providing an answer. The indices have been calculated by deflating the ratios of nominal values and volume indices with the price indices of the EU's gross internal product. The figures leave little room for misinterpretation. The sector's terms of trade have continually deteriorated with respect to the rest of the economy. During the period 1973-90, farmers received, on average, 4.7 per cent less annually per unit of value added 'sold'. It is worth noting that the real price decrease of a unit of value added was significantly less in the second subperiod than in the first. Although this may partly be due to the particular choice of the subperiods' initial and final years, a probably more important contributing factor was the significant drop in real prices of feed, energy and fertilizer during the eighties, which cushioned the effect of the restrictive price policies.

2.3.6   Agricultural income

From Tables 2.2 and 2.12 it can be calculated that real agricultural value added has decreased by about three per cent annually during the period 1973-90. Hence, real value added has decreased dramatically in the EU-9. However, before reaching any conclusion on the income position of the average agricultural household, two points should be noted. First, the three per cent reduction in the agricultural labour force over the period 1973-90, implies that there has been a modest increase in real value added per agricultural labourer, though this lagged behind the per capita increase outside agriculture. Secondly, real value added is not identical to household income. While it includes interest, rent and wages that the farmer has to pay, it excludes sources of income outside agriculture which are often quite substantial.

Table 2.13   Income composition of agricultural households, percentage

Income share from:	Farming	Non-farm sources
Luxembourg (1989)	66	34
France (1989)	62	38
Denmark (1988)	39	61
Germany, Fed. Rep. (1988)	47	53
Ireland (1987)	68	32
Italy (1988)	31	69
The Netherlands (1988)	77	23
United Kingdom (1986)	57	43

Sources: Eurostat (1992); Kuipers (1993).

Table 2.13 provides some information on this. Due to definition and other statistical problems the figures in the table must be considered as rough approximations only (see Eurostat (1992)). Nonetheless, the table clearly shows the importance of household income of non-farm origin. In Denmark, West Germany and Italy, agricultural households obtain less than fifty per cent of their total income from farm activities. In the other countries this share is higher but in all cases farming contributes less than eighty per cent to overall household income.

2.3.7   The changing role on the world market

Table 2.14   Self-sufficiency ratios, EU-9, for selected products

Product (group)	1973	1990
Wheat	.93	1.29
Coarse grains	.83	1.13
Sugar	.91	1.39
Oilseeds	.15	.51
Wine	.99	1.08
Beef	.96	1.11
Cheese	1.03	1.09
Butter	.98	1.21
Skimmed milk-powder	1.43	1.40

Source: Calculated from FAO, *Trade Yearbook* and *Production Yearbook*, CEC, *The Agricultural Situation in the Community*; see also Merbis (1995a).

The volume of total agricultural production increased on average by 1.5 per cent annually in the 1973-90 period (see Table 2.2). This may seem like modest growth, but because the growth of internal demand was even smaller, self-sufficiency ratios increased for nearly all products in the Community. Table 2.14 illustrates this for a number of products. With the exception of skimmed milk-powder, the internal consumption of which is largely determined by special subsidy programmes, self-sufficiency ratios for all products in the table were higher in 1990 than in 1973. For cereals,sugar, wine, butter and beef, self-sufficiency ratios crossed the 100 per cent value, causing the EU to experience a 'regime switch' from net importer into net exporter. Table 2.15 summarizes the evolution of the net trade position.

The regime switches were the outcome of relatively sluggish growth in internal production and a nearly stagnating internal demand. Two main tendencies lie behind the stagnating demand. First, demand for human consumption has hardly increased at all due to low population growth rates in most member states and a satiated per capita consumption. Secondly, and in a sense more importantly, despite growth of demand for marketable feed (see Table 2.7), the consumption of cereals as feed has decreased since 1973. As mentioned earlier, the CAP is mainly to blame for this shift in the feed mix.

Table 2.15   Net imports, EU-9, mln metric tons

	1973	1990
Wheat	3.0	-16.5
Coarse grains	13.1	-7.0
Sugar	0.5	-3.6
Oilseeds	8.3	10.4
Oilseed cake and meals	8.8	15.6
Wine	0.6	-1.0
Beef	0.2	-0.3
Cheese	-0.05	-0.4
Butter	-0.2	-0.1
Powdered milk	-0.5	-0.8

Source: Computed from FAO's Agrostat Supply Utilization Accounts.
Note: Due to differences in the procedure used for commodity aggregation, this table is not fully comparable with Table 2.14.

Table 2.16   Production quantities and EU-12's share in world production

	1982			1990		
	World (1000 mt)	EU-12 (1000 mt)	share (percent)	World (1000 mt)	EU-12 (1000 mt)	share (percent)
Wheat	459475	64625	14.1	601720	80190	13.3
Coarse grains	778725	82239	10.6	848035	78080	9.2
Oilseeds	203390	4421	2.2	250270	10430	4.2
Sugar	111000	18573	16.7	110820	17290	15.6
Milk, total	439800	114628	26.1	477565	109400	22.9
Butter	7380	2087	28.3	7775	1770	22.8
Cheese	12040	3895	32.4	14540	4770	32.8
Milk-powder	6345	2943	46.4	6295	2505	39.8
Bovine meat	45090	7200	16.0	51630	7700	14.9
Ovine meat	8010	858	10.7	9590	1180	12.3
Pig meat	52610	11477	21.8	69885	13435	19.2
Poultry meat	27900	5411	19.4	39870	6335	15.9
Eggs	28610	4354	15.2	34860	4760	13.7

Sources: CEC, *The Agricultural Situation in the Community*; FAO, *Production Yearbook*.
Note: Product composition of oilseeds is the same in the world and the EU.

Since imports of cereal substitutes such as protein cakes and meals and tapioca are not subjected to any import tax, they are cheaper than cereals, which are so strongly protected. Hence, cereals have increasingly been replaced in the feed mix by their cheaper substitutes. As a consequence, the net trade balance went from a shortage of 16.1 million metric tons in 1973 to a surplus of 23.5 million metric tons in 1990. Because these exports are subsidized, this development is not only expensive but has also provoked a lot of criticism from competing trade partners, especially the United States.

It is possible to put the problem of surpluses into a less dramatic perspective, by expressing its size in terms of global production. This is done in Table 2.16. The table shows that, except for oilseeds, cheese and ovine meat, the EU-12's shares in world production have decreased over the 1982-90 period. Milk quotas caused a decrease of more than three per cent in the EU's global market share for milk. With respect to the cereal surplus problem, it may be interesting to note that the total surplus in 1990 amounted to a mere 1.6 per cent of global cereals production (excluding rice; it is less than 1.2 per cent if rice is included).

Table 2.17   EU-12's share in world trade, percentage

	1980		1989	
	Import	Export	Import	Export
Cereals	11.6	8.8	3.1	15.0
Oilseeds	44.1	0.1	44.3	0.2
Sugar	6.4	13.8	6.9	17.8
Butter	13.3	57.4	8.8	43.7
Cheese	13.4	44.4	13.1	49.3
Other dairy products	0.1	60.0	1.3	50.6
Bovine meat	7.0	17.6	6.6	23.9
Ovine meat	37.0	0.3	29.8	0.8
Pig meat	10.0	20.1	4.0	23.5
Poultry meat	4.3	29.2	5.6	23.8
Eggs	2.5	20.5	9.3	30.4

Source: Adapted from Berkhout and Buck (1994).
Note: Cereals excluding rice; intra-EU trade is excluded.

In Table 2.17 exports and imports of the EU are expressed as shares in world trade. It appears that the EU has become an important exporter of cereals. It also plays a role of increasing importance with respect to a number of other products, like sugar, cheese, bovine meat. On the other hand the Community is losing ground on the markets for butter and other dairy products.

2.4   The CAP under siege

When the CAP was established, it was considered a necessary step towards economic integration (see Section 2.1). Because the regulations and interests of member countries were widely different at the time, the organizational schemes governing the common agricultural markets had from the outset the character of a complex compromise that did not fully satisfy any of the parties involved. Since the CAP rules were not seen as an immutable reality but rather as the object of permanent renegotiation, the discussion did not cease once the CAP came into effect.

And so the CAP provoked criticism from the very start. Price levels, the insulation of EU agricultural markets from the world market, the policy to strive for reasonable farm incomes via product-tied support, and many other controversial issues all became subjects of debate among policymakers, academics, farmers' organizations and other interest groups. At first the debate remained mainly an internal Community affair but as the role of the EU as an agricultural exporter became more important, these discussions increasingly became an international affair.

In order to set the scene for specific reform proposals, including those which led to the MacSharry reform and the GATT agreement, this section will present a brief survey of the main issues in the debate. The discussion will be informal. The points of contention will be considered more rigorously in Chapter 3. We start with an overview of the most widespread points of controversy. It is often said that the CAP is:

(a)   *Unfair to non-farmers*
      The budgetary cost of the CAP is too heavy and still increasing. The CAP keeps internal consumer prices for agricultural products at an artificially high level. This is unfair especially to lower income households. Farm households are not poor relative to non-agricultural households.

(b)   *Misallocating factors of production*

The CAP has led to a misallocation of resources within the EU, particularly between the agricultural and the non-agricultural sector but also within these sectors.

(c)   *Ineffective in providing income support*
Product-tied support is ineffective because large farmers benefit most.

(d)   *Distorting world markets*
Because it has provided disproportionate support, the CAP has resulted in artificial trade flows between EU and non-EU countries. For many products the EU market is virtually closed to imports from third countries. The CAP was a major contributing factor to disorder in many international agricultural markets in the last three decades.

(e)   *A barrier to market unity*
Despite the CAP, the aim of a single internal agricultural market has not yet been achieved.

(f)   *An administrative burden*
It is almost impossible to apply the CAP regulations fairly. Abuse and fraud are common practice.

(g)   *Causing environmental damage*
The CAP promotes an intensive and environmentally damaging method of production.

There can be no doubt that the CAP effectively insulates the EU agricultural market from the world market. In addition, the support schemes have raised internal prices of farm products well above the world market levels and agricultural production in the EU is increasing faster than consumption. Therefore, much of the criticism is easy to understand. The following sections will consider each of the points by turns.

2.4.1   Unfairness to non-farmers: budgetary and implicit costs

Community budget

The Community covers the direct costs of the CAP from the European Agriculture Guidance and Guarantee Fund (FEOGA). The FEOGA consists of two parts: the Guarantee Section, through which expenditures of the various market organization schemes are financed, and the Guidance Section, through which part of the expenditures resulting from structural policy measures are disbursed among the member states. Figure 2.4 shows how total Community expenditures have developed since 1973. A distinction is made between expenditures which are and are not related to CAP. The former is further subdivided into expenditures on behalf of the Guarantee Section and of the Guidance Section.

Figure 2.4 Budget outlays of the Community, billion ecu

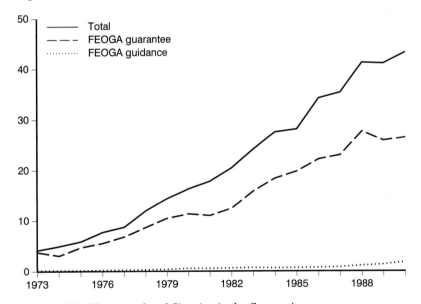

Source: CEC, *The Agricultural Situation in the Community.*

The figure displays the following trends:

(a)   Total Community expenditures rose rapidly: during the 1973-1990 period there was an average annual increase of 14.3 per cent. Total expenditures for 1990 amounted to 46.6 billion ecu.[17]

(b)   It is striking that the FEOGA plays such a dominant role in the overall budget. The share of FEOGA expenditures never dropped below 56 per cent. From both a budgetary and bureaucratic point of view, the EU is above all, a Common Agricultural Community.

(c)   Within the FEOGA the Guarantee Fund accounts for the lion's share of expenditures. The Guidance Section's share never exceeded five per cent, a clear indication of the minor significance of structural policies within the CAP.

(d)   Guarantee expenditures exhibit erratic behaviour. This is mainly due to the open-ended character of the regulations governing expenditures.

In order to pinpoint factors responsible for increasing expenditures one has to differentiate between farm products which are supported via refunds and variable levies at the border, and farm products supported via a system of deficiency payments (mainly oilseeds). Budgetary outlays for a product belonging to the first category approximately satisfy, for any CAP commodity, the following formula (here we disregard the storage costs of the intervention stocks):

$$E = (p^d - p^w) \, \alpha \, (q - x - v) + (p^d - p^s) \, (1 - \alpha) \, (q - x - v) \qquad (2.3)$$

where

E	budget expenditure on particular product
p^d	intervention price
p^s	internal price for products sold through special programmes
p^w	world market price

---

[17] Two qualifications are in order: (a) in the period under discussion the number of member states increased from 9 to 12 (see (CEC, *Financial Report on the European Agricultural Guidance and Guarantee Fund FEOGA, Guarantee Section*, various issues) and Court of Auditors, *Financial Reports*, various issues'); (b) the budget figures are in nominal terms, while there was an ecu inflation of about nine per cent during this period.

q	production level
v	intermediate use (mainly animal feed)
x	consumer demand
α	share of 'excess production' sold on world market
(1 − α)	share of 'excess production' sold on internal market through special programmes

For several products, total production (q) exceeded the total intra-EU demand (x + v) by a relatively small but growing margin over the period 1973-90. At the same time, the internal support price (p^d) was kept well above the world market price (p^w). Because of the negative effect of larger surpluses (q − x − v) on world market prices (p^w), the gap between internal prices (p^d) and world market prices (p^w) even widened. It follows that the growth rate of E must exceed the growth rate of q.[18] In other words: total expenditures have increased much faster than total production.

For products supported by means of deficiency payments, budgetary outlays follow the formula:

$$E = (p^d − p^w) \, q \tag{2.4}$$

If one disregards the effect of EU production q on world prices p^w, total expenditures increase in proportion to total production. In the eighties, however, the output level of products that are subject to a deficiency payment increased more rapidly than overall production; hence, the effect on total budget expenditures was more than proportional.

The cost to the consumer

The budget shows the size of the explicit transfers from the Community budget. Of course, these transfers are paid by the tax-payers, mainly non-farmers. The

---

[18] Collecting terms leads to: $E = [(p^d − p^w) \, α + (p^d − p^s) \, (1 − α)] \, (q − x − v)$. The growth rate is the sum of the growth rate of the terms in square brackets (which is nonnegative) and the growth rate of (q − x − v) which, around self-sufficiency exceeds the growth rate of q, by far.

non-farmers pay an even more massive (implicit) subsidy through their food bill. If the world market price were independent of the policies in the EU, and farm incomes had no impact on the EU supply and demand, it would be possible to measure this implicit subsidy directly as the difference between EU and world market prices multiplied by the quantity consumed. However, since such effects exist, one can only evaluate implicit subsidies by comparing the situation with and without the subsidy, while taking into consideration the effect of the abolishment of subsidy on supply, demand, trade etc., and for this one needs a simulation model.

Several estimates of implicit subsidies have been computed (see e.g. OECD (1989/1990) and Tyers and Anderson (1992))[19] and all come up with impressive amounts. These subsidies from the consumer to the farmer vary according to the quantities consumed. The lower income groups contribute more in relative terms, as they spend a larger share of their income on food.

2.4.2   Misallocation of factors of production

As internal prices of many agricultural products have been kept well above the world market level, the terms of trade of agriculture are distorted and this obviously affects the allocation of resources in the economy, keeping too many factors of production in agriculture. Moreover, because the support is unevenly distributed among products, there is also a misallocation of resources within the agricultural sector itself, not to mention the misallocation at the international level.

2.4.3   Product-tied support is ineffective and unfair

The sizeable implicit and explicit transfers to the farm sector are often justified as being necessary to guarantee reasonable incomes for farmers. They prevent a pauperization of the countryside and a marginalization of the farmers and rural areas within the overall economy.

---

[19] OECD (1989/90, p. 166) concludes that the average 1986-88 levels of agricultural support could have cost the OECD countries almost one per cent in lower real household income (72 billion US dollar at 1988 prices). Tyers and Anderson (1992, Table 7.7) predict a consumer gain in 1995 for the EU-12 of 25 billion US dollar at 1985 prices, when the industrial market economies introduce a phased 50 per cent reduction in agricultural protection.

According to the critics, however, product-tied income support is an ineffective mechanism for transfers. In addition to the welfare theoretical arguments to be discussed in Chapter 3, which state that direct income payments (lump sum transfers) have a less distortive effect on the allocation of the means of production, it is also argued that product-tied aid channels the bulk of support to large and, thereby, richer farmers, while the smaller farmers receive little support. Also, because small farmers are concentrated in the southern part of the Community, the support has a regional bias, a politically sensitive point. But even large farmers only profit to a limited extent from the support provided by the CAP. Because the land, in contrast with labour and capital, hardly lends itself to alternative uses, product-tied income support ultimately results in high land prices. Through inheritance agriculture loses a part of the value of land with each passing generation, so that a considerable part of the support eventually accrues to the non-agricultural sector. Therefore, although product-tied income support leads to a higher reward for the production factors, it does not necessarily mean a proportionally higher disposable income for the farmers, and certainly not in the long run.

Critics of the CAP also maintain that farm incomes cannot be raised in the long run through price support policies (see e.g. Tangermann (1989)). If agricultural prices are kept at an artificially high level, more people will remain in the sector, and any impact the support has on average farm income consequently vanishes.

But even if it were possible to raise farm incomes, statistical information suggests that it may be unnecessary to do so. If farm households were extremely poor, the explicit and implicit costs of the CAP could to some extent be justified on equity grounds. However, as shown in Table 2.18, on a per household base, disposable income in agriculture is, in all member countries, higher than the all-households average. However, this does not settle the issue completely.

First, agricultural households have, on average, more members than non-agricultural households implying that the relative advantage becomes less (in Italy and The Netherlands) or even reversed (in other countries) when income per household member is examined. Yet a per capita measure is questionable given that the age of household members matters and that there are associated

Table 2.18   Relative income position of farmers, percentage

Farm income relative to national average	Per household	Per household member
Luxembourg (1985)	143	94
France (1989)	121	95
Denmark (1988)	115	81
Germany, Fed. Rep. (1988)	110	63
Ireland (1987)	105	98
Italy (1988)	145	112
The Netherlands (1988)	263	178

Sources: Eurostat (1992); Kuipers (1993).
Notes: (a) National average = 100.
            (b) No figures were available for Belgium and the United Kingdom.

fixed costs in every household, which do not increase with the number of members. Secondly, the relatively favourable income position is related to the CAP and is affected by recent reforms. Thirdly, the table does not show the distribution within agriculture. It may well be that pseudo-farmers with a primary occupation outside agriculture distort the picture and anyway within agriculture 6.7 per cent of the farms generate 32 per cent of the value added.[20] Finally, the composition of non-agricultural income matters. The Eurostat data show that a significant part of farmers' income consists of social benefits, which may indicate that many are poor (to which one may retort that the non-farm sector also receives social benefits). In spite of all these qualifications the per capita figures are remarkable and call for further investigation.

2.4.4   The distorting effect on world markets

Despite the fact that EU exports of agricultural products have increased faster than its imports, the Community still remains a major net importer of agricultural products. In 1990 the EU-12 agricultural imports amounted to 71.2 billion ecu. This figure, corrected for intra-EU trade, is equal to 22.1 per cent of the total world trade in agricultural products. The value of agricultural exports was significantly smaller, amounting to 44.8 billion ecu. Nonetheless, the CAP

---

[20] Source: CEC, *The Agricultural Situation in the Community*, Report 1992, Table T/54.

is still often criticized for its highly protective character. Due to the system of variable levies,[21] potential exporters cannot gain access by reducing costs of production, any decrease in the offer price being fully offset by an increase in the levy.

Moreover, the CAP leads to artificial trade flows. As was mentioned previously, the use of cereal substitutes in animal feed was especially attractive to farmers located in the vicinity of a port of entry and in countries with positive MCAs. The resulting trade flows, mainly from Thailand, the United States and Latin America are ultimately dependent on the whims of the EU policymakers.[22] This is not conducive to the stability of international trade relations. The trade flows have also been blamed for having negative consequences on the environment in the exporting countries themselves. The tapioca monoculture in Northeastern Thailand has according to some reports depleted soil fertility (see van Amstel et al. (1986)) and Brazilian exports of oilseeds and meat have in some writings been related to the destruction of the rain forests (see Binswanger (1989) and Reis and Margulis (1991)).

2.4.5   The CAP and the pursuit of an internal market

A primary motivation behind the CAP was the pursuit of one large internal market for agricultural products. It was hoped such a market would ensure a rational development of agriculture and an optimal utilization of production factors. Section 2.2.4 explained that differences in monetary policies greatly frustrated attempts to realize the ideal of market unification. Until 1993 the trade

---

[21] In order to (partly) accommodate such criticism, the EU has, in the course of time, agreed to a number of preferential import agreements. Under the Lomé Convention, 66 African, Caribbean and Pacific countries are allowed to export, both duty- and levy-free, predesignated quantities of various agricultural products to the Community. Agricultural trade concessions have also been granted to most Mediterranean countries. These generally consist of reductions in import duties, albeit that such concessions are often limited to the off-season of the Community's own production and subject to quotas and minimum import prices. The EU has also entered into a number of bilateral agreements. Some of these, e.g. the concession to New Zealand to export butter to the EU under special conditions, have a historical background; others have been negotiated under the GATT.

[22] Due to concessions made in an earlier GATT round, however, and because of varying interests within the EU, it is difficult to erect (new) import barriers. Only with respect to tapioca (manioc) has the EU scored some degree of 'success': exporting countries have agreed to limit their exports to 6 million metric tons annually.

flows among member states occurred alongside border taxes or subsidies (MCAs). Quota regulations in the dairy and the sugar sector established on a national basis also run contrary to the principle of market unity. Thus, according to critics, the CAP was, and still is, inconsistent with its own objectives.

2.4.6   The administrative burden

The system of MCAs is not the only CAP-regulation that is not easily explained to the general public. The number of complex regulations has increased significantly over time and it appears that the entire body of CAP rules is difficult to control in any proper way. Abuse of subsidies has frequently been reported (see *The Official Journal of the European Communities*, various issues). According to some estimates, the total amount of subsidies incorrectly spent due to abuse and fraud could amount to many billions of ecu per year (see Tutt (1989)).

2.4.7   The effect on the environment

Like every other economic activity, farming has a number of side effects which do not carry a market price. In so far as these side effects relate to the environment, the CAP has stimulated methods of production and land use which damage the environment. Negative effects on the environment occur along three chains of causation:

(i)   High prices foster high production. A high production level can be attained by using more nonfarm inputs, i.e. extra fertilizer, pesticides, etc. The effect of these inputs on the ecological sphere is generally negative.

(ii) High prices also have an indirect effect on the environment. In the long run product-tied support results in higher land prices. High land prices in turn, hamper the conversion of agricultural land into land earmarked for forestry, nature conservation, wildlife and landscape preservation, as well as for other less environmentally hazardous uses (on the other hand when land prices are low it is less profitable to invest into it and more profitable to dump waste onto it).

(iii) Since internally produced feed grains are expensive, compared with imported substitutes (protein cakes and meals, tapioca, maize gluten feed, etc.), livestock farmers have replaced feed grains with these substitutes. This process has stimulated the development of specialized livestock farms, especially in countries with positive MCAs,[23] and in the vicinity of ports where these substitutes come into the Community, e.g. Rotterdam. A high concentration of animals does, however, imply a high production rate of manure. Consequently, in these areas manure has become an environmentally damaging waste product, instead of being considered a valuable fertilizer.

2.5 Four perspectives on reform and future of the CAP

The list of objections against the CAP is impressive. However, the critics have not only expressed objections. In the course of time they have also presented a number of reform proposals, some more radical than others. The CAP also has its defenders, who, while conceding that the scheme may need some reform, still want to maintain the basic principle that European agriculture must be regulated and to some extent insulated from the world market. As an introduction to the discussion of alternative proposals, we now return to the 'perspectives' mentioned in Chapter 1 and distinguish three medium term perspectives on European agricultural policy and one long term perspective. The book will evolve around an analysis of these viewpoints. Here we shall only describe them in relation to the subject of this chapter, the history of the CAP. In Chapter 3 we discuss their welfare theoretical implications and in Chapters 5-7 we analyze them in quantitative terms, through scenario simulations.

2.5.1   The free trade perspective
Although adherents of the 'free trade school' do differ concerning certain details, they share the conviction that the only real remedy for EU agricultural problems is a complete termination of all product-tied support. Radical free

---

[23] The difference in price between feed grains and grain substitutes was greatest in countries with positive MCAs.

traders propose the abolition of the CAP altogether. Free traders argue that an elimination of all product-tied support would result in a decrease in internal prices, more fluctuating prices within the Community and an increase in world market prices. The major consequences would be a reallocation of physical resources, both within the EU and worldwide, and the ceasing of the huge transfers within the EU from non-agriculture to agriculture. The reallocation of resources would take place at three levels.

First, within the overall EU economy there would be a shift of resources from the agricultural sector to the non-agricultural sector. Because agricultural product prices would decrease relative to non-agricultural product prices, labour and capital would migrate to non-agricultural sectors. The decrease in agricultural prices would also result in less intensive farming methods. Secondly, the change in relative prices would have allocative effects within the agricultural sector itself. Intensive livestock farmers who feed their animals cereal substitutes, but do not live in the vicinity of grain-producing areas, would lose their competitive advantage. As a result production would shift to the grain-producing areas. The change in relative prices would also stimulate production of mildly or non-supported products. Finally, it is believed that since the absence of support would prevent EU farmers from competing on international markets for most products, eliminating all product-tied support within the Community would, on balance, lead to an expansion of agricultural sectors in a number of third countries, but at the expense of the EU. The producers of cereal substitutes would be the main exception to the general picture.

The transfer effects would be twofold: if no support is granted, there is no need for taxpayers' money to finance a budget. Furthermore, if internal prices are brought to world market level, all implicit transfers vanish.

If we recall the above-mentioned points of criticism, the position of the free traders, who draw on welfare theory, can easily be understood. If all support were to be terminated, there would be important efficiency gains that would make it possible to relieve the pain for the farmers by direct income support. Because, in the longer run, land prices would decline and farms would increase in size and efficiency, the free traders consider such support as only necessary during a transition period. Whereas we shall see in Chapter 3 that matters are more complicated, when analyzed in welfare theoretic terms, in Chapter 6 we shall find that significant welfare gains can indeed be achieved, even if one does not reach full liberalization.

2.5.2 The interventionist perspective

Supporters of the interventionist perspective reject much of the criticism of the CAP by the free traders. They have little trust in the free market or in the 'patchwork reforms' implied by the defenders of the CAP. They believe that the CAP has relied too heavily on price policy as its main instrument and that this is the main cause of its failures. In general they agree with the principle of the free traders that economic policy should create conditions that make allocations more efficient but they do not believe that competitive markets will do so. And, more than the free traders, they emphasize distributional objectives. In their view a free trade regime would result in extremely low farm incomes, while a series of patchwork adjustments would not provide any solution to the sector's current surplus and income problems.

The majority of the interventionists points to technological progress as the source of all problems. They contend that technological progress is largely an autonomous process which induces a yearly increase of production of about 1.5 per cent. Because internal demand within the EU does increase more slowly, the imbalance between supply and demand unavoidably becomes larger. In principle this problem can be tackled from two sides: by means of price decreases, or by means of supply controls. Because of the low supply elasticity with respect to prices, however, using the price instrument would have a devastating effect on farm incomes. They therefore consider the price instrument unsuitable for solving the supply-demand imbalance and, instead of advocating an increasing role for the market, propose a more active supply control policy. It is only through supply control that the budget can be relieved without lowering farmers' incomes to unacceptably low levels. Moreover, supply control is also seen as a useful instrument for reducing environmental costs and mitigating the CAP's negative effects on world markets and, consequently, on agriculture in many developing countries.

Whereas the advocates of the free trade perspective constitute a rather homogeneous group whose proposals for reform are well documented in the literature, interventionists, who can be found in farmers' organizations, environmental groups, churches and, to a lesser degree, in academic circles, have presented a wide array of proposals, more often in political circles and in the press than in academic journals. We must therefore describe a spectrum of views and our references to published literature will necessarily be limited.

Closest to the free traders stand those who propose schemes like the ones currently implemented for sugar, that give producers guaranteed high prices up to a quota and world market prices for any production in excess of this quota but with quota set at a level that producers will in general want to exceed (see Blanford et al. (1989)). Then come interventionists who propose to follow a quota regime like the one implemented for dairy and give price guarantees up to the quota, with strong penalties for any production in excess of this quota. As will be explained in more detail in the next chapter, it is in principle possible to mimic free trade results (with transfers) by such schemes, provided the consumer and the feed industry pay the world market price and the quotas can be traded among producers. Interventionists prefer high prices-with-quotas to transfers for three reasons: first, because transfers are costly from an administrative point of view, particularly when the group of eligible farmers is large; secondly, and in a sense more curiously, because transfers make the support very visible and therefore, vulnerable (see e.g. Mansholt (1986)) and finally, because interventionists are convinced that environmental problems can be tackled more easily via quotas.

Many interventionists do not attach much importance to the welfare loss for the consumers, since their price elasticity is low anyway and because monopoly margins, which also cause welfare losses, are higher in other sectors. At the same time, the interventionists recognize the problem that quotas cannot be implemented easily for all products. For sugar and milk, where there is a nodal point in the market chain, a system of production quotas per farmer or processing factory can be employed. However, if such a nodal point does not exist, e.g. in the case of cereals, it is very difficult to enforce quota schemes because it is virtually impossible to determine which farmer has produced a particular quantity. In such a scheme, if the EU market price is above world market level, abuse of the system will follow. To avoid these problems, the use of land set-aside is proposed, as implemented in the MacSharry reform.

Of course, this brings the regulation one step further away from the free traders, to whom leaving a resource idle is hardly conducive to global efficiency. To this the interventionists will respond that the set-asides are needed as a second-best corrective measure, which will bring the EU export position closer to an efficient level, and that, in comparison, due to missing markets for environmental commodities, the free trade solution lies much further away from any international welfare optimum. Clearly, the two views are not likely to converge soon. A policy of supply controls in fact transforms European agriculture into a producers cartel that, like any other cartel, faces the problem of distributing quotas among producers. This could create serious problems at the Community level, as interests of member states diverge as the implicit rents from the quotas are distributed unevenly. This point will be discussed further in Chapter 6, where we report on outcomes from a cartel scenario.

The interventionist perspective also has another dimension: as it questions the importance of the free market arguments, it inevitably reopens the debate on the need for a 'common' policy. The increasing recognition of environmental problems in rural areas and of the importance of non-agricultural employment have somewhat shifted the concern away from a narrow farm price policy to a much broader rural policy. Such a rural policy is almost inevitably complex and is more efficiently implemented at the national and even at the regional level. There is also the more political aspect that rural policies involve direct transfers and it is doubtful that solidarity is sufficient at the Community level to mobilize these over a prolonged period. The solidarity with, and the political influence of, rural areas may be stronger at the national and at the regional level.

Few would advocate the return to a system of national food price policies. However, it is conceivable that the member states could maintain a system of common internal prices but give up the principle of 'solidarity' that all revenue and expenses of agricultural policy should be financed through the FEOGA. One could also imagine a system in which countries finance their own agricultural and rural policies, possibly with some, but this time explicit, aid from the

Community. In Chapter 6 we shall look into the consequences of such a financial renationalization of the CAP.

2.5.3   The bureaucratic perspective

It is the nature of criticism that it mainly comes from outsiders. So it was with the criticism of the CAP. It is not the policymakers, but rather, the farmers' organizations, environmentalists and the academic world who are constantly voicing their grievances against the CAP. Although it is difficult to determine the extent to which this criticism has affected the implementation of the CAP, the bureaucrats have in general successfully resisted pressures for radical reform as proposed by the free traders and interventionists.

In Section 2.1 it was argued that until 1984 the character of the CAP had hardly changed at all. And it was only because budgetary problems and pressures from third countries continued to worsen, that more drastic measures were taken such as the introduction of production quotas in the dairy sector and stabilizer regimes for other products. It should be stressed, however, that these measures were above all, reactions to concrete problems; they were at best indirectly inspired by the more abstract criticism of free traders or the adherents of the interventionist perspective. In practice, agricultural policy has been dominated by the bureaucratic perspective. Nonetheless, for the last couple of years the bureaucratic perspective has been losing ground, while the other perspectives have gained in popularity. The MacSharry reforms provide the clearest illustration of this, being more radical than all preceding reforms. They contain elements from both the free trade and interventionist perspectives. The shift in perspective is no accident. It coincides with a growing conviction that policies consistent with the bureaucratic perspective have failed. Chapter 5 investigates the grounds for this conviction in more detail.

2.5.4   A long term perspective

The three perspectives on reform of the CAP, free trade, interventionist and bureaucratic, have in common that they focus on trade and distribution issues, not on food security in the long term. Although, the free trader will argue that improved efficiency and flexibility provide the best safeguard for food security and the interventionist will say that controls are necessary to avoid environmental degradation and to ensure that technical progress moves in the appropriate direction. We will not be able to settle this debate but in Chapter 7 we present two scenarios which analyze some long term aspects, asking whether productivity growth and labour outflow from agriculture will eventually eliminate all income problems and need for support, and whether it is safe to assume that technical progress will be so significant that agricultural land may be devoted to other purposes in an irrevocable way.

2.6 Implications for the design of a policy model on EU agriculture

The discussion in the preceding sections has several implications for the specification of a policy model that can be used to analyze the relative merits of the various proposals. In this connection it is useful to distinguish between the two levels at which the debate on policy reform actually takes place.

The first level coincides with debates on policy changes in which the bureaucratic perspective prevails. The arguments are rather mundane and evolve around percentage changes of, say, cereal prices, butter exports or sugar quotas. Here the deliberate attempt is made to seek a compromise which encompasses the interests of various parties. Discussions in this sphere often lack transparency and theoretical underpinnings. However, they have the advantage of being very relevant as they are the expression of realities as perceived by policymakers.

The gap with the policy makers is much larger in discussions that take place at the second level, where the free trade or the interventionist perspectives prevail. Here a much larger role is reserved for economic theory and moral principles. Although debates on this level do have the advantages of transparency and consistency, they often take place at a great distance from where the actual decisions on agricultural policy are being taken.

Ideally, one would like to conduct an analysis of issues from all four perspectives within a single coherent framework. This would make it possible for policymakers to assess the consequences of alternative policy measures in terms of theoretical principles such as efficiency and equity. The same framework would also allow advocates of radical reforms to formulate proposals sufficiently specific to be relevant in policy decisions.

Clearly, it is impossible to achieve these objectives in a fully satisfactory way. However, a simulation model which is firmly embedded in the economic theory of efficiency and equity and which, at the same time, gives a realistic description of the current state of the EU agricultural sector, could certainly contribute to this purpose.

The need for welfare theoretical embedding almost tautologically leads to the choice for a general equilibrium model, as partial models or macro-econometric models do not lend themselves to formal welfare analysis. The other requirement is obviously more ambiguous since it is open to debate as to what exactly is meant by 'a realistic description'. Yet two points are, in our opinion, important in this respect. First, model variables should be defined in terms recognizable to bureaucrats and policymakers. To be explicit: the level of disaggregation should resemble the level chosen in Sections 2.2-2.4. The classification schemes should refer to individual countries, to concrete products and to explicit policies. Secondly, the model should be falsifiable, which means that time series information should be available on, at least, key variables.

This brings us back to our discussion in Chapter 1 of the four 'dimensions' of this study: the history and regulations of the CAP, the statistics on EU agriculture, economic theory and scenario simulation. There we gave the assurance that we would base ECAM, the 'fourth dimension', firmly on the other three. We also promised to report on sensitivity of the findings to specific assumptions, and finally, not to use this simulation model where we do not need it. Therefore, we shall now investigate how far welfare theoretic considerations not based on an applied model can take us in our analysis of the perspectives on CAP reform.

Chapter 3

Welfare analysis of CAP reform: a stylized model

Whereas the previous chapter described the perspectives on CAP reform as they appear in the public debate, this chapter will analyze them from a welfare theoretical angle. For the free trade perspective this is relatively straightforward, since welfare theory has traditionally advocated this view. However, the classical welfare theoretical results rely on several assumptions that rarely hold in practice. Hence, the policy maker faces the problem of choosing between reforms that make the assumptions come true, and interventions, by means of instruments such as indirect taxes and quantity rations, that seek to restore efficiency when these assumptions do not hold. In Sections 3.2 and 3.3, we shall compare the free trade and the interventionist perspectives on the basis of this problem. A second issue concerns the speed of adjustment in policy. Section 3.4 considers arguments against radical change in agricultural policy and this naturally introduces the bureaucratic perspective. Finally, Section 3.5 draws conclusions for the scenario simulations of Chapters 5-7, but first, to highlight the CAP-specific aspects, we present in Section 3.1, a simple model that already contains the CAP's main policy instruments and that may be viewed as a stylized version of ECAM.

3.1 A stylized version of ECAM

ECAM belongs to the larger class of Applied General Equilibrium (AGE) models.[24] Its stylized version provides an easy overview of the overall model

---

[24] A lucid exposition on general equilibrium theory can be found in Arrow and Hahn (1971). One of the first applied general equilibrium models was developed by Adelman and Robinson (1978). A description of the class of applied general equilibrium models to which ECAM belongs can be found in Fischer et al. (1988).

structure. It shows the model's theoretical underpinnings in general equilibrium theory and its aptitude for analyzing CAP reform.

3.1.1   Specification

The stylized version is specified by EU member state and refers to a single calendar year. In each member state, there are two sectors, a farm sector and a non-farm sector. The individuals in these sectors are referred to as farmers and non-farmers, indexed j, and $j \in J_1$ for farmers and $j \in J_2$ for non-farmers. Commodities are indexed k, and $k \in K_1$ for agricultural and $k \in K_2$ for non-agricultural commodities. We use vector notation to denote consumption x_j, production q_j, input demand v_j, the price received for output p^q and the input price p of commodities. Vectors of fixed resources are of dimension r and denoted by b_j.

Every farmer and non-farmer is represented in two roles, as a consumer and as a producer. As in most general equilibrium models, every consumer j will maximize his utility function $u_j(x_j)$ subject to a budget constraint:[25,26,27]

$$\max u_j(x_j)$$
$$x_j \geq 0$$
subject to   (3.1)
$$px_j \leq h_j$$

---

[25] We write ab for the inner product a·b. The variables under the maximand are the arguments of the optimization (in this case x_j). In addition quantity vectors are treated as column vectors and price vectors as row vectors.

[26] The utility function satisfies *Assumption C (consumer)*: every consumer j has preferences represented by a utility function u_j: $R_+^K \rightarrow R$ which is continuous, strictly concave, nonsatiated and homogeneous ($u_j(0) = 0$). Assumption C is standard, except that strict concavity is often weakened to strict quasi-concavity, to be introduced in Section 4.3.2.

[27] The consumer is assumed to pay the market price p. Taxes and subsidies on consumption will be introduced in Section 3.1.2.

Every producer j will maximize his net revenue from his firm, subject to the transformation constraint:[28,29]

$$\pi_j(p^q, p, b_j) =$$
$$\max \; p^q q_j - p v_j$$
$$q_j, v_j \geq 0$$

subject to

$$t_j(q_j, -v_j, -b_j) \leq 0$$

(3.2)

Consumer j's income consists of net revenue and (possibly negative) transfers

$$h_j = \pi_j(p^q, p, b_j) + T_j$$

(3.3)

Our main purpose in this section is to introduce price policies, stock adjustments and direct transfers. Although our focus will be on the subset of commodities to which the CAP applies, for simplicity of notation and to maintain vector notation, we do not distinguish between CAP and non-CAP commodities. This is possible because commodities for which there is say, only an import levy, can be treated as special cases. In this stylized version, we characterize the CAP as follows:

(a) Any surplus d is sold for intervention at given price level p^d [30]

$$d \geq 0 \perp p \geq p^d$$

(3.4a)

---

[28] The producer behaviour satisfies *Assumption P (producer)*: each producer supplies an output vector q_j using current inputs v_j and fixed resources b_j according to a transformation function $t_j: R^K \times R^K \times R^r \to R$, which is nondecreasing and strictly quasiconvex in $(q_j, -v_j)$; for given nonnegative prices p^q and p, the net revenue (or profit) function $\pi_j(p^q, p, b_j) = \max \; (p^q q_j - p v_j \mid t_j(q_j, -v_j, -b_j) \leq 0, q_j, v_j \geq 0)$ is compact-valued and nonnegative; it is positive whenever p^q is nonzero. Assumption P ensures that the producer (farmer or non-farmer) will always be able to derive positive income from his enterprise and that this income will eventually be bounded by the scale of the enterprise. In Section 4.3, this transformation function will be replaced by a set of constraints.

[29] The input price is taken to be equal to the market price.

[30] We use the notation $a \geq 0 \perp b \geq 0$ to represent $a \geq 0$, $b \geq 0$ and $ab = 0$.

(b)   A part of the surplus is exported, the remainder is kept in stock[31]

$$e = \tilde{e}(d) \tag{3.4b}$$

(c)   Imports are subject to a variable levy[32]

$$m \geq 0 \perp p \leq p^u \tag{3.4c}$$

(d)   The producer subsidy is fixed[33]

$$p^q = p + \zeta^q \tag{3.4d}$$

(e)   Transfers consist of grants received $T_j^0(p)$ minus a revenue tax[34]

$$T_j = T_j^0(p) - \tau\pi_j(p^q, p, b_j) \tag{3.4e}$$

(f)   The EU budget balances[35]

$$p^d (d - e - s_0) + (p^d - p) s_0 + (p^d - p^e) e + \zeta^q \sum_j q_j +$$
$$\sum_j T_j - (p^u - p^m) m = 0 \tag{3.4f}$$

Finally, a commodity balance has to be imposed, which requires intra-EU markets to clear:[36]

$$\sum_j x_j + \sum_j v_j + d = \sum_j q_j + s_0 + m \tag{3.5}$$

---

[31] This is a policy dependent function, whereby part of the surplus is kept in stock to avoid dumping on the international market or because the prices are expected to rise in the future. Sales of initial stocks on the intra-EU market may be accounted for by allowing for negative export values.

[32] Hence, the domestic price is equal to the given value p^u whenever a commodity is imported.

[33] The subsidy will be negative for excise taxes, like co-responsibility levies. The subsidy may also be taken to be proportional to prices p but in this stylized model we impose nominal price rigidities as they appear in the CAP.

[34] $T_j^0(p)$ is a given non-negative income transfer; this function is homogeneous of degree one in p.

[35] Value of stock increase + devaluation of initial stock + export refund + producer subsidy + direct income support - import levy = 0. Here all carryover stock is written off in one year; in ECAM stocks are valued at a book price.

[36] Note that there is no explicit demand for investment goods. For convenience, this demand is assumed to be included in x_j.

This completes the specification of model equations. The parameters and exogenous variables can be listed as:

p^d intervention price (stock purchase)
p^e (trade) export price
p^m (trade) import price
p^u tariff inclusive import price
ζ^q producer subsidy.

These prices are nonnegative and such that:

$$p^e \leq p^m$$
$$p^d \leq p^u.$$

Also given are:

b_j resources of j
s_0 initial stocks.

The stylized model is being solved for the variables:

d surplus
e exports
h_j consumer income
m imports
p market price
p^q producer price
q_j production by j
v_j input demand by j
x_j consumer demand by j
τ tax rate.

More formally, an allocation d^*, e^*, m^*, x_j^*, q_j^*, v_j^* supported by a price vector p^*, is an equilibrium solution of model (3.1)-(3.5). Under assumptions C and P,[37] this model has an equilibrium solution with (positive) prices p^*.[38]

If import prices are high and intervention prices are low, the commodity will not be imported or sold to intervention. Together, the EU budget balance, the complementarity conditions for prices and the commodity balance imply that the trade deficit will be zero: ($p^m m$ - $p^e e$ = 0).[39]

Based on the equilibrium values for a particular year, the resources b_j are updated (for instance to account for investments and for labour migration), policy parameters are adjusted and new initial stocks s_0 are computed, so that a solution can be obtained for the following year. In this way, a recursively dynamic scenario simulation can be performed. The scenario description will determine the time-path specified for the exogenous variables.

Consider, for example, a reduction in intervention price p^d. Unless this price is so low in (3.4a) that there are no sales to the intervention stock anyway, this will cause a loss to farmers, which may be compensated through an increase in direct income support ($T_j^0(p)$ in (3.4e)) or through an increase in producer subsidy (ζ^q).

3.1.2   The Negishi-format
The model (3.1)-(3.5) has the important property that its equilibrium solution will be consistent: individual consumers satisfy their budget constraint and total demand does not exceed supply. This is an advantage of using a general equilibrium model in a descriptive context. Another advantage is that the general equilibrium model has a clear normative content, which makes it possible to compare actual performance of agriculture under the CAP with a possible, less distorted situation. It is more convenient to conduct such welfare analysis after

---

[37] See footnotes 26 and 28.

[38] This is only ensured if income transfers $T_j^0(p)$ are sufficiently small to avoid the problem that the tax rate needed to finance it could make some consumer's income negative. A proof of existence could proceed as in Fischer et al. (1988), chapter 2.

[39] In ECAM we allow, of course, for the trade deficit to reach its historically observed value. If the tax rate is kept fixed, the condition of EU budget balance (3.4f) is relaxed, so that the trade deficit may be nonzero.

writing the stylized model in an alternative format, known as the Negishi-format (Negishi (1972)). We emphasize that this format is only an alternative mode of presentation of precisely the same model.

The Negishi-format specifies the general equilibrium model as a welfare program with an objective function that is linear in utility and that contains additional linear terms for indirect taxes (distortions).[40] These parameters are adjusted so as to satisfy restrictions specified outside the welfare program that depend on optimal values and Lagrange multipliers of this program. A usual restriction is that every consumer should satisfy his budget constraint.

The constraints represented within the program - the commodity balances, the transformation functions and the restriction on the trade deficit - define the space of feasible allocations. Hence, the welfare program may be written as:[41]

$$\max \sum_j \alpha_j u_j(x_j) - \xi^u m + \xi^d d + \xi^q \sum_j q_j$$
$$d, m, q_j, v_j, x_j \geq 0$$

subject to (3.6)

$$\sum_j x_j + \sum_j v_j + d = \sum_j q_j + s_0 + m \qquad (p)$$
$$p^m m \leq p^e \bar{e} \qquad (\rho)$$
$$t_j(q_j, -v_j, -b_j) \leq 0 \qquad (\psi_j)$$

Values of parameters ξ^q, ξ^d, ξ^u and $\bar{e}$ are chosen such that:

$\xi^q = \rho\zeta^q$	(producer subsidy)	
$\xi^d = \rho p^d$	(cost of intervention)	(3.7a)
$\xi^u = \rho(p^u - p^m)$	(import levy)	
$\bar{e} = \tilde{e}(d)$	(export function)	

and positive welfare weights α_j are such that every consumer satisfies his budget constraint, i.e. the value of consumption is equal to income after tax:

---

[40] For a representation of distortions in a welfare program see also Ginsburgh and Waelbroeck (1981) and Fischer et al. (1988), chapter 3.

[41] Variables in brackets on the right-hand side of the constraints denote Lagrange multipliers.

$$px_j = (1-\tau)\,\pi_j(p^q, p, b_j) + T_j^0(p) \qquad\qquad (3.7b)$$

where $\tau = 1 - \Sigma_j\,(px_j - T_j^0(p))/\Sigma_j\,\pi_j(p^q, p, b_j)$ is obtained from optimal values in (3.6).

Equations (3.7a)-(3.7b) define "feedback relations" to the welfare program (3.6): the parameters of program (3.6) are adjusted until these conditions are satisfied. We verify that the solution will be an equilibrium which fully coincides with the solution of (3.1)-(3.5). To show this, we assume differentiability of utility and transformation functions and write the Kuhn-Tucker conditions of (3.6) as:

(i) $\alpha_j\,\partial u_j/\partial x_j \le p$ $\perp$ $x_j \ge 0$

(ii) $\xi^q + p \le \psi_j\,\partial t_j/\partial q_j\ \perp$ $q_j \ge 0$

(iii) $\psi_j\,\partial t_j/\partial v_j \le p$ $\perp$ $v_j \ge 0$

(iv) $p \le \xi^u + \rho p^m$ $\perp$ $m \ge 0$

(v) $\xi^d \le p$ $\perp$ $d \ge 0$

Condition (i) is a first-order condition for the consumer; (ii) and (iii) are first-order conditions for the producer. Welfare weights can be scaled so that $\rho = 1$. Then, appending restrictions (3.7) to these first-order conditions, one finds that (3.1)-(3.5) and (3.6)-(3.7) are equivalent: they define the same model in two different formats. Format (3.1)-(3.5) is often referred to as the Arrow-Debreu format[42] and format (3.6)-(3.7) as the Negishi-format.

3.2 Free trade

The Negishi-format is particularly suited for welfare analysis because it provides a convenient format to express the two Welfare Theorems (Section 3.2.1) and because it makes it possible to formulate reforms of the CAP that would, under the assumptions of the stylized model, yield welfare improving results (Section 3.2.2).

---

[42] This is the format that is commonly used in theory (see e.g. Arrow and Hahn (1971)).

3.2.1 The Welfare Theorems

As discussed in the previous chapter, agricultural economists have often opted for a free trade perspective and pointed to the welfare cost of the CAP. In their view support to agriculture is at best justified to maintain an equitable income redistribution, but in that case support should be given through a lump sum transfer and not through prices. In this section, we first repeat the classical arguments against protection and then discuss several lines of theoretical investigation which lead to less radical conclusions: conditions may prevail under which support to agriculture is not only required for social equity but also for economic efficiency.

To introduce the Welfare Theorems, we use the model (3.6)-(3.7), keeping all the ξ-terms in (3.6) equal to zero. Then, if one also assumes all surplus to be exported ($e = d$) the model reduces to:

$$\max \Sigma_j \, \alpha_j \, u_j(x_j)$$
$$e, m, q_j, v_j, x_j \geq 0$$

subject to (3.8)

$$\Sigma_j \, x_j + \Sigma_j \, v_j + e = \Sigma_j \, q_j + s_0 + m \qquad (p)$$
$$p^m m - p^e e \leq 0 \qquad (\rho)$$
$$t_j(q_j, - v_j, - b_j) \leq 0 \qquad (\psi_j)$$

for welfare weights α_j such that:

$$px_j = (1-\tau) \, \pi_j(p^q, p, b_j) + T_j^0(p) \qquad (3.9)$$

Now, under assumptions P and C, the First and Second Welfare Theorem hold:
(i) Any competitive equilibrium is Pareto-efficient.
(ii) Any Pareto-efficient allocation can be obtained in a decentralized way as a competitive equilibrium, with transfers among consumers.

There are also two useful corollaries.

(iii) Any welfare optimum in (3.8) is Pareto-efficient.

(iv) The welfare optimum (3.8) defines a competitive equilibrium with transfers.

Points (i)-(iv) summarize the basic relations between welfare optimality, Pareto-efficiency and competitive equilibrium, as implied by the Welfare Theorems. The Welfare Theorems have far-reaching policy implications, also for the CAP. Originally, most attention was given to the first theorem which shows that a competitive equilibrium possesses specific properties. Since many economists considered the competitive assumptions to be unrealistic, they did not find the first welfare theorem a very powerful tool. Over the past decade or two, attention has shifted to the second theorem, which implies that the rather uncontroversial problem of welfare maximization, restricted by assumptions on preferences and technology, can only be decentralized through prices if the agents behave competitively. In view of the generally perceived need for decentralization through markets, economists could now turn the assumptions on competitive behaviour, the realism of which they previously had a hard time defending, into powerful policy guidelines: competitive conditions should be created, if they did not exist already.

If the underlying assumptions are accepted, the welfare theorems have the following consequences for government policy :

(a) Price fixing, say by a government, cannot yield a Pareto-superior outcome when compared with a situation without such an intervention. This is the basis for the free trade arguments.

(b) Income transfers to consumers may be desirable socially (Second Welfare Theorem) but Pareto-efficiency can be maintained without such transfers; such transfers should be given through a direct payment, not through price intervention.

(c) There is no need to support producers. Any producer who makes a loss at competitive prices should not produce, and anyone who can make a profit should be allowed to produce as much as he likes. Thus, there should be no subsidies, no production quotas, no constraints on the utilization of land etc.

(d) Producers should maximize profit. Any rule of conduct that is incompatible with profit maximization is Pareto-inefficient. Therefore, only future profits matter; losses or debt incurred in the past should not affect producer decisions.

These are strong and clear guidelines, which essentially advocate free competition. They have exercised decisive influence on policy advice currently given by economists.

3.2.2   Welfare improving reforms

The model (3.8)-(3.9) describes an extreme case without any distortion, whereas in welfare program (3.6) distortions enter through ξ-terms in the objective. Moreover, there is a restriction on exports in (3.6) which does not appear in (3.8). Therefore, the optimal value of $\sum_j \alpha_j u_j(x_j)$ will, for the same α_j's, tend to be higher (and never lower) in (3.8) than in (3.6). This shows the (weak) Pareto-superiority of non-intervention. The Negishi-formulation makes it possible to specify a piecemeal reform that does not eliminate all distortions and that allows one to compensate all losers. To compute these compensation payments, we can solve model (3.6)-(3.7) prior to reform and then introduce the prevailing utilities as lower bounds on the utilities of all consumers except consumer 1 and bring their welfare weights to zero. This generates a program which maximizes $\alpha_1 u_1(x_1)$ plus the ξ-terms in the objective of (3.6). Now consider a proportional reduction of all these ξ-terms. This will usually lead to an increase in $\alpha_1 u_1(x_1)$ and never to a reduction. Hence, such a proportional reduction of all ξ-terms is a (weakly) Pareto-improving reform, even if it is piecemeal. This provides in addition to the policy conclusions from the Welfare Theorems, a technique for specifying welfare improving, partial reforms that start from distorted conditions, such as those created by the CAP.

3.3 Interventionism

So far, our discussion has followed the straight path of welfare analysis and arrived at conclusions that support the free trade perspective. However, although the Welfare Theorems have often been invoked in support of free trade policies, they merely prove the equivalence between a centralized allocation and a (decentralized) competitive equilibrium. Formally, they justify intervention through quantity rationing as much as free trade. We will now present welfare theoretical arguments in favour of intervention. These are formulated as objections against particular assumptions of the competitive model. These objections in turn result in a rejection of some of the guidelines of Section 3.2.1 and hence of the free trade position. Although all interventionists do not necessarily advocate support to agriculture, here we shall pursue our discussion of Section 2.5.2 and restrict attention to those who do. We group their arguments into three categories.

First, interventionists have often expressed their doubt that support can be given through transfers, without high administrative costs. They assert that price support, as it exists under the CAP, may be more efficient than direct transfers. We shall see in Section 3.3.1 that such a price policy does not necessarily cause misallocation of resources. For this, we present a modification of the stylized model in which substitutability is restricted so much that no welfare loss occurs. We also show that if there only is substitution on the production side, then production quotas can restore efficiency.

Secondly, a competitive equilibrium may be inefficient if there are external effects, and may not even exist if there are indivisibilities. In Section 3.3.2, we discuss how taxes and quotas can be used to restore efficiency in such cases.

Finally, the competitive equilibrium assumes that all agents take prices as given and according to the Welfare Theorems they should, but what if the others do not follow this rule of conduct? Producers on other sectors may be able to restrict their supply or segment markets. Governments in other countries may keep on protecting their agricultural or some other sector. Even in the GATT negotiations on free trade policy changes towards free trade are often used as 'commodities' to be exchanged at the best possible price against concessions in other sectors. In Section 3.3.3 we briefly review the arguments for intervention that are derived from the theory of imperfect competition and from the 'new' theory of international trade, which basically says that as long as other sectors and countries do not operate according to the rules of perfect competition

European agriculture may perhaps be well advised to deviate from these rule also.

3.3.1 Price policies and quotas to avoid direct transfers

Drawbacks of direct transfers

The reasons for preferring price support above direct income transfers may be summarized as follows. First, price policies are generally believed to be more easily implemented and administrated than lump sum transfers. The administrative cost of tax collection and of redistribution to the intended recipients may be substantial. Price policies do not require registration of information about individual producers or consumers. Secondly, few direct transfers are truly lump sum. Income tax, for example, is not on the availability of manpower (employment plus leisure) but only on employment. It thus operates like an excise tax on labour supply and amounts to a price intervention that may be more distorting than, say, a subsidy on food exports.[43] Finally, direct transfers to farmers are far more visible to the consumer/taxpayer than an implicit price subsidy that results from border protection, especially when it is a levy on imports. Of course, this point does not give a welfare theoretical justification but it is most likely the main reason why in the past farmers organizations have been so reluctant in accepting schemes of direct income support.

Efficient price policies

Under the assumptions of the Welfare Theorems price policies will in general cause inefficiencies. However, under specific, albeit restrictive assumptions, they may not cause any inefficiency, so that they can be used to achieve

---

[43] Nonetheless, some transfers are lump sum: for example, profits from state-owned firms that are redistributed to households on the basis of, say, age or past events are in principle lump sum. In the ECAM-scenarios - particularly the decoupling scenario in Chapter 6 - transfers will be specified in this way.

distributional objectives. To show this, we amend the stylized model (3.1)-(3.5) as follows. First, assume that the consumer is so wealthy that his food consumption is perfectly inelastic, i.e. that it appears as part of committed demand $\bar{x}_j$ and that food demand in excess of commitment does not raise utility, for all consumers except consumer 1 (all additional income is spent on non-food items). The consumer problem (3.1) may then be written as:

$$\max u_j(x_j - \bar{x}_j)$$
$$x_j \geq \bar{x}_j$$

subject to   (3.1′)

$$px_j \leq h_j$$

where $\bar{x}_j$ is a given, nonnegative commitment. For this consumer it does not matter whether income redistribution to farmers is achieved through an income tax or through a higher consumer price.

Secondly, we turn to the producer. The sectoral profit function $\pi_j(p^q, p, b_j)$ as specified in (3.2) may also be obtained from profit maximization by several farms. We consider, for every j, n_i farms of type i, $i \in I_j$, which compete for resources b_j:

$$\pi_j(p^q, p, b_j) =$$
$$\max \Sigma_{i \in I_j} \pi_i(p^q, p, r_i/n_i)n_i$$
$$r_i \geq 0, n_i \geq 0, \text{ all } i \in I_j$$

subject to   (3.10)

$$\Sigma_{i \in I_j} r_i \leq b_j$$

where π_i is the restricted profit function of farm type i with fixed factor r_i/n_i, $\pi_i(.)$ is taken to be homogeneous and concave, nondecreasing in resources,[44] and where:

r_i the vector of resources used by farms of type i

---

[44] Note that n_i enters like a costless input.

n_i the number of farms of type i, which is set endogenously and taken to be real-valued,

p   the vector of input prices,

p^q the vector of output prices,

b_j the given resource availability.

Under the prevailing assumptions, the profitable farms will produce and the unprofitable ones will not, as is required by the welfare theorem. This picture remains unaffected when we introduce (possibly discounted) setup cost, $c_i(p)$ incurred independently of the scale of production, to be subtracted as $n_i \, c_i(p)$, an additional term in the objective of the program. Higher setup cost will lead to a smaller number of firms, i.e. to concentration, but otherwise the welfare propositions remain valid, as long as the number of farms n_i is real-valued (this amounts to a perfect divisibility assumption that will be relaxed below).

Now assume that the choice of the individual producer is constrained to the extreme: farm-group i owns given stocks of physical assets k_i, which it may use, rent out, or leave idle, with a fixed input demand γ_i, yielding a fixed output mix β_i; program (3.10) now becomes:

$$\pi_j(p^q, p, b_j) =$$
$$\max \Sigma_{i \in I_j} \, \pi_i n_i$$
$$n_i \geq 0, \text{ all } i \in I_j$$

subject to   (3.11)

$$\Sigma_{i \in I_j} \, k_i n_i \leq b_j \qquad\qquad (\mu)$$

for given unit profits $\pi_i = p^q \beta_i - p \gamma_i - c_i(p)$ for all $i \in I_j$.

Problem (3.11) is a linear program with activities n_i that will leave idle (i.e. set $n_i = 0$) all farm types that make losses (have negative π_i) and possibly also some farms that use the resources less effectively. Note that nontradeable resources can be represented by defining farm-type specific entries in b_j and k_i. The first-order conditions imply:

$\pi_i = \mu k_i$ whenever a farm type is active ($n_i > 0$)   (3.12a)

and

$\pi_i \le \mu k_i$ otherwise ($n_i = 0$)   (3.12b)

Consider now a solution at free trade prices for outputs and inputs. We introduce a subsidy on value added i.e. we tax inputs and subsidize outputs at a flat rate τ. This will obviously lead to a rise in farm income, at the rate τ. In (3.12a) shadow prices μ will also rise at this rate and in (3.12b) the same set of firms will remain inactive.

In short, the modified stylized model (3.1′, 3.11, 3.3-3.5) shows that if there is no substitution within every firm's technology and within every consumer's utility from food, it is possible to provide income support through price subsidies without distorting the allocations.

Moreover, all resources in the vector b_j are farm-type specific, a farm will be fully active as soon as its net profit π_i is positive. In this case any type of price support can be given without causing distortions, as long as it does not make profits positive for an otherwise unprofitable farm.

Of course, the non-substitution assumptions made here are extreme. However, empirical studies of price liberalization (see Goldin and Knudsen (1990)) have only found modest welfare gains and advocates of price support to agriculture often invoke the limited scope for substitution. In the EU the consumer demand for food is price inelastic and the share of foodstuffs in total household expenditures is modest (15.1 per cent for the EU-12 in 1990, exclusive of beverages and tobacco).[45] The EU farmer has little choice in the short run because rotation constraints as well as past investments in specialized equipment restrict his options. Perhaps more importantly, the labour supply and the land availability are inelastic in the short term.

Although these points suggest that the welfare gains from liberalization will be limited, they do not settle the issue because it is generally recognized that there is significant substitution among animal feeds and within product groups, and because agricultural price policies may lead to over-investment in

---

[45] Source: CEC (1992) *The Agricultural Situation in the Community.*

agriculture. Also, as indicated in Table 2.13 the opportunities to combine family employment outside agriculture with the farming activity may not be as limited as is often believed.

Quantity constraints to correct for price distortions

Even when the non-substitution assumptions do not hold, channelling income support via the producer price will not cause inefficiencies, provided the appropriate quantity constraints (quotas) are introduced. In terms of program (3.10), solving it at first-best prices yields net supplies for each farm-type that can be used as quotas. Solving it again, but now at subsidized prices and with quota constraints will lead to the same allocation, e.g. if the subsidy rate is the same for all activities. But other schemes are also possible, like setting the quota at a lower (infra-marginal) level based for example on production in a previous year. Then, if the planner's model is correct, and if there is no direct effect of income on production, the producer will base his production decision on the marginal returns that prevail at first-best prices, and there will be no distortion.

Another reason for using quotas arises when price signals cannot be given. The Welfare Theorems in fact prove the equivalence between a central allocation through quotas (the welfare program) and a competitive equilibrium. Hence, they also justify quantity rationing. Clearly, those in favour of policy interventions on food markets in the EU will rarely go as far as proposing that the consumer should be rationed. Their proposals for introducing quotas will usually be restricted to the spheres of production and international trade.

The quotas can take various forms. They may be expressed as bounds in quantity terms that are imposed on individual producers and that no producer should exceed. They may also take the form of what is known in the EU as a maximum guaranteed quantity (see Tangermann (1989) and De Gorter and Meilke (1989)), a two-price system whereby the producer receives a high guaranteed price for quantities up to the quota limit and a (prohibitively) low price for production in excess of the quota. Such schemes are in principle all equivalent methods of rationing the individual producer, though the practical implementation is not the same for all schemes.

Of course, there are many difficulties in the modalities of implementation of quantity rationing schemes: how to measure the level of output for commodities like feeds that are produced on the farm itself; how to avoid producers selling on the market output in excess of the quota ('black milk') and how to ensure that output supplied by a producer originates from his land, if the consumer price is above world market level. As an aside we mention that, if there is price support and efficiency is maintained through producer specific quotas, a reform that makes the quotas tradeable among producers will in general cause inefficiencies to occur, and not bring a welfare gain. This is because if subsidized prices are 'arbitrary' relative to the first-best prices and quotas become tradeable, essentially non-productive assets become valuable and this may lead (see (3.10)) to a restructuring that further orients the allocations according to the 'wrong' prices. In practice, the policy change also creates new collaterals and this will favour producers with large initial assets. Moreover, it promotes the outflow of revenue from agriculture via inheritance and outmigration.

However, the main problem with quotas is that it is virtually impossible for the authorities to compute their levels correctly, that is in an optimal way.[46] This is a basic weakness of many interventionist views. Whereas a free trader makes proposals to improve procedures and institutions (markets should exist, property rights respected, monopoly avoided, excise taxes should be reduced etc.), interventionists often find themselves in the more vulnerable position where they have to prove that the proposed levels of taxes, subsidies and quotas are indeed optimal .

3.3.2   Interventions to cope with external effects and indivisibilities

External effects

---

[46] The implementation of an infra-marginal scheme is somewhat easier but in this case there is an equity problem. Giving a high price for a small initial quota say, the milk production of the first cow, is like an equal lump sum transfer to all dairy farmers. But if the quota is larger, small farmers receive less.

Interventions through taxes, subsidies and quotas are not only imposed as a substitute for direct transfers but also as additional signals to maintain Pareto-efficiency in the presence of external effects. Here we consider the two situations which are particularly relevant for environmental policies: non-excludability and non-rivalry.

Excludability is ensured if it is possible to exclude those who do not pay from enjoying the commodity (no theft or self-service). Non-rivalry means that the commodity does benefit several consumers at the same time. The farmer who pollutes the groundwater with manure from his livestock operation, uses a natural resource. This usually causes an excludability problem, because the farmer does not have to go to the market to obtain access to the groundwater resource that he uses up. He can use the groundwater freely unless emission constraints are effectuated (either through taxes or through quotas) and this obviously requires extensive and costly monitoring. If this makes the transaction costs very high it will not be possible to achieve decentralization through competitive markets and intervention will be needed.

The requirement of rivalry is not satisfied when many users benefit at the same time from a given demand. The 'visual services' rendered by landscapes are to some extent non-rival, but not fully, as many visitors of overcrowded tourist resorts may report. The property of non-rivalry appears in a clear way in relation to environmental awareness. Many find resource depletion a discomforting thought and derive utility merely from the knowledge that natural resources are being conserved (the same stock of resources enters the utility function of several agents and is not used up in the process). For non-rival goods, competitive markets cannot be organized since the consumer cannot buy the commodity as an individual.

In the EU, these problems have led governments to approve extensive environmental regulation and monitoring mechanisms. The farmer is increasingly seen as a polluter who has to pay rather than being supported. On the other hand, he is also seen as the keeper of the rural landscape who should be rewarded for his services. However, since there is no market for environmental services, it is difficult to determine the desirable level of these payments. In such a vacuum, the earlier 'green' lobby for higher agricultural prices could transform itself into an equally green lobby for higher environmental prices,[47] this time without any foreign competitors to provide a yardstick for the calculation of the implicit subsidy. These difficulties are not only problematic for the interventionists. They also undermine the position of the free traders, because when markets are missing for some commodities, price liberalization may exacerbate the misallocation of resources and create a false illusion of increased efficiency, with less farmers and higher value added per farmer as biased indicators.

In principle all these problems can be addressed by taxes as substitutes for market prices and in the longer term by creating markets for environmental resources. In this respect there is not much disagreement between the free traders and the interventionists. Yet environmentalists often disregard the more fundamental problem concerning the distribution of property rights over environmental resources among individuals. The taxes attribute a price paid for the use of natural resources, but paid to whom? Agricultural policies tend to identify the farmer and the government as sole beneficiaries: the farmer enjoys a tax rebate that redistributes part of the proceeds from environmental taxes to the polluter (to avoid massive bankruptcy) and the government receives the remainder. This implies that the farmers and the government are seen as the rightful owners of the groundwater, fresh air, etc., and such a view should at least be subject to political debate (see also Keyzer and Tims (1994)).

Indivisibility of the farm

Interventions are also needed when there are important indivisibilities in technology. In agriculture, the indivisibility of the farm may have to be accounted for. The indivisibility can be represented in the modified stylized

---

[47] There is more at stake than the payment for the use of natural resources within the EU, because 'fair' competition has to be maintained between domestic producers who operate in an environmentally friendly way or who pay for the damage which they cause and foreign producers who do not. The current WTO rules do not permit the use of an import tariff as a corrective measure, but 'eco'-labelling whereby the consumers receive information on the mode of production is not excluded. However, under the guise of product information, this may introduce a new type of protectionism that could be very harmful to developing countries that cannot comply with all the standards and even if they do, cannot prove it.

model (3.1', 3.11, 3.3 - 3.5) through the integer-valuedness of n_i. Of course, if the number of identical farms in each farm-type is large, the approximation of the integer variable n_i by a real number makes little difference and the problem of indivisibility can possibly be disregarded. However, it is not obvious that many farms belong to the same group i, because of the heterogeneity introduced by the spatial nature of land: even two farms with identical equipment and land quality distribution are located at different places. If one of the two decides to give up its operations, the other may not be interested in buying the land, unless the parcel is adjacent to the own farm.[48] Indivisibility may create serious efficiency problems particularly when many farmers decide to terminate their operations, as may be the case in the aftermath of a reform.

Once the variable n_i is treated as an integer, problem (3.10) becomes a mixed integer program. Then, profit maximization by the individual farm may not lead to an equilibrium: non-profitable farms would wish to cease their operations, but once inactive they might face factor prices at which it would seem attractive to produce.[49]

In the optimum of a centralized profit maximization (like in (3.10)), or of a social welfare maximization, some farms would be closed and some land consolidation transactions would be performed. A decentralized solution would also provide lump sum subsidies that should help covering the setup costs of socially desirable farms that are not profitable. A welfare program can thus be seen to come up with regional programs of farm restructuring, that may be supplemented with some direct income support.

Unfortunately, the extent to which local indivisibilities do in fact justify support is not well understood as yet and is known to depend heavily on the specifics of the farms considered. At any rate, the argument does not justify price support: any transfer should be given lump sum. Setup costs only amplify the distortion resulting from price support (and from compensation per hectare as given under the MacSharry reform). The support will raise the rents on

---

[48] The indivisibility occurs if setup costs have to be incurred on the parcels, otherwise it is possible to treat n_i as a real variable.

[49] Hence, the problem is that equilibrium may fail to exist, not that a given equilibrium would be inefficient.

factors and distort resource allocation even further, intertemporally and among sectors. To reach more specific conclusions a spatially disaggregated analysis is required which in detail describes the technology and the setup costs of individual farms. ECAM is not equipped for this task, be it in its stylized or in its detailed form. Yet the welfare theoretic framework has the virtue of expressing the micro-issue of land fragmentation in the same terms as the sectoral issue of CAP reform and to indicate relations between the two.

Indivisibility of rural households

The indivisibility of the (farm) household may also have important implications. Development economists have learned to recognize poverty traps. Impoverishment at regional level will often be characterized by a deterioration of capital stocks, infrastructure and limited innovation which by itself leads to a downward spiral of depression. Keynesian theory has emphasized the importance of such mechanisms and a sudden fall in agricultural prices would definitely depress rural areas in the short term. The welfare theorems would suggest to cure this through greater price flexibility and factor mobility: let labour move out of the depressed areas and shift to more profitable activities.

This neglects the positive relationship between labour productivity and consumption that used to be central in the nineteenth century classical tradition that sees labour as a produced factor and consumption as an input. Then, it is not only true that consumption is high because labour productivity is high but the converse also holds. This relationship was examined in what has become known as the efficiency wage theory (see Stiglitz (1976), Dasgupta and Ray (1986)). We feel that the concept is relevant in the debate on the future of European agriculture because it provides a theoretical framework for the view that a drastic fall in farm prices could eventually hamper farm (labour) productivity. Impoverished rural areas would also lose their capacity for innovation.

However, the theory does not conclude that government should always subsidize poor regions. In terms of the stylized model, the efficiency wage relation may be represented as follows. The transformation function would depend on consumption of the farm household. As before, we assume that the transformation function is strictly quasiconvex, nondecreasing in its arguments. The household model is now:

$$\max u_j(x_j)$$
$$x_j, q_j, v_j \geq 0, \pi_j$$

subject to

$$px_j \leq (1-\tau) \, \pi_j + T_j^0(p)$$
$$\pi_j = p^q q_j - pv_j$$
$$t_j(q_j, - v_j, - b_j, - x_j) \leq 0$$

In the absence of taxes ($T_j^0(p) = 0$ and $p^q = p$) the farm household will be able to look after itself: it will anticipate the productive effect of its consumption and this leads to an efficient allocation in which no support is needed for efficiency reasons, whatever the price level.

In case the farm household has to give up a significant part (here τ) of its income, say for taxes or for servicing of past debt, its consumption may reach some critical level below which Pareto-efficiency is lost. Then, an income supplement (say a tax-waiver or subsidized education) would allow the farmer to improve his labour productivity and lead to Pareto-superior outcomes. Moreover, even in the absence of income taxes, indivisibilities of the farmer's household may cause setup costs that are similar to those of the farm as a production unit and in this case the earlier discussion on indivisibilities applies: transfers and regulated access may be necessary even when tax rates are not very high.

As in the indivisibility of the farm, the main problem in dealing with indivisibilities in the household is that it requires solving a very detailed model in which all agents are represented separately. This, of course, cannot be implemented on a real world scale. The theory only serves to provide archetype illustrations of the type of interventions that may be required. It does not lead to models from which socially optimal policies can be derived.

3.3.3   Imperfect competition

The welfare theorems assume that all agents take prices as given. This means that they do not have the power (or do not use the power) to behave as monopolists. Farmers in the EU have often advocated price support to agriculture as a second-best policy to rebalance relative prices with respect to monopolistic non-agricultural sectors, particularly the input supplying and output processing sectors which link agriculture to the rest of the economy, and to achieve 'fair' competition with other countries.

Of course, farmers incomes could benefit from a market protection that would enable them to operate as a cartel with supply controls on the production and the import side, with the EU consumer as the main loser. The CAP itself has sometimes been described in this way and in Chapter 6 we shall follow that route but here we ask the question whether imperfect competition could benefit the EU in its totality, including its consumers, and perhaps even be Pareto-improving for the world as a whole. In other words, is there any justified reason for deviating from the rule that all governments should see to it that everyone operates under perfect competition, taking prices as given and abstaining from any action that seeks to influence price levels. In the international trade literature, the advocates of imperfect competition have seen their numbers rise spectacularly in the past decade. Here we can only give a brief sketch of the issues involved.

Cournot competition

Traditional theory of (Cournot) imperfect competition has argued that large exporters should perhaps levy an export tax in order to restrict the supply by their own producers and make the foreign customers pay more. Although, in reality, agricultural exporters tend to subsidize rather than tax their exports, the set-aside schemes and the production quotas on sugar and dairy in the CAP are intended indeed to limit exports. Whether such a policy will be effective depends on the reaction of the importers and on the relative size of the exporter. Theoretically, the importers could retaliate by taxing imports in order to capture part of the rent on quotas. Bagwell and Staiger (1990) show that such a strategy may lead to an outcome of complete autarky.

For food products this is a most unlikely sequence of events. Export taxes would raise international prices and subsequent import taxes would increase the domestic price even more. Then social pressures would call for an import subsidy rather than a tax. As to the relative size, a small exporter cannot expect his supply restriction to have a significant impact. As was seen in Section 3.2, commodity taxes, tariffs and quotas will not bring welfare gains, relative to the free trade situation, to the country that imposes them. Although, for many products, the EU has become a relatively important player on the international markets (recall Table (2.17) in Section 2.3.7), it hardly has monopoly power because even for products like dairy, where the EU's market share is quite significant, the competing exporters could eventually fill the gap if EU exports fall. Hence, a unilaterally imposed export quota is not an effective instrument to raise international prices.

Chamberlin competition

The 'new' international trade theory tries to explain why exporters tend to subsidize. Some authors focus on monopolistic (Chamberlin) competition between exporters whereby these try to increase their market share by reducing the price. In their widely debated article Brander and Spencer (1988) show that a subsidy may be the best choice for the exporting country. However, the outcomes from models of imperfect competition crucially depend on the assumptions made with respect to preferences, technology and anticipations. Neary (1994) describes a model of a subsidy game in which it appears that only firms that would be profitable without export subsidies should receive support.

More generally, the competing exporter can be expected to react in order to maintain his share. For example, the EU has in the past used its export refunds to augment its market share, but this has been a very costly proposition. In fact it was little more than a way to dispose of surpluses, that failed to achieve any reduction in export volumes by the competitors. Quite on the contrary, as a reaction the US created an Export Enhancement Program (USDA

(1988)) to match the EU policy. The clients were obviously the main winners in the process.

Market segmentation

Another strand of imperfect competition literature focuses on market segmentation. If there is no perfect substitute on the demand side and the sector has to produce with significant setup costs, then producers should seek market segmentation and sell at a high price on selected, smaller segments in order to cover the setup costs and at low prices on other, large segments in order to exploit the returns to scale. Such a policy is proposed, in particular for high-tech products (Japanese electronics are often taken as an example), because of their high setup costs in research and development and their spin-offs to other sectors in the economy (Tyson (1992) and Salvatore (1993)). The national government can help the market segmentation by restricting access to the domestic market through import quotas and other barriers. This maintains competition between the producers with setup costs but at the same time enables them to recoup a significant part of their setup costs from the domestic consumer.

For EU agriculture this line of reasoning is of lesser relevance, again because agricultural exports have almost perfect foreign substitutes. However, there are some similarities. One may interpret the CAP as charging the domestic consumer of agricultural products for the setup up costs of the rural households and the rural infrastructure.

The creation of free trade zones (like NAFTA in North America and the expanded EU in Europe) is also in full accordance with 'new trade' theory, since in this context free trade only means that impediments on bilateral trade are reduced. It is a step towards a customs union (harmonization of trade barriers with respect to third countries) and eventually an economic union (policy on fair competition) but it does not lead to abolishment of protection against imports from third countries: the larger the domestic market that is being charged a high price, the more the high-tech firm can exploit its returns to scale.

Managing trade negotiations and reforms

So far, we have only mentioned arguments providing gains to the country that practices imperfect competition. According to the new trade literature, trade policy may also serve as an instrument to make the markets more competitive because threatening with an import restriction can break a deadlock in trade negotiations, and ensure that all parties abide by the agreed rules of competition. This is known as 'managed trade' sometimes also known under the euphemism of 'fair trade'. The adherents of managed trade view trade negotiations as a marketplace where everyone is trying to obtain the highest return on concessions: access to the home market for one high-tech commodity say, Japanese electronics, may be traded for access of US rice to the Japanese market. They see it as an important limitation of the Second Welfare Theorem and the associated free trade view that it only expresses an ideal that may be announced as a final aim at the beginning of trade negotiations but that does not specify how negotiations should be conducted.

To the general public, the Uruguay Round has indeed made the impression of an immensely tedious, interminable process. This has been especially frustrating for powerful nations. During the Round they were not able to exercise their power through sanctions, because this would spoil the climate of the negotiations, while after the negotiations they are bound by the agreement that has been reached and cannot use their power either. When the agreement that was eventually reached is violated, sanctions can only be effectuated after elaborate procedures for settling disputes. Moreover, in the GATT context every country always has the option to apply non-tariff barriers for some time and wait until others retaliate or the GATT panels force it to lift the barrier. Hungerford (1991) shows that it may be optimal for a country to pursue such a strategy.

The difficulties in reaching and enforcing multilateral agreements have contributed to the popularity of bilateral managed trade, particularly for the powerful as it enables them to conclude bilateral treaties and retaliate promptly to impose sanctions when there is a violation. However, it is not clear that the managed trade approach works better. Sanctions may provoke retaliation, whereas the Uruguay Round Agreement seeks to limit such a spiraling process through detailed and binding rules and procedures for settling disputes and for imposing sanctions, within an agreed time-calendar.[50] If these prove effective, bilateralism will become less tempting. What remains is that agriculture is now an intrinsic element of trade negotiations. Liberalization of agricultural trade will in the future not only depend on the conditions that prevail on agricultural markets, and policy measures may be implemented for agricultural commodities that serve objectives for other markets.

Implications for the CAP

We conclude that the 'new' theory of imperfect competition and international trade may go a long way in describing how the CAP operates in practice. Clearly, the CAP may be viewed as an arrangement of market segmentation between the European consumer, the high price zone, and the foreign consumer, the low price zone. In this arrangement the quotas on production and the set-aside schemes serve to control exports to avoid oligopoly wars with competing exporters. The prohibitive import tariffs (the so-called Community preference) do not only enable the Community to shield off foreign competition, they also provide the opportunity for granting import quotas on preferential terms (i.e. with lower tariffs) as part of trade negotiations. Hence, the system equips the Community with a rather powerful set of instruments that has evoked the image of a 'Fortress Europe'. Be this as it may, in the end the price is paid by the European consumer and by the foreign exporter who is denied access or has to pay an import levy. In spite of all the sophisticated arguments, the 'new' theory fails to provide a satisfactory justification for price support. As far as agriculture is concerned Fortress Europe is strong but inefficient.[51]

---

[50] See Section 5.3.6 for a further discussion of these procedures.

[51] For other sectors the image of the Fortress seems less appropriate. Grilli (1995) shows that its walls are porous because in spite of various protective measures and of the recession in the early nineties, the imports from third countries have increased significantly. Moreover, the policy measures to protect a specific non-agricultural product do not consist of tariff walls but of highly targeted anti-dumping actions that are 'laser beam-actions' against a particular country or firm that should serve as deterrent for others (Messerlin (1995)).

3.4 The bureaucratic perspective

A sequence of corrective actions

We have surveyed various arguments in favour of interventions other than lump sum transfers. There could be price support if substitution is limited or if lump sum transfers are costly. Quantity constraints could be added to the package to correct for price distortions, to cope with external effects and indivisibilities in the farm technology as well as in the farm household. Yet the discussion inescapably points to a basic problem of every interventionist approach, which is that one does not know how to determine the optimal levels for taxes, subsidies, quotas and transfers. It is now generally accepted that even the most refined and elaborate optimization model does not allow to compute these values accurately.

The officials who originally formulated the CAP have never claimed that its policy instruments would lead to first-best outcomes. The CAP has been developed within a bureaucratic perspective as a sequence of corrective steps that introduced new instruments to correct for undesirable consequences of earlier ones, navigating between free trade and interventionism. The CAP started with a price policy as a means to support farm incomes but the non-substitution conditions of Section 3.3.1 did not hold and higher farm prices triggered an increase in supply that had to be disposed of in some way. Initially, the CAP used foreign trade as the main adjustment mechanism, first reducing its imports of cereals and bovine meat and gradually turning into an exporter. Short term imbalances were absorbed by intervention stocks. As the foreign markets became increasingly satiated, quantity constraints were added to the arsenal of instruments, for dairy and more recently via set-asides for oilseeds and cereals. Finally, food surpluses, budgetary pressures and trade conflicts brought about reforms that took the free trade arguments more seriously. In the bureaucratic perspective this is only a natural sequence of gradual corrections.

Policy scientists who have studied the CAP can offer a multitude of explanations as to why the policy has been so complex and its change so slow by pointing to the various interest groups and to the need for compromise. Here we will pursue our discussion from the welfare theoretic angle and abstain from trying to explain policy through interest group politics as is commonly done in the 'public choice'-literature (see e.g. Mueller (1989) or Swinnen and Van der Zee (1993)). We take the CAP as given and do not try to arrive at an endogenous representation of the political processes that led to it.

Gradualism or shock therapy?

Whereas the bureaucratic perspective always tends to opt for gradualism, the Welfare Theorems in principle advocate shock therapy whereby the first-best conditions are brought about at once. Shock therapy has often been advocated in the context of economic reform of the formerly centrally planned economies. Some free traders use the same arguments in relation to CAP-reform.

The reforms of centrally planned economies require a transition to a completely new legislative system. The task of designing a system that meets the needs of a particular country is gigantic and cannot be successful if the rules change permanently. Also, investors have to make long term decisions and cannot do so if price distortions are extreme. Finally, the pre-reform situation is characterized by huge consumer subsidies that are largely covered through money creation. The resulting inflation cannot be stopped unless all the subsidies are cut drastically. Then, gradualism is hardly an option.

To express this argument in terms of the stylized model, we must consider the dynamics of the variables and interpret this model in a multi-period context. So far, we have only presented the model (3.1)-(3.5) in a static, single-period context, with given resource levels b_j. Under the intertemporal interpretation, there is a finite time horizon T and commodities carry a time index $t = 1, ..., T$. Consumers make intertemporal plans at the beginning of $t = 1$; their budget constraint is a wealth constraint; prices are discounted to $t = 1$; producers maximize a discounted stream of profits. The Welfare Theorems hold, provided that at the beginning ($t = 1$) all markets exist (for $t = 1, ..., T$). Since in this model all agents have perfect foresight it is clear that fast reform that abolishes all distortions at once will yield higher welfare than a gradualist approach. This is a basic argument for shock therapy.

However, the reasoning again presupposes that lump sum transfers can be given and that all appropriate interventions are effectuated. Also, model (3.1)-(3.5) does not specify explicitly the adjustment lags that are due to liquidity constraints, short term indivisibilities, etc. These would call for specific policy measures during a transition period (see Kydland and Prescott (1982)). More importantly, the general equilibrium model has been criticized as being inherently static since it does not describe how equilibrium prices come about and therefore does not show which signals and mechanisms are needed to achieve equilibrium. In Section 3.3.3 we concluded that the model was not suited to describe the 'dynamics' of trade negotiations. Here we see that it should not be used to describe the short term dynamics of economic transition. In this sense gradualism is a critique of free trade and interventionism and seems to provide some welfare theoretical justification for the bureaucratic perspective.

When compared with the reform of previously centrally planned economies, CAP reform is only a minor operation. This makes it possible to implement it in stages. Whether a gradual change is economically desirable will depend on the importance of the short term adjustment costs. At any rate transition measures have to be introduced to avoid hardship for the farming community and to gain a minimum of acceptance of the reform among farmers.

In our view, the main lesson concerning shock therapy to be learnt from the welfare theoretical model is that predictability is important. The entrepreneurs should not make their choices on investment and migration under wrong assumptions. A clear and credible timepath of future taxes, subsidies and compensation payments should be announced and adhered to. The MacSharry reform in some sense reflects this principle. After many years of 'stabilizers', whereby support prices were reduced following overproduction in the previous year, the new CAP defines a timepath at least until 1996.

3.5 Consequences for the perspectives on reform

In view of the various objections mentioned in Section 3.3, it becomes difficult to base a pure free trade position on welfare theory alone. Welfare theory provides some support for specific interventions. There may for example be a case for regulation of the land market (local indivisibility), there are obviously very good reasons to impose constraints on pollution of the environment, and there exist valid theoretical arguments in favour of regional development programs. Though the theory does not prove that such interventions are needed, it does not reject them either.

Hence, two approaches are possible. One is to elevate the principle of free trade to a moral status and condemn any deviation from it. Then, the objections are interpreted as obstacles to be removed by policy (avoiding indivisibility, creating markets etc.). This approach greatly simplifies the policy discussion, since it enables the reformers to proceed in small steps but unfortunately, until the final aim is reached, this process may lead through highly undesirable states. Therefore, we conclude that, although it is difficult to determine which level and type of intervention is appropriate, the interventionist arguments cannot be discarded so easily.

At the same time we recognize that there is a danger in treating the free trade and the interventionist perspective so evenhandedly. Here we want to quote Krugman's evaluation of strategic trade policy (Krugman (1990, p. 233)):

> 'Strategic trade policy is, without doubt, a clever insight. From the beginning, however, it has been clear that the attention received by that insight has been driven by forces beyond the idea's intellectual importance. The simple fact is that there is a huge external market for challenges to the orthodoxy of free trade. Any intellectually respectable case for interventionist trade policies [...] will quickly find support for the wrong reasons. At the same time, the profession of international economics has a well developed immune system designed precisely to cope with these outside pressures. This immune system takes the form of an immediate intensely critical scrutiny of any idea that seems to favour protectionism.'

Krugman's statement does not only apply to strategic trade but also to the other interventions that we have considered: the models can provide the basis for an intellectually respectable argument that finds support for the wrong reasons. However, while agreeing with Krugman's view and even extending it to the other topics, we must add that the external market for non-interventionism is also large. Even the proponents of strategic export policy like to preach free trade to potential importers. There are specific interests associated with both views, in particular because the free traders are seldom serious on the issue of compensation of losers.

Therefore, we shall in the sequel follow the alternative approach of studying specific interventions through a simulation model. We recognize from the outset that it will not be possible to derive optimal levels of policy interventions from any simulation model, whatever its level of sophistication and refinement. For example, the optimal setting of production quotas at farm level requires detailed information on the technology of the farm concerned which is not available, and this is fortunate because the collection of such information would be a hindrance to the farmer and very distortionary by itself. In our view, the practical approach is to develop a more aggregated policy simulation model that can be used to analyze alternatives to the prevailing policy i.e. to the CAP after the MacSharry reform.

ECAM is such an empirical model. It does not have the capability of generating policy recipes. Its role is 'reduced' to that of an analytical framework but since it is embedded in general equilibrium theory, it will at every stage allow to identify assumptions which cause inefficiencies. The next chapter will report in detail on the specification of this model. In Chapter 5 we study the implications of the MacSharry reform that will serve as our reference scenario. In Chapter 6 we return to the free trade and interventionist viewpoints, for which we define scenarios as variants of the MacSharry reform.

Chapter 4

ECAM: an agricultural model of the EU-9

Since the conclusions reached in the welfare assessment of the previous chapter are too general to be conclusive, the analysis has to be supplemented with a more quantitative assessment. For this, the stylized model must be developed into an applied general equilibrium (AGE) model. We describe the main steps of this process (Section 4.1) and their implementation in the context of EU agriculture (Section 4.2). The AGE model has become a widely used tool, that has been described elsewhere; for surveys of AGE models, see Manne (1985), De Melo (1988), or Gunning and Keyzer (1995); principles of construction of AGE models are treated in Dixon et al. (1992) and Shoven and Whalley (1992). Kehoe (1991) gives an excellent treatment of many theoretical and computational aspects. Brooke et al. (1988) and Codsi et al. (1992) document two useful software packages.

However, the analysis of the CAP calls for specific extensions of the standard framework. While buffer stocks and quantity constraints that appeared in the stylized model of the previous chapter, already extend the basic framework, ECAM mainly distinguishes itself from other (recursively dynamic) AGE models through its representation of agricultural supply, in particular its explicit treatment of pastures and other non-marketed green fodders, which have been neglected in most other studies. Section 4.3 describes in some detail the mathematical program of agricultural supply which constitutes the core of the agricultural side of the model. This section is rather technical and assumes some familiarity with mathematical programming. It may be skipped. Section 4.4 concludes with an overview of the model and with some remarks on the experience gained in construction and use of ECAM. Two annexes complete the model description: Annex 4A describes the model validation, while Annex 4B reports in general terms on the sources of data and the methods of estimation that were used.

4.1 Applied general equilibrium modelling

Applied general equilibrium models are the numerical counterparts of theoretical models such as the stylized model (3.1)-(3.5). Construction of an applied model requires (a) the choice of a classification for agents and for commodities, (b) specifying the model in an algebraic form, (c) collection of statistical data for all its variables, (d) specification of functional forms for the consumption, supply, input demand and exports and estimation of the parameters of these forms, and finally, (e) incorporating the model within a computer program that can solve it, i.e. that can compute the values for the endogenous variables, given numerical values of exogenous variables and of parameters of functions. We discuss these tasks in turn.

4.1.1   Choice of classification

In applied models one has to choose not only a classification of consumers and firms but also a commodity classification. This is one of the most decisive steps in applied modelling. To keep the costs involved in checking of data, parameter estimation and monitoring of simulation results manageable, the detail of classification will have to be limited. To choose a meaningful classification, detailed information on the economy is essential.

At this point it must be recognized that all applied general equilibrium models suffer from problems involved in the representative agent construction: aggregation of individual net trades does not preserve micro-economic properties other than continuity, homogeneity and adding up. This is a fundamental problem from which any level of aggregation suffers. The best one can do is to choose the representative agents 'wisely':[52] when their number is too small the

---

[52] In partial models, say of consumer demand it is possible to avoid such aggregation: one may represent a continuum of consumers or model all consumers separately which appear in the original data set. For a further discussion see Kirman (1992).

misspecification becomes excessive and when it is too large the model becomes intractable.

The general equilibrium formulation implies that one must represent all consumers and all firms albeit in a simplified way. Hence, the non-agricultural sector must be covered even if the main interest is in agriculture. In the EU, where the agricultural sector is relatively small this may seem an unacceptable limitation. It is indeed pointless to try to represent all the effects of agricultural policies on the non-agricultural sector and the danger is real that one ends up modelling the non-agricultural sector with a small agricultural appendix. It will be discussed below how this difficulty has been addressed in ECAM.

4.1.2　The stylized model in algebraic form

As a further step towards functional specification the consumer and producer problems (3.1) and (3.2) have to be expressed as functions of the variables exogenous to the problems. For consumers this is the Marshallian demand function $x_j(p, h_j)$. The supply function $q_j(p^q, p, b_j)$ and the input demand $v_j(p^q, p, b_j)$, derived from the profit function $\pi_j(p^q, p, b_j)$, solve the producer problem. This enables us to substitute the Marshallian demand functions and the supply functions within commodity balance (3.5).

$$\sum_j x_j(p, h_j) + \sum_j v_j(p^q, p, b_j) + d = \sum_j q_j(p^q, p, b_j) + s_0 + m \tag{4.1}$$

Although equations (3.3) and (3.4a)-(3.4f) are unchanged, we repeat them here as equations (4.2) and (4.3)-(4.8), for convenience. The income equation is:

$$h_j = \pi_j(p^q, p, b_j) + T_j \tag{4.2}$$

The CAP is characterized as follows:[53]

(a)　Any surplus d is sold for intervention at given price level p^d

$$d \geq 0 \perp p \geq p^d \tag{4.3}$$

---

[53] Recall that we do not distinguish between CAP and non-CAP commodities. This is possible because commodities for which there is say, only an import levy can be treated as special cases.

(b)   A part of the surplus is exported, the remainder is kept in stock

$$e = \tilde{e}(d) \tag{4.4}$$

(c)   Imports are subject to a variable levy

$$m \geq 0 \perp p \leq p^u \tag{4.5}$$

(d)   The producer subsidy is fixed

$$p^q = p + \zeta^q \tag{4.6}$$

(e)   Net transfers T_j consist of grants received $T_j^0(p)$, minus a revenue tax

$$T_j = T_j^0(p) - \tau\pi_j(p^q, p, b_j) \tag{4.7}$$

(f)   The EU budget balances

$$p^d (d - e - s_0) + (p^d - p) s_0 + (p^d - p^e) e + \zeta^q \Sigma_j q_j +$$
$$\Sigma_j T_j - (p^u - p^m) m = 0 \tag{4.8}$$

for given

b_j	resources of j
p^d	intervention price (stock purchase)
p^e	(trade) export price
p^m	(trade) import price
p^u	tariff inclusive import price
s_0	initial stocks
ζ^q	producer subsidy

with endogenous variables

d	surplus
e	exports
h_j	consumer income
m	imports
p	market price
p^q	producer price
T_j	net transfers received by j
τ	tax rate

and function specifications for

 $\tilde{e}$ exports of the EU
 q_j production by j
 T_j^0 transfer function for j
 v_j input demand by j
 x_j consumer demand by j
 π_j profit of j.

4.1.3   The Social Accounting Matrix (SAM)

Given a solution for model (4.1)-(4.8), it is possible to assign, in quantity as well as in monetary terms, numerical values to every supply and demand item, in each commodity balance and in each budget constraint. These values constitute the basic elements of a Social Accounting Matrix (SAM). Often a SAM is written in value terms only. It is (like an input-output table) organized to highlight the flow of payments by commodity between agents. A simple SAM is shown in Table 4.1.

The correspondence between Table 4.1 and equations (4.1)-(4.8) can be explained as follows. Every term in the table (production, input etc.) refers to a sub-matrix of the SAM. Every row of the SAM denotes a source of funds and every column a destination. For example, in accordance with equation (4.2), every consumer j earns an income from profits π_j and from (possibly negative) direct transfers T_j; since his demand satisfies a budget equation, this income is spent on demand px_j, which appears in the column for consumers. Every firm j earns its income from production (the firms-row) and spends it on inputs (the firms-column) as well as on dividend payments (profits). Government has, as in equation (4.8), revenue from indirect taxes and from foreign savings (the trade deficit) and spends on net transfers and stocks (the net demand for stocks is $p(d - e - s_0)$). Finally, the external sector sells imported commodities on the EU market, buys exports and pays the foreign savings to the government. Although the trade deficit ($p^m m - p^e e$) is zero in the stylized model, it is introduced here for later reference. When all the matrices have thus been filled, the commodity balance will also hold in value terms (input plus consumption plus stocks plus exports being equal to production plus indirect tax plus imports).

In this SAM, all price wedges from (4.3) appear as indirect taxes in the commodity column. Obviously, since the entries are derived from balance equations, the row and column totals are equal.

Table 4.1   Structure of the SAM for the stylized model

	Commodities	Firms	Consumers	Government	External
Commodities		Input	Consumption	Stocks	Exports
Firms	Production				
Consumers		Profits	Net transfers		
Government	Indirect tax				
External	Imports				Trade deficit

Once a SAM (in monetary terms) has been obtained, point-estimates of initial quantities in (4.1)-(4.8) can also be derived, provided one also has estimates of prices.[54] By construction, the model will fully replicate the SAM when fed with the exogenous values that appear in the SAM. Hence, such a base year solution does not provide any new information for the period covered by the SAM.[55]

4.1.4   Parameter estimation and model validation

Full system econometric estimation of the parameters in equations (4.1)-(4.8) is very difficult for various reasons. First, there are identification problems since the number of endogenous variables is very large. Still, one could attempt to

---

[54] In many applications prices are set equal to unity in the base year; the disadvantage of such an approach is that price and quantity results cannot be compared directly with published data. A more serious drawback is that the information contained in price differences e.g. on transport costs is likely to be lost. For example, if wheat is produced in different locations, any interregional price difference will be attributed to product heterogeneity rather than to transportation costs, even if the products are in fact physically identical.

[55] It does provide consistency checks and this is an important difference from non SAM-based models. When the outcomes of the model do not coincide with those of the SAM, one may be able to identify the error by comparing all row and columns totals. There are two possible sources of differences: either the SAM violates model restrictions (like non-negativity of income) or the model does not follow the SAM structure (due to a programming error or a difference in design).

instrument for at least some of these endogenous variables but this is rarely done, in part because, in an AGE model, the number of candidate instruments is very limited. Secondly, the model contains complementarity conditions which cause severe estimation problems because they impose restrictions on the distribution of disturbance terms. Thirdly, a general equilibrium model does not allow rejection of variables on statistical grounds (like dropping commodities with insignificant demand elasticities). Fourthly, full system estimation is hampered by lack of data. This severely limits the scope for a more than rudimentary treatment of the intertemporal correlation of disturbances. Finally, the model contains many lagged dependent variables. This calls for the application of time series methods which is very difficult here because the number of variables is large and because there are many nonlinearities.

Although full system estimation cannot be performed, it is possible to estimate components of the model, e.g. consumer demand, or net supply separately. Such a modular approach has been followed in the estimation of the parameters for ECAM. However, since the modular approach disregards simultaneity and lagged endogeneity, it is insufficient to calibrate the full model. The crucial step of calibration and validation is then the final tuning phase, during which the full model is run over a historical period and parameters are adjusted to improve the fit. Usually parameters which were obtained on the basis of very few observations are adjusted first and the more robust coefficients are left unchanged as much as possible.

This informal (and time-consuming) procedure did, nevertheless, lead to rejection of some specifications. It also led to a model which appears to replicate the past with reasonable accuracy but, clearly, this ability to reproduce historical evidence may not be a proof of validity, since there is a large number of parameters which can be adjusted to achieve this. The comparative strength of the model is that it maintains an elaborate theoretical structure under alternative simulations. This makes this model suitable for policy analysis, more perhaps than for projections.

4.1.5   Model solution

The model (4.1)-(4.8) is a nonlinear complementarity problem. On each market either a price or a quantity (d, m, or e) is adjusting but one does not know in advance which case (regime) applies. This makes model solution more complex than if the regimes were known, because then only a set of nonlinear equality constraints would have to be solved.

To solve ECAM, a nonlinear complementarity algorithm has been used, which exploits the property of the model that there are, in practice, only few changes in regime and most prices are fixed by the CAP, so that stock and trade are the adjusting variables. Further details can be found in Keyzer (1989b) and Overbosch (1992). Of course, policy analysis requires more than simply printing the main endogenous variables of a particular model. Outcomes must be presented in a form which enables policy analysis. Here the applied general equilibrium model has a comparative advantage in that consistent accounts can be presented at various levels, ranging from income expenditure accounts for separate consumers and firms, to supply utilization accounts (commodity balances), government accounts and balances of payments. In short, it can produce a time series of SAMs under alternative policy scenarios.

4.2   From stylized model to application

It is in principle possible to implement the stylized model according to the five steps listed. Yet to make the model policy relevant, these steps need further elaboration. A more detailed specification is required not only of the policies themselves but also of structural relations in the agricultural economy of the EU. We discuss six issues: the agent and commodity classification, the aggregation of supply utilization accounts, the treatment of exchange rates, consumption, the specification of non-agricultural supply and, finally, the specification of agricultural supply.

4.2.1   Agent and commodity classification

ECAM distinguishes nine EU countries: Belgium-Luxembourg, Denmark, France, West Germany, Ireland, Italy, The Netherlands and the United Kingdom.

In each country there are two sectors, a farm sector and a non-farm sector. The people in these sectors are referred to as farmers and non-farmers, respectively, indexed j = 1, ..., J, (where $j \in J_1$ for farmers and $j \in J_2$ for non-farmers). As in the stylized model, farmers and non-farmers are represented in their roles as producers and as consumers.

Of course, a specification which includes all twelve member states would be preferable. However, limited data availability has so far prevented the incorporation of models for Greece, Portugal and Spain. Table 4.2 lists the percentage share in EU-12 production covered by the EU-9.

Table 4.2   Shares of EU-9 in production of EU-12, 1990, percentage

Wheat	91
Coarse grains	78
Rice	68
Sugar	82
Oilseeds	81
Vegetables, roots	77
Fruits and nuts	59
Milk	91
Bovine meat	91
Ovine meat	67
Pork	84
Poultry	81
Eggs	83

Source: FAO, Agrostat, Supply Utilization Accounts.

The table shows that EU-9 specification covers the agricultural production of the EU-12 to a great extent, particularly for the main CAP commodities, cereals, milk and bovine meat. It could also have been informative to disaggregate the national farm sectors by region or by type of farm. Again limitations concerning data availability and model size were the main factors preventing this.

The specification of a suitable commodity classification is a very important and difficult task in applied modelling. We mention three issues. First, one must decide on the level of aggregation of the non-agricultural commodities. Clearly, in a model which focuses on agriculture the non-agricultural commodities will have to be represented in an aggregate way. ECAM only distinguishes two non-agricultural commodities for each country: one which is internationally tradeable and one which is not. Secondly, one must decide on how to treat commodities that are not exchanged on markets, either because they remain within the agricultural sector (e.g. green fodder), or because they are treated as fixed factors (the vector b_j in equation (3.2); here land, labour and physical capital) or because they are absent from the model altogether (say, financial assets). This point is more easily discussed in the context of the specification of agricultural supply. Finally, the aggregation of agricultural commodities must be dealt with. This is the issue which we shall now discuss.

In a farm model, the problem of commodity aggregation is relatively straightforward because the list of commodities that are actually traded at farm level provides the basic information and only a decision on grouping of commodities, like rapeseed and sunflower seed into oilseeds is required. In an AGE model that also has to describe consumer demand and international trade, it is necessary to follow all outputs along their processing chains, from the farm to the border (and vice versa for inputs). Some part of the oilseed production may, for example, be processed into oils and cakes and then exported.

A separate representation of all processed products would lead to an intractably long list of commodities. A list of manageable size can be obtained by treating the processed commodities as consisting of raw materials plus a non-agricultural commodity called 'processing'; the price paid, say by the consumer will then consist of a raw material component and a processing margin (possibly supplemented by a tax). This approach has been followed for all agricultural commodities in ECAM.

The conversion of raw materials proceeds as follows. The crops and livestock products of the farm are split into marketed commodities before they reach the consumer: oilseeds into oils and cakes, sheep into meat, fats, wool and hides etc. Some commodities have multiple use. Sugar is for example refined and then consumed directly or as an input into soft drinks. This is represented by having the consumer of soft drinks buy a composite commodity, which consists of fruits, processing and sugar. The consequence of all this is that several commodity classifications will coexist within the same model. At farm-level there will be a classification in terms of crops and livestock. The market will clear in terms of processed raw materials and the end-users will buy composite goods. Hence, in ECAM there are three commodity classifications:

Table 4.3a   List of cropping and livestock activities

1.	Wheat	13.	Non-consumable potatoes
2.	Coarse grains	14.	Other vegetable products
3.	Rice (paddy)	15.	Pasture grass
4.	Sugar beet	16.	Foddermaize
5.	Oilseeds	17.	Other roughage
6.	Consumable potatoes	18.	Dairy cows
7.	Vegetables and pulses	19.	Layinghens
8.	Temperate fruit	20.	Non-dairy cattle
9.	Non-temperate fruit, nuts and spices	21.	Sheep and goats
10.	Grapes	22.	Pigs
11.	Olives	23.	Poultry
12.	Hops, fibers, tobacco	24.	Fish

Table 4.3b   List of exchange commodities

1.	Wheat	11.	Carbohydrate products
2.	Coarse grains	12.	Coffee, tea and cocoa
3.	Rice	13.	Butter
4.	Sugar	14.	Dairy products, excluding butter
5.	Fats and oils, excluding dairy	15.	Bovine and equine meat
6.	Protein feeds, excluding dairy	16.	Ovine meat
7.	Temperate fruits and vegetables	17.	Pig meat
8.	Subtropical fruits and nuts	18.	Poultry meat and eggs
9.	Wine	19.	Fish
10.	Industrial crops	20.	Non-agricultural, tradeable
		21-28	Non-agricultural, non-tradable

a consumer classification for composite goods (Table 4B.3 in Annex 4B), a classification for processed raw materials (Table 4.3b), to be referred to as the exchange classification and a farm-gate classification of crops and livestock (Table 4.3a).

Figure 4.1 Physical flow of a commodity in ECAM

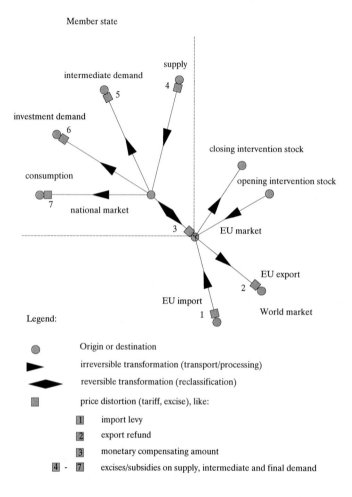

Figure 4.1 shows the flow (or commodity balance) of a single processed raw material. It originates from imports or from the farm (after 'splitting'). It then moves via the market to the consumer who uses it as part of composite goods, to the intervention stock, to an export destination, or back to the farm as an input say, as a compound feed.

The three commodity classifications are linked through mappings. For example, let q_j^f and p_j^f denote the intensity and gross revenue of crop and livestock activities performed by farm j and let the constant[56] matrix M_j^f perform the mapping from these crops and livestock activities to the exchange commodities. Then the following relations hold:

$$q_j = M_j^f \, q_j^f \tag{4.9a}$$
$$p_j^f = p_j^q \, M_j^f \tag{4.9b}$$
$$p_j^q = p^q \tag{4.9c}$$

In (4.9a) the outputs from productive activities are split into exchange commodities. Equation (4.9b) builds up gross revenues as composites of market prices (as usual, price vectors are taken to be row vectors); equation (4.9c) indicates that national prices of exchange commodities are, so far, taken to be equal across countries but this assumption will be relaxed later on. For consumption, input demand and tariff inclusive imports and exports similar mappings have been defined using the market price p instead of the producer price p^q.

This eventually leads to the lists for crop and livestock activities and for exchange commodities: most categories are more or less self-explanatory but, to clarify the relations between the two lists, it may be added that oilseeds (5) are, at exchange level, split into fats and oils (5) and protein feeds (6), dairy cows yield butter (13) and other dairy products (14). Slaughtering of cattle (20) yields bovine meat (15), fats (5), protein feeds (6) and hides which appear as industrial crops (10); similar splittings apply to other livestock activities. Carbohydrate products include starch potatoes, (imported) manioc and byproducts from sugar production, like molasses and dregs from brewing and distilling.

---

[56] The mappings can be looked at as non-square input-output matrices. Hence substitution can be introduced by making them price dependent. In ECAM the mappings are fixed (or time-dependent), except for consumption where the value shares are taken to be fixed. This implies a Cobb-Douglas technology, (as opposed to a Leontief technology) for the processing activity.

4.2.2   The procedure for aggregation of physical quantities

It is a distinguishing characteristic of agricultural statistics that commodity balances are available for almost all raw and processed agricultural commodities. These are commonly referred to as supply utilization accounts (SUA). There exist for every country of the EU more than six hundred of such balances, which are available as time series of about thirty years, starting in 1961. These balances are obviously a valuable source of information for equilibrium models but the richness of this data source calls for an aggregation procedure. Aggregation proceeds in two stages.

In the first stage aggregation is performed along every processing chain. Consider for example the items of a supply-utilization account for wheat and for wheat flour: production, consumption, input use, import and export, and possibly other items. If wheat is chosen as the unit of measurement of raw material in which wheat flour has to be expressed, then, if one disregards all byproducts from wheat milling, all items of the commodity balance for wheat flour have to be divided by the extraction rate (flour per unit of wheat). In the first stage of the aggregation the flour export in wheat-equivalent is then added to the wheat export, and similarly for imports, consumption and input demand. Flour production is not added to wheat production, in order to avoid double-counting and it is deducted from the total input use. This yields a consolidated account for wheat and wheat products measured in the raw material unit wheat.

In the second stage of the aggregation the quantities are expressed in a common unit of measurement, like metric tons and then summation is performed over the commodities which belong to the same group. For example, in ECAM barley and oats belong to the marketed commodity coarse grains.

These two stages of processing only deal with quantities of agricultural product. Information on the quantity of non-agricultural product which is involved in the processing has to be derived from other sources, usually price information. The difference between the unit value of, say, sugar consumption and the raw material cost of sugar is then (after correcting for consumer taxes or subsidies) treated as input of processing services. When a unit value has been attributed to all quantities in an aggregated commodity balance, one may derive a commodity balance in value terms, which is as we have seen a central component of a SAM.

4.2.3   Green and budget ecus

The stylized model assumes that all prices are expressed in the same currency and that the prices are, like in (4.9c), equal across member states. Since the supply and demand relations in the stylized model are homogeneous of degree zero in prices, real outcomes are unaffected by changes in national exchange rates. In ECAM all values are expressed in ecu using market exchange rates. These are called budget ecu to distinguish them from the green ecu. The green ecu is a unit of measurement which is used in the CAP to set common price bands for intervention and import levies (the prices p^d and p^u in the stylized model).[57] A country-specific conversion rate is subsequently used to express the green rate prices in budget ecu. This leads to country specific price bands which are implemented through tariffs and subsidies on trade among member states (the monetary compensating amounts, MCAs). The MCAs have gradually been reduced from 1987 onwards and abolished in 1992 (see Section 2.2.4). The green ecu still exists but it now keeps a parity to the budget ecu which, in principle, is not country specific.[58] This leads to the following equations:

$$p_j = p \; K_j$$
$$p_j^q = p^q \; K_j$$

where p and p^q are set in green ecu and the diagonal matrix K_j converts these to budget ecu (clearly K_j will be the same for two consumers or firms in the same country).

However, this leaves one difficulty in modelling the regime. Note that the levy on imports is measured as $(p^u - p^m)$, where p^u is measured in green ecu and p^m in budget ecu. The actual levy at the external border of the EU is in budget ecu and therefore varies among member states. The difficulty is that in the

---

[57] In practice (and in ECAM) the green ecus are even commodity specific.

[58] However, it remains a decision of the agricultural ministers to set the green rates and to define what is to be used as a market rate. Hence, in practice there still is some degree of country specificity.

stylized model the external trade is not specified by country and in fact the CAP and the MCAs are designed to make the trader indifferent (if one disregards transport costs) as to the country which imports or exports. Hence, external trade cannot realistically be represented for member states separately. To resolve this problem the levies in ordinary (non-green) monetary units are recovered as Σ_j (p_j - p^m) m_j, where m_j is the vector of positive net purchases by agent j and the same applies for export refunds and the valuation of intervention stocks.[59]

4.2.4   Consumption

A specification of consumer demand functions $x_j(p, h_j)$ that is compatible with the utility maximization problem (3.1) can be obtained by application of Shephard's lemma from duality theory (see e.g. Varian (1992)). First, consumer expenditure is obtained by deducting savings and direct taxes from income.[60] Let $\tilde{h}$ denote the resulting consumer expenditure. We consider the expenditure function which is dual to the utility function $u(x)$:[61,62]

$$c(p, \tilde{u}) = \min (px \mid u(x) \geq \tilde{u}, x \geq 0)$$

where $\tilde{u}$ is chosen such that $c(p, \tilde{u}) = \tilde{h}$, the income of the consumer. By assumption C this expenditure function is concave, homogeneous of degree one and nondecreasing in p and convex increasing in u, and $c(p, 0) = 0$ (hence, the condition $c(p, \tilde{u}) = \tilde{h}$ defines a unique utility level $u^*(p, \tilde{h})$; this is the indirect

---

[59] The intervention stock creates a minor additional complication. The stocks are in fact held in specific countries whereas the regulations are designed to make the (often private) stockholders indifferent as to which country this is. In ECAM it is postulated that the past distribution D_j of stocks over agents is maintained (D_j is a diagonal matrix with element D_{jk} as the share of the stock of commodity k kept by j). Only the non-agricultural sector keeps stocks. This makes it possible to value stocks in ecu prices p_j. The stocks add a term Σ_j (p_j - p^u) D_j (d - e - s_0) to the expression for levies.

[60] In ECAM, a fixed savings rate is used. This simplification is of lesser importance because the emphasis lies on the demand for food which is relatively income inelastic anyway. Investments are taken as a (time-dependent) fraction of income. In this section we disregard investments in order to facilitate exposition.

[61] For notational convenience, we drop the subscript j and we also write p instead of the consumer price p^c. In ECAM a tax-ridden price is used and, as discussed in Section 4.2.1, there is a mapping from marketed to consumed commodities.

[62] The consumer demand is expressed on a per capita basis, so that income and consumption are in fact divided by the population. We do not show this explicitly, to keep notation simpler.

utility function). By strict concavity of $u(x)$[63] the expenditure function is also differentiable and by Shephard's lemma the consumer demand function can be recovered as:

$$x(p, \tilde{h}) = \partial c(p, \tilde{u})/\partial p, \text{ where } \tilde{u} = u^*(p, \tilde{h}) \tag{4.10}$$

When as in ECAM the number of commodities is relatively large it is advisable from an econometric point of view to impose more structure on the expenditure function, so as to avoid spurious correlations. Therefore, a two-level specification has been adopted, whereby the expenditure function is written in nested form as:

$$c(p, \tilde{u}) = C(P(p), \tilde{u}) + p\bar{c}, \text{ where } \tilde{u} = u^*(p, \tilde{h})$$

The nesting appears in the first term on the right-hand side. $P(p)$ is a price index for an aggregate commodity (which is concave, nondecreasing and homogeneous of degree one) and $C(P, \tilde{u})$ is an expenditure function expressed in aggregate prices. The term $p\bar{c}$ denotes committed demand, which is fixed (or time-dependent). The consumption function is obtained through the chain rule as:

$$x(p, \tilde{h}) = \partial C(P, \tilde{u})/\partial P \ \partial P(p)/\partial p + \bar{c}, \text{ where } \tilde{u} = u^*(P(p), \tilde{h} - p\bar{c})$$

The term $\partial C(P, \tilde{u})/\partial P$ computes the demand for aggregate commodities and $\partial P(p)/\partial p$ determines the (uncommitted) demand within each commodity group per unit of aggregate commodity.[64]

---

[63] In ECAM the assumption of strict concavity is relaxed to strict quasiconcavity. This does not change the properties of the expenditure function and Shephard's lemma also holds in this case.

[64] In ECAM the function $P(p)$ is a Cobb-Douglas price index and the expenditure function for aggregate commodities $C(P, \tilde{u})$ has a flexible form and is specified as an Almost Ideal Demand System (see Deaton and Muellbauer (1980)). Estimation proceeds as follows: first one estimates a linear expenditure system (L.E.S.) for each commodity group separately. This gives the price index function $P(p)$ and the committed demand for each group. Then, one computes a time series of values of uncommitted expenditures $\tilde{h} - p\bar{c}$ and of aggregate prices $P(p)$, which serve to estimate the system for aggregate commodities. The main issue in the latter system is to ensure that the expenditure function is concave in P for a sufficiently wide range of prices. See Diewert and Wales (1987) for a discussion on the problem of maintaining concavity in flexible forms. Further details on the estimation procedure and results can be found in Michalek and Keyzer (1992).

4.2.5   Non-agricultural supply

The aggregation for each EU member state of all non-agricultural production into one tradeable and one non-tradeable commodity is obviously a gross simplification. This calls for an equally stylized representation of the supply of these two commodities. The supply of the tradeable good is treated as a given endowment which grows according to an exogenous trend and the supply of the non-tradeable is assumed to adjust to domestic demand. Hence, the treatment of the non-farm sector can be said to be semi-exogenous because it abstracts from endogenous supply response due to capital accumulation as well as from reallocation between the agricultural and the non-agricultural sectors. Moreover, the prices are also almost exogenous: the price of the tradeable commodity follows international inflation and the price of the non-tradeable commodity is set through markup pricing (with a time dependent markup rate).[65] Finally, recall that savings and investment are specified through time dependent fractions and therefore virtually exogenous.

This simplified treatment of the non-agricultural sector gives ECAM a place somewhere between an agricultural model and an economywide model. It may even cast doubt on the appropriateness of choosing a general equilibrium methodology but this choice can in our view be justified as follows.

First, the semi-exogenous treatment brings the obvious advantage that one does not need to spend excessive effort on data collection and modelling of a sector which is not the focus of the study.

Secondly, the semi-exogenous representation is partial in the appropriate sense of the term because it is embedded in a non-partial theory and explicitly makes some variables exogenous, thus maintaining theoretical compatibility with an original general equilibrium specification. Partial models which are formulated outside the general equilibrium framework tend to adopt assumptions which make them incompatible with a general equilibrium formulation even if the classifications of commodities and agents were to be extended to cover the entire economy.

---

[65] A markup operates like an excise tax which is redistributed to the owners of the firm rather than to the government.

Thirdly, the accounts produced by the model are complete. This makes it possible to show the agricultural sector and its budgetary cost in an economywide perspective.

Fourthly, several linkages between the farm and the non-farm sector, for example the impacts through agricultural processing, input demand and migration, can be represented in this partial context also. The general equilibrium framework shows how a possibly more elaborate representation of these relations could be incorporated in a future version of the model, so that it becomes feasible gradually to develop ECAM into a more comprehensive model in a way which avoids methodological inconsistencies.

Finally, the approach ensures a consistent treatment of non-agricultural prices as they affect the decisions of consumers and firms. It provides for example a treatment of inflation which avoids money illusion. This is important in the context of the CAP with its green and budget ecu-rates and the divergent rates of inflation between member states.

We conclude that the semi-exogenous treatment of the non-agricultural sector should not be seen as a weakness of ECAM but as an illustration of the flexibility of the applied general equilibrium methodology.

4.2.6   Agricultural supply

The agricultural supply component constitutes the core of ECAM, as it does in many agricultural sector models. There exists a wide range of models of agricultural supply, with linear programs at one end and supply functions at the other. The linear program has the advantage that it can incorporate large scale systems of commodity balances, for marketed commodities as well as for on-farm 'commodities' (like labour or manure). This makes it relatively straightforward to account for engineering information and other a priori restrictions. The main limitation of the linear program is that its response to changes in objective coefficients and resource levels is not continuous, so that outcomes can be 'wild', and that it cannot be validated using available econometric methods (this is in part due to the discontinuity of its response).

Supply functions take supply to be determined by prices and possibly other variables. The functions are continuous and econometric estimation is relatively straightforward but little a priori information is incorporated and no balance constraints are being maintained. Most importantly, the supplies do not satisfy any restriction derived from the micro-economic theory of the firm (like profit or revenue maximization) unless they follow from duality theory, but this again makes the econometrics more difficult.

The nonlinear programming model which serves as the agricultural supply component in ECAM may be seen as an attempt to combine the advantages of the two approaches. It has been designed to fulfil the following six requirements. First, it must have a micro-economic interpretation. Secondly, its response to changes in parameters must be continuous. Thirdly, its unknown parameters have to be. estimable by econometric methods. Fourthly, it must maintain essential balances, like the constraint on land availability. Fifthly, it must allow for the representation of crop-specific input requirements. Finally, it must contain some device to represent rigidities in allocation due to unaccounted inputs. We shall now describe a supply program that fulfils these requirements.

4.3 The agricultural supply program

We start from the agricultural supply program (3.2), according to which every farmer $j \in J_1$ maximizes his profit:[66]

$$\pi_j(p^f, p, b_j) =$$
$$\max \ p^f q_j^f - p v_j$$
$$q_j^f, v_j \geq 0$$

subject to   (4.11)

$$t_j(q_j^f, -v_j, -b_j) \leq 0$$

where the fixed factors b_j, which include land, labour and physical capital are adjusted between periods in a way unspecified as yet. The advantage of this formulation is that it is very compact and nevertheless incorporates important

---

[66] We write the farm outputs in terms of the crops and livestock activities, making use of the mapping M_j^f of equations (4.9a)-(4.9b) and we define the transformation function accordingly.

aspects of the farmers' behaviour like rationality and indifference with respect to the level of absolute prices.

This is a nonlinear program and due to the strict quasiconvexity of the transformation function t_j, its response to changes in its parameters (p^f, p, b_j) is continuous and obviously in accordance with micro-economic principles, so that the first two requirements listed in the previous section are satisfied. However, it does not possess sufficient structure to meet the other requirements. In Section 4.3.1 we will focus on the problems involved in meeting the third requirement (parameter estimation by econometric methods) without giving up the others. In Section 4.3.2 we propose a specification for the crop sector which will be applied to a mixed crop-livestock farm in Section 4.3.3. The fixed factors land, labour and capital are introduced in Section 4.3.4. Finally, their adjustment is described in Section 4.3.5.

4.3.1   Primal and dual approaches

If the coefficients of the transformation function t_j are known, one can solve the program directly. This is the so-called primal approach. However, if the coefficients are not known, they must be obtained from econometric estimation. It is difficult to apply regression methods directly to mathematical programs. Therefore, the practice of the implementation of nonlinear programs like (4.11) is to specify explicit functions for supply and input demand which inherit as many of the properties of the mathematical program as possible. This is the dual approach. By Hotelling's lemma, supply and demand functions can be specified as:[67]

$$q^f(p^f, p, b) = \partial\pi(p^f, p, b)/\partial p^f$$
$$v(p^f, p, b) = - \partial\pi(p^f, p, b)/\partial p \tag{4.12}$$

To implement this approach a functional form has to be specified for $\pi(p^f, p, b)$, which is convex in (p^f, p), concave in b and continuously differentiable in (p^f, p). By Hotelling's lemma (see Varian (1992)), differentiation leads to (4.12),

---

[67] For convenience, we shall in this section drop the subscript j.

the system for which the parameters must be estimated. However, this approach has some drawbacks.

First, it does not enable the imposition of any a priori information say, on balance requirements or on other technical relations like yield functions. Hence, it will lead to supply and input demand functions which do not satisfy balance constraints, say on land use, feed requirements or capacity bounds. Secondly, the approach is not modular. All supplies and input demands that relate to the same resources must be estimated simultaneously in one single system. Finally, the profit maximizing formulation suffers from the practical limitation that all inputs and all outputs must be accounted for through purchases and sales. In applications it is impossible to fulfil this requirement particularly on the input side where demand for financial assets like insurance is seldom represented (this is the problem alluded to in connection with the last requirement of Section 4.2.6).

4.3.2   A mixed primal-dual program for the crop sector

The agricultural supply component of ECAM attempts to overcome some of these limitations through a mixed primal-dual approach (see also Keyzer (1989a)). This approach seeks to maintain important properties of a (primal) mathematical program by decomposing it into subproblems, linked through constraints with known coefficients. The constraints with known coefficients enable the imposition of a priori information and the decomposition makes it possible to estimate separate modules. As will be seen it also provides an option for dealing with missing inputs.

In order to describe the approach we consider a special case of program (4.11). After some reformulation it will constitute a basic building block of the national agricultural supply programs in ECAM. In this section we only specify the program for a crop producing farm. To make the a priori information explicit, the transformation function of (4.11) is replaced by a set of constraints. We consider n crops indexed h, and K inputs indexed k. Let y_h denote the crop yield per hectare, a_h the number of hectares and f_{hk} the input of commodity k per hectare of crop h. Land is the only fixed resource and we impose the land balance $\sum_h \delta_h a_h \leq b$, where δ_h is the given and positive land requirement of crop h (here $\delta_h = 1$ but we introduce the parameter because it will not be equal to unity when we consider livestock). We define two technical constraints: a yield function $y_h = \tilde{y}_h(f_{h1}, ..., f_{hK})$ and a rotation constraint $g(a_2, ..., a_n) \leq a_1$ which describes the imperfect substitution among crops. The functions $\tilde{y}_h(\cdot)$ and $g(\cdot)$ satisfy the following assumptions:

Assumption Y (yield function): The yield function $\tilde{y}_h(f_{h1}, ..., f_{hK})$ is $R_+^K \to R_+$, continuous, strictly quasiconcave and monotonic. The function is uniformly bounded above ($\tilde{y}_h(f_{h1}, ..., f_{hK}) \leq \bar{y}_h$, where $\bar{y}_h$ is a technological maximum) and $\tilde{y}_h(0, ..., 0)$ is positive for some h (natural fertility).

Assumption G (rotation function): The rotation function $g(a_2, ..., a_n)$ is $R_+^{n-1} \to R_+$, continuous, monotonic and homogeneous of degree one. It is also convex and has strictly concave isoquants.

The formulation of the yield function is not restrictive as it even allows for increasing returns. The rotation constraint is a generalization of the linear constraints which appear in many agricultural programming models. The linear case is obtained if one defines: $g(a_2, ..., a_n) = \max_{h=2, ..., n}(\gamma_h a_h)$ where γ_h is the minimal area under crop h per hectare of crop 1.[68] Obviously, the choice of crop 1 as numéraire crop is restrictive and more elaborate constraints can be formulated (which have been implemented in ECAM). The coefficients γ_h are usually set as a calibration device in most programming models. The mixed primal-dual approach enables to estimate these parameters statistically and to consider a nonlinear constraint.

Program (4.11) may now be written as:

---

[68] For some crops (e.g. temperate fruits and horticultural products) acreages are set exogenously through trends. For pastures, part of the acreage is set through exogenous trends. This is to account for pasture land that is unsuited for crop cultivation.

$$\pi(p^f, p, b) =$$

$$\max \sum_h p_h^f q_h^f - \sum_k p_k v_k$$

$$a_h, f_{hk}, q_h^f, v_k, y_h \geq 0, h = 1, ..., n \text{ and } k = 1, ..., K$$

subject to   (4.13)

(i) $q_h^f = y_h a_h$

(ii) $v_k = \sum_h f_{hk} a_h$

(iii) $\sum_h \delta_h a_h \leq b$

(iv) $y_h = \tilde{y}_h(f_{h1}, ..., f_{hK})$

(v) $g(a_2, ..., a_n) \leq a_1$

In this program, constraints (i) and (ii) define total output and input, constraint (iii) is the land balance, equation (iv) specifies the yield function and (v) the rotation constraint. Problem (4.13) is a convex program, which is feasible because any land allocation which satisfies the land balance is feasible. The program is bounded because the yield is bounded. In any optimum the land balance will hold with equality (because some positive yield can be achieved without current input). The program defines a profit function. The mixed primal-dual approach now proceeds in three stages which decomposes this problem into successively smaller subproblems. In the last step we will find it necessary to modify (4.13) in order to make the decomposition complete.

First, we note that the strict quasiconcavity of the yield function implies that the producer will minimize his cost of achieving given crop yields. Hence, we may, for every h, define the cost function:

$$c_h(p, y_h) =$$

$$\min \sum_k p_k f_{hk}$$

$$f_{hk} \geq 0, k = 1, ..., K$$

subject to   (4.14)

$$\tilde{y}_h(f_{h1}, ..., f_{hK}) \geq y_h$$

This makes it possible to use Shephard's lemma and obtain the crop specific input demand functions $f_{hk}(p, y_h)$.

Secondly, the producer will also choose the yield which maximizes his revenue per hectare. Hence, he will solve, for every h:

$$\tilde{\rho}_h(p_h^f, p) = \quad \max \quad p_h^f y_h - c_h(p, y_h) \qquad\qquad (4.15)$$
$$y_h \geq 0$$

Here there is no need to estimate a separate function, since the parameters of the cost function fully characterize the problem. If one now defines $\rho_h = \tilde{\rho}_h(p_h^f, p)$, then program (4.13) may be rewritten in terms of crop areas only as:

$$\tilde{\pi}(\rho, b) =$$
$$\max \Sigma_h \rho_h a_h$$
$$a_h \geq 0, h = 1, ..., n$$

subject to $\qquad\qquad\qquad\qquad\qquad\qquad\qquad\qquad$ (4.16)

$$\Sigma_h \delta_h a_h = b \qquad\qquad\qquad (\phi)$$
$$g(a_2, ..., a_n) \leq a_1$$

where ϕ is the (positive) Lagrange multiplier associated with the land balance. It follows from the homogeneity of degree one of the function g and the linearity of the land balance constraint that $\tilde{\pi}(\rho, b) = \phi b$, so that all net revenue accrues to land.

Finally, in the third stage one solves (a modified version of) program (4.16). Here, one has the choice between four options. The first option is to follow the primal approach, which amounts to solving (4.16) directly. This is only possible if the coefficients of the function $g(\cdot)$ are known. The second option is to apply duality, but this will cause violation of the land balance because the functional form chosen for the profit function does not incorporate this restriction.[69] There are two further options, either to maintain the land balance through the shadow price on land or to introduce a residual cost. We discuss them by turns.

Maintaining the land balance through the shadow price on land

The third option is to treat the shadow price ϕ as a rental price. The value of ϕ would be adjusted until the linear constraint is satisfied:

$$\tilde{\pi}(\rho - \phi\delta) =$$
$$\max \Sigma_h \ (\rho_h - \phi\delta_h) \ a_h$$
$$a_h \geq 0, h = 1, ..., n$$

subject to

$$g(a_2, ..., a_n) \leq a_1$$

However, this approach is not workable, because the program is unbounded, so that no profit function exists. One therefore needs a different decomposition and for this one may for example choose the maximum attainable profit per unit of the numéraire commodity. One then solves for relative crop areas $\tilde{a}_h = a_h/a_1$, h = 2, ..., n in:

$$R(\rho_2 - \phi\delta_2, ..., \rho_n - \phi\delta_n) =$$
$$\max \Sigma_{h \neq 1} \ (\rho_h - \phi\delta_h) \ \tilde{a}_h$$
$$\tilde{a}_h \geq 0, h = 2, ..., n$$

subject to   (4.17a)

$$g(\tilde{a}_2, ..., \tilde{a}_n) \leq 1$$

---

[69] There may be good reasons to settle for this, because one may not want to impose the balance constraint so strictly, in view of errors in the data and in the model. Hence, since there is no hope for a perfect fit anyway, it depends on the specification of the disturbance term whether for example the land balance is to be imposed strictly in estimation. Even primal production models unavoidably miss some constraints which are reflected in the statistical data and the dual models are bound to be worse in this respect.

We know that ϕ must be set so as to ensure that land absorbs all net revenue: $(\rho_1 - \phi\delta_1) a_1 + \Sigma_{h\neq 1} (\rho_h - \phi\delta_h) a_h = 0$. Therefore, ϕ must in (4.17a) be chosen so that:

$$(\rho_1 - \phi\delta_1) + R(\rho_2 - \phi\delta_2, ..., \rho_n - \phi\delta_n) = 0 \tag{4.17b}$$

Hotelling's lemma can now be applied to obtain $\tilde{a}(\rho, \phi)$ and the area under crop 1 is determined so as to satisfy the land balance. Unfortunately, this approach has important disadvantages. First, there is the practical difficulty that the shadow price ϕ is not observable. It has to be obtained from (4.17b) for every parameter value during the (maximum likelihood) estimation process, which is cumbersome. Secondly, the allocation is heavily influenced by the value of the constant δ, and it may be undesirable to let this constant affect allocations so much. Finally, one may expect the revenue function to be nondifferentiable at points where $\rho_h - \phi\delta_h = 0$ for some h, in which case Hotelling's lemma does not apply. Therefore, it is difficult to estimate the parameters of this system, although it maintains the land constraint.

A residual cost

We now consider the fourth option which requires a modification of problem (4.16) that makes it possible to apply the mixed primal-dual approach in an easy way. For this, we associate to the area under the numéraire crop an additional cost R, which absorbs all net revenue. The resulting program is:

$$\tilde{\pi}(\rho, b) =$$
$$\max \Sigma_h \rho_h a_h - Ra_1$$
$$a_h \geq 0, \, h = 1, ..., n$$

subject to $\tag{4.18}$

$$\Sigma_h \delta_h a_h = b \qquad (\phi)$$
$$g(a_2, ..., a_n) \leq a_1$$

where R is set so that $\phi = 0$. Since $\tilde{\pi}(\rho, b) = \phi b$ and $\phi = 0$, it follows that $\tilde{\pi}(\rho, b) = 0$. In this formulation the rotation constraint is no longer to be interpreted as a purely technical requirement but as a representation of input requirements not explicitly accounted for in the model. In the absence of this constraint the program would allocate all land to the most profitable crop. The reason for not doing so in practice is not only that some technical requirements prevent this but also that the cropwise cost accounting is incomplete. For many important inputs like labour, machinery, insurance the cost data are not crop specific and for some they are not even recorded at the level of the farm. Program (4.18) explains the diversification as resulting from requirements for such unallocated and possibly unmeasured inputs. It attributes all profit to a residual input which is complementary to the numéraire crop. Note that the formulation shows similarity with the quadratic objective function that corresponds to maximization of expected quadratic indirect utility (see Hazell and Scandizzo (1979)), where product diversification (portfolio) is due to risk aversion.

The allocation problem can now be decomposed in two parts, one for relative acreages and one scaling equation to meet the land constraint. The relative acreages can be obtained easily as the shadow price on land is zero. In order to specify revenue maximization per unit of the numéraire crop we define relative net revenue $\tilde{\rho}_h = \rho_h / \rho_1$ and relative area $\tilde{a}_h = a_h / a_1$ for $h \neq 1$. Program (4.18) may then be written in three parts as:

$$\tilde{R}(\tilde{\rho}) =$$
$$\max \Sigma_{h \neq 1} \tilde{\rho}_h \tilde{a}_h$$
$$\tilde{a}_h \geq 0, \ h = 2, \ ..., \ n$$
subject to $\hspace{5cm}$ (4.19a)
$$g(\tilde{a}_2, \ ..., \ \tilde{a}_n) \leq 1$$

and

$$\Sigma_h \delta_h a_h = b \hspace{5cm} (4.19b)$$
$$a_h = \tilde{a}_h \, a_1, \text{ for } h = 2, \ ..., \ n \hspace{3cm} (4.19c)$$

where $\tilde{a}_h$ is optimal in (4.19a). The value function $\tilde{R}(\tilde{\rho})$ in (4.19a) is now a standard revenue function. The residual cost R is equal to the total net revenue per hectare of crop one: $R(\rho) = \rho_1(\tilde{R}(\rho_2/\rho_1, ..., \rho_n/\rho_1) + 1)$. Hence, $\tilde{R}(\tilde{\rho})$ may be given the interpretation of the markup rate in a constant returns to scale technology. Application of Hotelling's lemma gives the function $\tilde{a}(\tilde{\rho})$ which can be estimated and which has been used in ECAM.[70] Given these optimal $\tilde{a}$'s, constraint (4.19c) can be substituted into (4.19b) to compute acreages a_h.

Finally, we note that program (4.18) may be rewritten in an equivalent form as a single program (without feedback conditions on parameters):

$$\tilde{\pi}(\rho, b) =$$
$$\max \Sigma_h \rho_h a_h$$
$$a_h \geq 0, h = 1, ..., n$$

subject to $\qquad\qquad\qquad\qquad\qquad\qquad\qquad\qquad\qquad$ (4.20)

$$\Sigma_h \delta_h a_h = b \qquad\qquad (\phi)$$
$$g(a_2, ..., a_n) \leq a_1$$
$$\Sigma_h \rho_h a_h \geq R(\rho)a_1$$

As in (4.16) $\tilde{\pi}(\rho, b) = \phi b$, but the important difference with (4.16) is that the two constraints at the bottom fully determine the set of feasible a_h's, up to a scalar.

4.3.3   A program for the crop and the livestock sector combined

Structure of the program

Each national production model in ECAM consists of a program for a representative farm with a crop and a livestock sector. Land is the limiting resource b in the crop sector and operating capacity (to be defined in Section 4.3.4) is the limiting resource in the livestock sector. In this section the two sectors are only linked through the demand for animal feed. In Section 4.3.4 the

---

[70] ECAM uses the indirect addilog functional form: $\tilde{R}(\tilde{\rho}) = \Sigma_{h \neq 1} \alpha_h (\tilde{\rho}_h)^{(\sigma_h + 1)}$. This leads to the relative acreage function: $\tilde{a}_h = \beta_h (\tilde{\rho}_h)^{\sigma_h}$, where $\beta_h = \alpha_h(\sigma_h + 1)$. The parameter α_h is taken to be a function of $\tilde{a}_{h,t-1}$.

operating capacity available for livestock will be seen as a second channel of interaction because it will depend on the availability of fixed factors (land, labour, equipment) as well as on the operating capacity requirements of the crop sector.

As before, agricultural activities carry the subscript h, with h = 1, ..., n for crops and h = n+1, ..., N for livestock; the associated index sets are C = {1, ..., n} and L = {n+1, ..., N}, respectively and H = C ∪ L. Two types of crops have to be distinguished: green fodders (including roughage, with index set G) and marketed crops (with index set M). Green fodders remain within agriculture and are usually produced on the farm which uses them. Pastures, fodderbeets and fodder maize are important sources of green fodder. Markets for green fodders are not well developed and are characterized by high transportation margins, due to the bulkiness of the products. Therefore, green fodders are represented in ECAM as nontraded crops which have a value because they substitute for feeds purchased on the market, like coarse grains.

Let $w = \Sigma_{h \in G} (y_h a_h)$ denote the production of green fodders measured in energy units. The green fodders are assumed to be distributed among livestock activities according to a distribution function that satisfies:

Assumption W (green fodder distribution): Green fodder is distributed among livestock activities according to the function $w_h(w, a_{n+1}, ..., a_N)$, which is nonnegative, continuously differentiable, homogeneous of degree one, concave, increasing in w and such that $\Sigma_{h \in L} w_h(\cdot) \leq w$.[71]

The distribution rule is supposed to represent the imperfect substitution among alternative uses of green fodder which is due to the limited tradeability of the green fodders among farms as well as to the variation in suitability of land types, some being well suited say for sheep grazing only, while others are suitable for cattle grazing as well. It is also assumed that, for a given livestock herd there is decreasing returns to green fodder supply because of the limited

---

[71] The analytical form used is a linear system: $w_h = \eta_h(w - \Sigma_{i \in L} \theta_i a_i) + \theta_h a_h$, for every h ∈ L. where all η_h and θ_h are nonnegative and $\Sigma_h \eta_h < 1$ (as a representation of decreasing returns).

absorption capacity of green fodder by animals.[72] Energy requirements by livestock activity h are determined according to a feed requirement function.[73]

Assumption M (feed requirement): The feed requirement function $m_h(y_h)$ is continuous, increasing for $y_h \leq \bar{y}_h$ and infinite for $y_h > \bar{y}_h$.

It is assumed that the feed requirements which are not satisfied from green fodder must be purchased on the market.[74] Hence, the net purchase of feed is:

$$z_h = m_h(y_h)a_h - w_h(w, a_{n+1}, ..., a_N), \text{ for every } h \in L \qquad (4.21)$$

The cost function for livestock production will not be specified as in (4.14) for crops. It consists of three parts, $c_h^0(p, y_h)a_h$ for non-feed inputs (like fuel) and $c_h^1(p)z_h$ for the purchased feeds[75] and $p^w w$ for green fodders, where p^w is the price of green fodder. The green fodder purchased by the livestock sector will have to be paid to the crop sector so that the two cancel out and are absent from the objective of the program of the two sectors combined.

---

[72] Although time series data are available on the surfaces under green fodders, the production on this land is not recorded systematically, so that it has to be imputed from the feed requirements of the animals. For this an energy balance (in time series form) has been set up for each livestock activity in each member state. The total requirement for green fodder is then obtained residually and the yields are derived from there. The decreasing returns property in assumption W is to be understood in the sense that the marginal productivity on greenfodder will lie below the average productivity.

[73] The feed requirement function is specified as: $m_h = \kappa_h + \varepsilon_h y_h$ for $y_h \leq \bar{y}_h$ and infinite otherwise, for every $h \in L$. The slope parameters ε_h are nonnegative. The intercepts κ_h are positive and time-dependent; it may be interpreted as a maintenance requirement. The feed requirement is expressed in energy units.

[74] The relevant commodities are wheat, coarse grains, milk and compounds of carbohydrates and protein feeds.

[75] The cost function has been specified as: $c_h^1(p) = \Sigma_k p_k \gamma_{hk} + \delta_{h0} \Pi_k (p_k)^\delta hk$, with $\delta_{hk} \geq 0$ and such that $\Sigma_k \delta_{hk} = 1$, where k is the index of the (feed) commodity purchased. This leads to a linear expenditure system: $p_k v_{hk} = (\delta_{hk} (c_h^1(p) - \Sigma_i p_{ik} \gamma_{hi}) + p_k \gamma_{hk}) z_h$. This specification assumes that the composition of purchased feeds does not vary with the animal yield.

The program also contains yield functions for crops which satisfy assumption Y[76] and distinct 'rotation'-functions are specified for crop and livestock activities:

Assumption G2 (rotation function for crops and livestock): The rotation function $g_C(a_2, ..., a_n)$ and $g_L(a_{n+1}, ..., a_N)$ are continuous, monotonic and homogeneous of degree one. Moreover, they are convex and have strictly concave isoquants.

We adopt the approach of program (4.18) and introduce residual costs R_C and R_L which absorb all profits in the crops and livestock sectors, respectively. We are now ready to write the mathematical program as:

$$\max \sum_{h \in M} p_h a_h - \sum_{h \in G} c_h(p, y_h)a_h - R_C a_1 +$$
$$\sum_{h \in L} (p_h^f y_h a_h - c_h^0(p, y_h)a_h - c_h^1(p)z_h) - R_L a_{n+1}$$

$a_h \geq 0$, all $h \in H$; $y_h \geq 0$, all $h \in G$; $y_h, z_h \geq 0$, all $h \in L$, $w \geq 0$

subject to   (4.22)

$$\sum_{h \in C} \delta_h a_h = b_C \qquad\qquad (\phi_C)$$
$$g_C(a_2, ..., a_n) \leq a_1$$
$$\sum_{h \in L} \delta_h a_h = b_L \qquad\qquad (\phi_L)$$
$$g_L(a_{n+2}, ..., a_N) \leq a_{n+1}$$
$$z_h \geq m_h(y_h)a_h - w_h(w, a_{n+1}, ..., a_N)$$
$$w = \sum_{h \in G} y_h a_h$$

where R_C and R_L are set so that $\phi_C = 0$ and $\phi_L = 0$.

Decomposition of the program

---

[76] A linear technology is assumed with a (time-dependent) maximum yield $\bar{y}_h$. For marketed crops the net revenue maximization (4.15) is $\tilde{p}_h(p_h^f, p) = \max ((p_h^f - \sum_k p_k \alpha_{hk})y_h \mid 0 \leq y_h \leq \bar{y}_h)$. This reduces to $\tilde{p}_h(p_h^f, p) = (p_h^f - \sum_k p_k \alpha_{hk})\bar{y}_h)$ whenever the net revenue is positive. When the net revenue is negative the yield will be set to zero but one may as well set it equal to $\bar{y}_h$, since the overall program will then set $a_h = 0$ (unless it is the numéraire crop). For green fodder and livestock the yield is also at a bound, as will be explained in footnote 79.

To implement the mixed primal-dual approach like in (4.19), (so as to avoid the estimation of the parameters of the (primal) rotation function), this program has to be decomposed. It can indeed be partitioned into a crop and a livestock program, as follows. We assume that $z_h > 0$, so that feed is purchased on the market for all livestock activities. Then, the marginal value p^w for green fodder can be obtained as shadow price for the last equation in program (4.22) as:

$$p^w(p, w, a_{n+1}, ..., a_N) = \Sigma_{h \in L} \ c_h^1(p) \ \partial w_h(w, a_{n+1}, ..., a_N)/\partial w$$

Hence, for green fodders a net revenue per hectare $(p^w y_h - c_h(p, y_h))$ can be computed, and a net revenue maximizing yield can be determined, for every $h \in G$, in a way similar to (4.15) as:[77]

$$\tilde{p}_h(p, w, a_{n+1}, ..., a_N) =$$
$$\max p^w(p, w, a_{n+1}, ..., a_N)y_h - c_h(p, y_h) \qquad (4.23)$$
$$y_h \geq 0$$

For given net revenues,[78] the cropping decisions can now be determined according to (4.18), using (4.19). We can now specify the program of the livestock sector separately, charging it with a price p^w for its green fodder purchases:

---

[77] Hence, if a linear technology is assumed the yield determination can proceed like for marketed crops. See footnote 76.

[78] The net revenue in general depends on $(w, a_{n+1}, ..., a_N)$ but in the linear expenditure specification the value of p^w depends only on (known) prices, since $\partial w_h/\partial w$ $(= \eta_h)$ is constant. Therefore, the green fodder price can be computed outside the program. Hence the linear expenditure system makes it possible to solve the crop and the livestock allocations separately.

$$\max \sum_{h \in L} (p_h^f y_h a_h - c_h^0(p, y_h)a_h - c_h^1(p)(m_h(y_h)a_h - w_h(w, a_{n+1}, ..., a_N)))$$
$$- p^w w - R_L a_{n+1}$$

$$a_h, y_h \geq 0, \text{ all } h \in L, w \geq 0$$

subject to $\qquad\qquad\qquad\qquad\qquad\qquad\qquad\qquad\qquad$ (4.24)

$$\sum_{h \in L} \delta_h a_h = b_L \qquad\qquad (\phi_L)$$

$$g_L(a_{n+2}, ..., a_N) \leq a_{n+1}$$

The constraints are as in (4.18) and as before R_L can be set so as to absorb all profits. However, in order to enable implementation of a revenue function as in (4.19), we still need to reformulate the objective in the standard form. First, we define the net revenue that would prevail if all livestock were to consume purchased feed only:[79]

$$\psi_h = p_h^f y_h - c_h^0(p, y_h) - c_h^1(p) \, m_h(y_h)$$

Secondly, we define relative net revenues and activity levels $\tilde{\psi}_h = \psi_h/\psi_{n+1}$ and relative livestock numbers $\tilde{a}_h = a_h/a_{n+1}$ for $h = n+2, ..., N$. Finally, we also define normalized values for c_h^1, p^w and w: $\tilde{c}_h^1 = c_h^1/\psi_{n+1}$, $\tilde{p}^w = p^w/\psi_{n+1}$ and $\tilde{w} = w/a_{n+1}$. Now, the equivalent of (4.19) may be written as:

$$\tilde{R}_L =$$
$$\max \sum_{h > n+1} \tilde{\psi}_h \tilde{a}_h + \sum_{h \geq n+1} \tilde{c}_h^1 w_h(\tilde{w}, \tilde{a}) - \tilde{p}^w \tilde{w}$$
$$\tilde{a}_h \geq 0, \text{ all } h > n+1, \tilde{w} \geq 0$$

subject to $\qquad\qquad\qquad\qquad\qquad\qquad\qquad\qquad\qquad$ (4.25)

$$g_L(\tilde{a}_{n+2}, ..., \tilde{a}_N) \leq 1 \qquad\qquad (\phi_L)$$

To analyze the properties of this program, we use the Kuhn-Tucker conditions:

---

[79] The function $c_h^0(p, y_h)$ is specified as $(\sum_k p_k \alpha_{hk})y_h$. The net revenue maximizing yield is then determined in: $\psi_h(p_h^f, p) = \max ((p_h^f - \sum_k p_k \alpha_{hk})y_h - c_h^1(p)m_h(y_h) \mid 0 \leq y_h \leq \bar{y}_h)$. Due to the linearity of the function m_h this problem also will find its optimum at $\bar{y}_h$ (or at zero).

(i) $\tilde{\psi}_h + \sum_{i \in L} \tilde{c}_i^1 \partial w_i / \partial \tilde{a}_h = \phi_L \partial g_L / \partial \tilde{a}_h,$ for every $h > n+1$

(ii) $\sum_{i \in L} \tilde{c}_i^1 \partial w_i / \partial \tilde{w} = \tilde{p}^w$

$$(4.26)$$

Condition (4.26ii) holds by definition of $\tilde{p}^w$. Therefore, the optimum is fully characterized by condition (4.26i), which implies that marginal net revenue may be defined as:[80]

$$\tilde{\rho}_h = \tilde{\psi}_h + \sum_{i \in L} \tilde{c}_i^1 \partial w_i / \partial \tilde{a}_h, \text{ for every } h \in L \qquad (4.27)$$

This makes it possible to apply (4.18) and (4.19) as for crops.[81]

Solution procedure

Once the parameters have been estimated the mathematical program for agricultural supply can be solved numerically in the following sequence, starting with the crop sector.[82]

Crops:

(i)   Compute net revenues $\tilde{\rho}_h$ using (4.15) for marketable crops, (4.23) for green fodders.

(ii)   Determine the relative activity levels $\tilde{a}_h$ as $\partial \tilde{R}_C / \partial \tilde{\rho}$ (applying Hotelling's lemma as in (4.19)).

(iii)   Scale activity levels to satisfy the resource balance.

---

[80] This leads to a specification in which the marginal net revenue may depend on variables (w and $\tilde{a}_h$) that are set in the program. Then, the problem becomes a mathematical program with feedback (recall the Negishi-format of Section 3.1.2). However, in the linear expenditure specification there is no such feedback. First, the variable $\tilde{w}$ disappears from the objective of the problem. Secondly, the net revenue is $\tilde{\rho}_h = \tilde{\psi}_h + (\tilde{c}_h^1 - \tilde{p}^w)\theta_h$, where θ_h is the committed demand. This implies that, committed demand has to be valued at the price of green fodder and uncommitted demand at the unit cost of purchased feed. It also implies that all net revenues can be computed outside the program, so that the livestock program can also be specified according to (4.18) and (4.19) using as numéraire value the net revenue ρ_{n+1} rather than ψ_{n+1} and this is in fact the specification used in ECAM.

[81] We recall that the linear expenditure system for green fodder allocation enables to compute net revenue in (4.27) as depending on prices only, so that the crop and livestock allocation can be solved for separately. In general, iterative adjustment is required.

[82] Prior to this calculation all parameter values have been adjusted and yields have been set at their bound $\bar{y}_h$.

(iv)   Compute outputs as $y_h a_h$.

(v)   Apply Shephard's lemma to recover input demands.

Livestock:

(vi)   Distribute roughage production among animals.

(vii)   Compute net revenues ρ_h using (4.27).

(viii)   Perform the steps (ii)-(v) for livestock.[83]

If the computation of net revenue depends only on prices p^f and p, then this procedure can be executed recursively. Otherwise an iterative adjustment is required to make the feedback variables which determine net revenues coincide with the values obtained in (i)-(viii). The linear distribution rule for green fodder would indeed, by itself, lead to a recursive procedure. However, there is a further complication: production quotas.

The CAP involves production quotas for milk and sugar. These have been implemented as additional inequality constraints in program (4.22). The Lagrange multipliers μ_h associated with these constraints are like input prices for additional commodities. Hence, in the computation of net revenue, the term $p_h^f y_h$ must be replaced by $(p_h^f - \mu_h) y_h$. After this modification, steps (i)-(viii) can be executed but the variables μ_h must be adjusted iteratively until the quota restrictions are satisfied.

4.3.4   The full program with land, labour and capital

The agricultural supply program (4.22) takes land b_C and livestock operating capacity b_L as given. Here, we relate these variables to the fixed factors land, capital and labour (A, K, and E) according to an aggregate transformation function which is separable between outputs and inputs:

$$F(Y_C, Y_L) - G(A, K, E) \leq 0$$

---

[83] Consider the demand for purchased feed which will result from this calculation. Its energy content may not be equal to the energy requirement $(m_h(y_h) - w_h))$. This deviation can be interpreted as an efficiency loss due to imperfect substitutability but numerical tests with ECAM show that the difference is minor.

where Y_C and Y_L are aggregate output indices of the crop and livestock sectors and where the function $F(Y_C, Y_L)$ is convex increasing and homogeneous of degree one, and $G(A, K, E)$ is concave increasing and homogeneous of degree one.[84]

The output indices are specified as production indices $Y_C(\bar{y}_1 a_1, ..., \bar{y}_n a_n)$, $Y_L(\bar{y}_{n+1} a_{n+1}, ..., \bar{y}_N a_N)$. These are taken to be linear, with fixed positive weights v_h.[85] For livestock, the requirements δ_h of operating capacity b_L are set at $\delta_h = v_h \bar{y}_h$, so that $b_L = Y_L$, by definition. It would seem preferable to treat factor inputs of labour and capital in a crop specific manner, together with current inputs but this is not possible because very little data is available on labour and capital inputs by activity and, moreover, the valuation of these inputs is problematic: recall that it was the impossibility of allocating fixed factors to crop and livestock activities that led us to adopt the residual-cost specification (4.18).

The supply program (4.22) can now be extended to incorporate the transformation function. For this we make use of the net revenue maximizing formulation (4.20). We start from given net revenues which have been computed according to (4.15), (4.23) and (4.27) for marketable crops, green fodder and livestock respectively (possibly accounting for production quotas). The extended program is:

$$\Pi(\rho, p, A, K, E) =$$
$$\max \Sigma_h \rho_h a_h$$
$$a_h \geq 0, \text{ all } h \in H, Y_L \geq 0$$

subject to (4.28)

---

[84] In ECAM the function $F(Y_C, Y_L)$ is taken to be CES-convex: $F(Y_C, Y_L) = (\alpha Y_C^\rho + (1-\alpha)Y_L^\rho)^{1/\rho}$, with $\rho > 1$ for convexity. The function $G(1, K/A, E/A)$ is also taken to be CES but concave and with decreasing returns: $G(1, K/A, E/A) = (\beta(K/A)^{-\mu} + \gamma(E/A)^{-\mu})^{-\lambda/\mu}$, with $0 < \lambda < 1$ for decreasing returns and $\mu > -1$ for concavity.

[85] We use the base year net revenues (in base year prices) as weights: $v_{h,t} = \rho_{h,t}/\bar{y}_{h,t}$, $t = 0$.

$$\sum_{h \in C} \delta_h a_h = A \qquad\qquad (\phi_C)$$

$$g_C(a_2, \, ..., \, a_n) \leq a_1$$

$$\sum_{h \in C} \rho_h a_h \geq R_C(\rho)a_1$$

$$\sum_{h \in L} \delta_h a_h = Y_L$$

$$g_L(a_{n+2}, \, ..., \, a_N) \leq a_{n+1}$$

$$\sum_{h \in L} \rho_h a_h \geq R_L(\rho)a_{n+1}$$

$$F(Y_C(a_1, \, ..., \, a_n), \, Y_L) \leq G(A, \, K, \, E)$$

This program is decomposable, because all cropping decisions are set according to the first three constraints.[86] Therefore, one may solve for crops first and then consider the problem for livestock, treating Y_C as a given parameter. For livestock, the value function of program (4.20) may be used to obtain a more compact form. Let $\tilde{\pi}_L(\rho, \, 1)$ be the net revenue per unit of Y_L defined like in (4.20). Problem (4.28) then reduces to:

$$\max P_L Y_L$$
$$Y_L \geq 0$$

subject to $\qquad\qquad\qquad\qquad\qquad\qquad\qquad\qquad$ (4.29)

$$F(Y_C, \, Y_L) \leq G(A, \, K, \, E)$$

for given Y_C, where $P_L = \tilde{\pi}_L(\rho, \, 1)$. For positive P_L, this is a trivial problem, and, therefore, Y_L can be computed directly from the transformation function. However, the problem becomes non-trivial when we allow for investment.

4.3.5 Resource adjustment

Since all production factors can be considered to be variable in the long run, they can in principle be represented as current inputs in an intertemporal model

---

[86] We must emphasize the importance of the equality sign in the land balance. It may happen that the shadow price ϕ_C becomes negative, because the marginal productivity in the crop sector is too low. However, we do not elaborate on this case because in model simulations with ECAM the variable ϕ_C remains positive.

with a given time horizon of say T years (as discussed in Section 3.4). When faced with a complete set of prices for current as well as future inputs and outputs, the producer will use capital, labour and land so as to maximize the present value of returns. Hence, in such a setup land outflow, labour migration and capital investment follow from competition for scarce resources. One advantage of such a formulation is that it is fully compatible with general equilibrium theory. A formulation which is intertemporally optimal also has the advantage that it ensures time consistency: if price expectations are realized, all producers stick to their original plans.

However, this only holds for a plan drawn up at $t = 0$ until a fixed end-year T; hence, there may be time inconsistency if a new plan is made at $t = 1$ until T+1. Therefore, time inconsistency can only be avoided if the planning horizon in the model is much longer than the simulation horizon and in principle it has to be infinite. As implementation of infinite horizon models remains problematic (see Keyzer (1991)), it may not be practical to use intertemporal optimization. There are also empirical reasons for not following an intertemporal optimization approach in the representation of EU agriculture. First, a realistic specification of intertemporal behaviour involves the representation of individual farmers and the differences between them, as in model (3.10). Even such a disaggregated model may be of limited value because there are many discrete and often irreversible choices which have to be accounted for, particularly in relation to the non-agricultural use of land and to migration; investment decisions are affected by uncertainty, liquidity constraints and life cycle considerations (see Phimister (1993)). These issues cannot be addressed through intertemporal extensions of the agricultural supply program. Secondly, in a model where the non-agricultural sector is semi-exogenous, the absorption of fixed factors outside agriculture cannot be made fully endogenous. Therefore, a more partial approach has been adopted, which we will now describe.

Land

Land outflow from agriculture is specified through a time trend. Two general reasons for keeping factor outflow exogenous have already been given. For land, there is the further justification that in several EU member states it is a government decision whether land is to be reserved for agricultural purposes or may be devoted to other uses.

Labour

The specification of labour supply in agriculture distinguishes between demographic rate of change g_t and a migration rate m_{jt} (recall that $j \in J_1$ for farmers):

$$E_{jt} = (1 + g_{jt-1} + m_{jt-1}) \, E_{jt-1}, \text{ for every } j \in J_1 \qquad (4.30)$$

Total employment E_{jt} equals the sum of two working populations: young (0-55 years) and old (55+). For the second cohort (55+) migration equals zero by assumption. Both agricultural age classes have their own participation ratio (the ratio of employment over population), which can be obtained from the average national participation ratio and the age distributions of agricultural employment and total population. Then the demographic rate of change g_{jt-1} of agricultural employment is, for both age classes, equal to the sum of the growth rate of the corresponding total population cohort and the age specific participation ratio. Outmigration applies only to the cohort 0-55 and is specified according to:

$$m_{jt} = M_j(H_{j+1,t}/H_{jt}, \, E_{j+1,t}/E_{jt}), \text{ for every } j \in J_1 \qquad (4.31)$$

where H_j is the per capita income.[87] The function M_j is increasing in its arguments. It is formulated in the Todaro-tradition (Todaro (1976) and Linnemann et al. (1979)) and can be derived from diffusion models. Hence, migration rises with income disparity and also depends on the relative size of employment in both sectors (for more details, see Folmer (1993)). The population levels which affect the consumption and utility calculations can now

---

[87] The subscript j+1 refers to the non-farmer associated to farmer j. In ECAM the values of E_{jt} are updated for natural growth before they are entered into this equation and the function M_j is linear in logarithms. The population which migrates out of agriculture obviously becomes non-agricultural.

be recovered through division of the sectoral labour force by the sectoral participation rate.

Capital

A simple way to avoid time inconsistency in capital accumulation is to treat capital in the agricultural sector as being rented from the non-agricultural sector at a rental rate $r(p)$ (which includes interest charges and depreciation). The capital stock is then obtained by solving for given agricultural employment E and land area A, the extension of program (4.29), and hence, of the full program (4.28):

$$\max P_L Y_L - r(p)K$$
$$K, Y_L \geq 0$$

subject to $\qquad\qquad\qquad\qquad\qquad\qquad\qquad$ (4.32)

$$F(Y_C, Y_L) \leq G(A, K, E)$$

for given Y_C.[88]

4.4 The dynamic structure

It would in principle be feasible to replace the original producer model (3.2) by the full model (4.28) extended with a capital investment as in (4.32). All interactions would then be simultaneous. However, this would insufficiently account for planning lags in agricultural production and for gestation lags in investments.

Therefore, in ECAM a more differentiated dynamic structure has been implemented. A one-year production lag has been assumed in the crop and livestock allocation component (4.28) with the qualification that feed composition can adjust instantaneously. Hence, in terms of the stylized model,

---

[88] In ECAM some flexibility constraints which keep changes in capital stock within reasonable bounds had to be imposed as well.

it is with given agricultural supply and given intermediate and investment demand for non-agricultural commodities by the farmers that the market equilibrium is solved in every year of simulation. The resulting incomes then affect migration and investments and, given the announced prices and subsidies for the following crop-year, the allocation problem is solved again for each member state. This yields the new values for the market equilibrium calculation, and so on. The following steps summarize this computational scheme:

(i)   Land outflow and labour migration
(ii)   Crop and livestock allocation
(iii) Investment
(iv)   Policy adjustments
(v)   EU-market equilibrium

4.5   Experience gained from ECAM

The value of ECAM depends mainly on its usefulness in policy analysis and this can only be judged on the basis of the policy scenarios that will be discussed in subsequent chapters. However, the model has now been operational for several years and experience has been gained not only in the process of its construction but also of its maintenance and use. In this section we will report on this and successively discuss the experience in terms of data requirements, econometric estimation and the model specification itself.

Data requirements

Applied general equilibrium models are considered to be very 'data hungry'. The construction of a social accounting matrix is in particular a data intensive process. The ECAM-project started with the construction of a complete SAM for the base year 1982 (see Folmer et al., 1988). This was a time-consuming and laborious task, not only because of the large amount of data that had to be processed, but also because of the large number of inconsistencies between them. This SAM served as the basis for initializing the model and since it was impossible to update it fully over a series of years it also served as a source for processing coefficients, commodity mappings and tax rates. Tax rates have been adjusted over time on the basis of time series data but no such series are available for processing margins. This posed a problem when it came to running the model over the period 1982-90, the main years for calibration. Some processing coefficients led to unreasonable prices, so that the coefficients had to be adjusted. Hence, it appeared that the processing coefficients in the SAM depreciated rather quickly and this casts some doubt on the usefulness of a very detailed treatment of the processing margins in the SAM. It is our tentative conclusion that the processing level of the agricultural commodities represented in the model should be kept as close as possible to the raw material level, especially for agricultural production and for international trade. This can be achieved by treating the demand, say for processing in agricultural imports as part of the non-agricultural imports.

Besides these problems with processing margins on trade and production, the other data requirements have not been excessive. Time series data on crop yields, crop areas, intervention prices etc. are readily available and are more easily fitted within a disaggregated model like ECAM than in an aggregated model.

Econometric estimation

All behavioral components of the model have been estimated by econometric (maximum likelihood) methods. This was also a time-consuming process. As discussed in Section 4.1.4, the modular approach for estimating parameters has the attraction that it is more easily manageable than the simultaneous equations approach. However, because it is essentially static, the method is insufficient to ensure a good fit for the model as a whole when it is simulated over a historical period. This has also been our experience. The initial estimates provide a reasonable fit in the initial years but they need adjustments to generate a good dynamic behaviour. This was particularly the case for the crop and livestock allocation models and for investments. In our view the econometrics of the separate modules mainly serves as a device to reject inappropriate specifications and to provide first round estimates of parameters.

Specification

With respect to model specification it is our overall conclusion that the general formulation given in this chapter is sufficiently rigorous to lead to a coherent model and yet sufficiently flexible to make the model suitable for the different conditions which prevail in the various member states. Also, when in the future more data becomes available on crop specific inputs, for example for labour, these can be incorporated relatively easily and would significantly improve the quality of the model.

However, some of the functional forms could have been chosen differently. The linear expenditure system of feed purchases appears, for example, to allow insufficient substitution between cereals and protein feeds. The linearity of the yield relations is also debatable, although here the alternatives do not seem very promising, because at the national level it is very difficult to disentangle the growth in yields (and the related change in input requirements) due to substitution by the farmer from the change due to technological progress.

Among the further limitations in the specification of ECAM we mention the following. First, the model only applies to the EU-9. Although this covers a large fraction of the supply of CAP-related commodities, models for the other three members, as well as for the EFTA countries that have joined the EU in 1995 must be incorporated in the near future. Secondly, there is a single representative farmer in each country. Although the model could be disaggregated to a level with several representative farmers, it is not clear that this would significantly improve the capability of explaining national supply response, and further, this extension is not a minor task. Thirdly, the relations with future members, associated countries and other countries with preferential arrangements could be made more explicit. Finally, in the present version all international prices are exogenous and therefore unaffected by EU policies; this is unrealistic. While the scenarios that will be described in subsequent chapters, rely on exogenous adjustments in international prices, depending on the policy that is pursued, it would be useful to link ECAM to a model of international trade, or if no such model is available, to develop trade models for important EU partners like the US.

In the future development of ECAM, efforts should be made to overcome these limitations. Fortunately for the econometricians, the MacSharry reform introduces many variations in prices, especially for animal feeds. This will help in strengthening the reliability of the empirical estimates. Surveys are now also available that allow the representation of income distribution within countries. Moreover, initial steps have already been made to extend the coverage of ECAM to the EU-15.

Annex 4A

Model validation

A main step in model validation is to assess how well the model can track the past. This Annex describes the procedure that was followed to validate ECAM. Applied modellers must always navigate with great care between the disclaimer that their model is not meant to predict the future and the claim that it has practical relevance nonetheless. AGE-modellers and other builders of large scale models find themselves in even more dangerous waters because their models contain various parameters that were estimated for model components separately, or were obtained from calibration. We cannot circumvent all these problems, but rather than stating in general terms that the model has been calibrated over a given historical period and turning to future simulations right away, we describe in this annex how ECAM has been validated. Section 4A.1 discusses the general approach, while Section 4A.2 reports on results.

4A.1 The approach to validation

When comparing ECAM outcomes with observed facts as reported in the official statistics, it is important to realize that we are not particularly interested in replicating the details and only want to focus on the main tendencies. A model that reproduces all statistics with great accuracy will usually be one that has used up so many degrees of freedom that its forecasts are very poor. There are also more CAP-specific reasons not to aim for a perfect replication of the past. We mention three.

First, the CAP consists of an extensive and complex set of measures and regulations, which in some instances are changing by the day. Obviously, in modelling the CAP one has to abstract from many such details. The second point relates to the deterministic nature of ECAM simulations, which do not account for random shocks caused, say, by animal diseases or fluctuations in rainfall. Simulated crop and animal yields only give averages over time, and consequently model outcomes deviate from statistical observations. The third point concerns the availability and quality of the data. The construction of a complete social accounting matrix for the base year 1982 requires that data from various sources had to be adjusted so as to fit within a consistent framework. For years beyond 1982 much of the data used for 1982 was not available (sometimes it was available but not processed). Hence, it is simply not possible to check the 'fit' for all variables.

The model validation was part of a calibration exercise and proceeded as follows. If the difference between the time path of a model variable and the observed development was considered too large, first the underlying data base was checked for logical mistakes. This sometimes led to the detection of errors, for example concerning the assumptions with respect to data aggregation, analytical specification or estimation procedures. Occasionally this has led to changes in function specifications and parameter estimates (e.g. in agricultural investment). For a description and justification of the main adjustments made in this way, see the references in Annex 4B. If, after this second step, the result was still unsatisfactory, estimated values of some model parameters were changed in a more ad hoc way. Clearly, the adjustments were not done in an arbitrary way, but only to make the model fit better. Parameters that were found to be robust in econometric estimation were left untouched. Parameter adjustments were tolerated if they could be based either on non-quantitative and patchy quantitative information, that was not used in the estimation procedure, or on knowledge that structural changes had occurred after the sample period of estimation. For example, in the allocation model of animal feeds, a shift from cereal substitutes back to cereals (due to the price fall under the MacSharry reform) has been introduced through a forced substitution between committed quantities (see Folmer et al. (1990)).

4A.2   Comparison of model outcomes with published statistics

The standard computer output of a simulation run contains about 250 pages,

Table 4A.1   Production quantities, EU-9, 1982-90

	Production Annual growth rate		Acreage mln ha, average		Animal stocks mln heads, average	
	(1)	(2)	(1)	(2)	(1)	(2)
Wheat	3.1	2.9	12422	12346		
Coarse grains	-0.1	-0.1	13044	12709		
Rice	3.4	3.7	202	211		
Sugar beet	1.0	1.0	1781	1669		
Oilseeds	13.8	15.4	2617	2613		
Veg., fruit, potatoes	1.4	1.4	3050	2832		
Grapes	-0.2	-4.2	2181	2212		
Dairy cows	-0.3	-0.7			24.0	23.0
Laying hens	0.1	-0.3			277.6	261.6
Non-dairy cattle	0.5	0.6			53.9	50.5
Sheep and goats	4.0	3.3			57.6	58.1
Pigs	1.4	1.6			80.0	79.6
Poultry	3.2	1.7			514.7	568.1

Columns:
(1)   ECAM results
(2)   Computed from FAO's Agrostat Supply Utilization Accounts, FAO (1992).
Note: Veg., fruit, potatoes denotes vegetables, temperate fruit and consumable potatoes.

showing volume and value accounts for all products and for each of the nine member states[89], condensed versions of the national accounts, value added of agriculture and non-agriculture, a summary of consumer expenditures etc. In short, the output consists of a complete social accounting matrix for each year the model is solved. Here we only present results on selected variables. We show nine tables. These cannot fully be confronted with statistical information due to the lack of available data. Therefore, the comparison between ECAM calculations and data from published statistics is occasionally incomplete. The historical simulation period refers to 1982-1990.

Table 4A.1   Production[90]

---

[89] Figures for Belgium and Luxembourg are combined.

[90] The computations based upon FAO's Supply Utilization Accounts are documented in Merbis (1995a).

The validation effort has focused on the crop and livestock allocation, to ensure that production tracks at the EU level. The ECAM base run shows modest growth rates of agricultural production for most commodities. For some products production even declined. Oilseeds were a remarkable exception, as in the period 1982-1990 oilseed production increased on average by 15 per cent a year. The background of these developments has already been discussed in Chapter 2 and the model appears to reproduce these trends reasonably well.

Table 4A.2   Production quantities, 1982-90, period average and annual growth rate

	Wheat				Oilseeds			
	Mln metric tons		Annual growth rate		Mln metric tons		Annual growth rate	
	(1)	(2)	(1)	(2)	(1)	(2)	(1)	(2)
Belgium-Luxembourg	1299	1257	3.4	3.6	18	20	3.9	11.5
Denmark	2534	2321	10.1	16.0	693	533	11.7	11.3
France	29622	28951	2.7	3.5	3548	3599	11.2	11.3
Germany, Fed. Rep.	10614	10201	3.5	2.8	1077	1047	13.6	16.4
Ireland	496	476	4.1	5.7	0	11	-	-
Italy	8760	8684	-1.3	-1.3	1236	1268	26.7	32.3
The Netherlands	855	961	-2.1	1.3	24	36	-10.3	-2.0
United Kingdom	14306	12637	6.5	3.9	1046	964	8.4	10.6
	Cattle				Pigs			
Belgium-Luxembourg	322	317	1.7	1.6	716	761	2.3	2.4
Denmark	196	229	-1.5	-1.7	1079	1109	2.5	2.6
France	2075	1863	-0.1	-0.1	1900	1741	2.7	1.4
Germany, Fed. Rep.	1589	1618	1.6	2.4	3260	3264	-0.1	0.8
Ireland	446	437	0.8	4.4	124	147	0.4	0.5
Italy	643	1216	0.8	0.8	1230	1220	3.8	2.3
The Netherlands	536	503	-0.2	3.1	1695	1448	2.7	4.0
United Kingdom	1043	1054	0.2	0.4	1079	975	0.2	-0.1

Columns:
(1)   ECAM results
(2)   Computed from FAO's Agrostat Supply Utilization Accounts.

Table 4A.2   Production by member state

Striking differences in growth performance between member states can be observed for the four commodities listed. For example, wheat production in Denmark increased by some 10 per cent per year, according to ECAM, while in Italy there was an average annual decline of 1.3 per cent. Since the developments of production at member state level are more erratic than at EU level, the discrepancies are necessarily larger, especially for the smaller countries. Yet the differences were found acceptable, and appear to cancel out at the level of the EU-9.

Table 4A.3   Consumption and intermediate demand, EU-9, 1982-90, annual growth rate

	Consumption		Intermediate demand	
	(1)	(2)	(1)	(2)
Wheat	1.8	0.7	4.6	5.1
Coarse grains	2.6	1.7	-3.5	-2.0
Sugar	0.7	-0.5	2.7	7.8
Fats and oils	0.6	2.5	0.3	-1.4
Protein feeds	-	-	2.1	6.5
Carbohydrates	-	-	0.4	-1.2
Wine	-0.2	-1.7	2.7	n.a.
Butter	-0.7	-1.1	-2.1	0.0
Other dairy	1.6	2.2	-2.3	-1.9
Bovine meat	-0.4	0.3	2.4	n.a.
Ovine meat	1.1	0.8	3.3	n.a.
Pig meat	1.8	2.0	3.0	n.a.
Poultry meat and eggs	1.6	0.6	-1.1	0.6

Columns:
(1)   ECAM results
(2)   Eurostat supply balance sheets for wheat, coarse grains and bovine meat and FAO's Agrostat Supply Utilization Accounts for the other commodities.
Note: In column (2) fats and oils and protein feeds only from crushing oilseeds; carbohydrates covers only manioc, starch potatoes and byproducts from breweries and sugar processing. In column (1) sugar only refers to refined sugar from sugar beet, while in column (2) it covers sugar in all products.

Table 4A.3   Consumption and intermediate demand.
The model distinguishes between three types of internal demand: consumption, intermediate use and stockpiling. Stock adjustments can hardly be tuned, as in practice changes in stocks (exports, subsidized consumption) are mainly determined by unpredictable policy decisions. Therefore, we do not report them here.

Table 4A.3 compares statistical figures on consumption and intermediate demand (in case they are available) with model outcomes. In general the differences are not excessive in the cases where the statistics are defined in a way similar to the model variable. In cases were discrepancies look more serious, they can be explained by differences in definition.

The consumption pattern is in line with developments described by the statistics. The growth rates reflect the demand effect of a slowly growing population, of the low price and income elasticities of demand, and of the changes in preferences, away from animal fat, wine and bovine meat. Developments in intermediate demand (feed, seeds and waste), are dominated by feed demand. The feed use of wheat has increased at the expense of coarse grains.

Table 4A.4   Net imports, EU-9, three-year average, 1000 metric tons

	1982/84		1985/87		1988/90	
	(1)	(2)	(1)	(2)	(1)	(2)
Wheat	-12110	-13855	-8926	-14120	-15738	-18685
Coarse grains	2895	2610	-4885	-7555	-9359	-9130
Sugar	-4081	-4310	-4716	-4210	-3975	-4705
Protein feeds	10210	4335	11005	5246	11207	5460
Carbohydrates	22990	6200	24880	6135	23791	6075
Butter	-170	-270	-372	-340	-718	-290
Other dairy	-9930	-10505	-13630	-10840	-14294	-11560
Bovine meat	-128	-260	-445	-255	-450	-285

Columns:
(1)   ECAM results
(2)   Eurostat Supply balance sheets for wheat, coarse grains and bovine meat and FAO's Agrostat Supply Utilization Accounts for the other commodities.
Note: See also the note in Table 4A.3 on the definition of the cereal substitutes.

Table 4A.4   External trade
The excess of production and committed import over internal demand is exported to third countries, either directly or after a period of stockpiling. In the eighties EU-9 imports declined and exports increased. The differences in Table 4A.4 with respect to protein feeds and carbohydrates can be explained from differences in product coverage.

Table 4A.5   Net cereals trade by member state

In Table 4A.5 the trade figures for cereals are shown by country. Since net trade is the balancing item of two relative large quantities, we find the differences acceptable. We also note that Eurostat's commodity balance for wheat and coarse grains has been consolidated in a way different from ECAM.

Table 4A.5   Net cereals imports, three-year average, 1000 metric tons

	1982/84		1985/87		1988/90	
	(1)	(2)	(1)	(2)	(1)	(2)
Belgium-Luxembourg	2879	1810	2573	1820	2538	1880
Denmark	-837	-1055	-1494	-1385	-1851	-2575
France	-20285	-23785	-24791	-27450	-27861	-30510
Germany, Fed. Rep.	1462	2355	2296	475	-523	-1060
Ireland	275	209	195	278	164	-40
Italy	5365	3837	5095	4742	5711	4040
The Netherlands	3865	3198	3725	3035	3557	3064
United Kingdom	-1940	-2395	-1607	-3181	-6833	-2824

Columns:
(1)   ECAM results
(2)   Eurostat supply balance sheets.

Table 4A.6. Protection on production.

Third countries criticize the CAP most for its protectionist character. Although it is easy to establish that there is protection, it is difficult to agree on a single measure for it (see Guyomard and Mahé (1994)). One measure is the ratio of an internal (tariff inclusive or border) to an external (world market) price. Although this ratio has the advantage of simplicity and transparency, serious objections can be raised against it. First, the rate of protection suffers from an index problem, since it is calculated for each commodity group as an index with traded quantities as weights. This gives rise to the problem that commodities with a high degree of protection will not be represented adequately, since their weight will be small. Secondly, all ratio measures are static and do not measure the welfare loss which they cause. Of course, a model like ECAM overcomes this limitation to some extent, as it calculates welfare under alternative scenarios but severe limitations remain because the price data used for each commodity group also suffer from the index problem. Thirdly, and this objection is easier to address, the ratio between internal and external prices disregards non-border measures like producer and consumer subsidies.

Table 4A.6   Measures of protection on production, three-year average, percentage

	1982/84		1985/87		1988/90	
	(1)	(2)	(1)	(2)	(1)	(2)
Wheat	30.	25.	60.	44.	60.	37.
Coarse grains	31.	27.	52.	48.	57.	41.
Sugar	75.	51.	115.	64.	84.	48.
Fats and oils	25.	-	26.	-	33.	-
Oilseeds	-	38.	-	60.	-	59.
Butter	49.	-	57.	-	41.	-
Other dairy	49.	-	64.	-	41.	-
Milk	-	43.	-	66.	-	59.
Bovine meat	17.	47.	25.	50.	30.	53.
Ovine meat	35.	60.	47.	66.	59.	74.

Columns:
(1)   ECAM results
(2)   OECD, PSE data base. Protection is defined as PSE-support divided by production value cum PSE-support. PSE-support is defined as sum of levies, transfers, reduction of input costs other than feed, general services, national support and other PSE.

To avoid some of these problems, we have opted for another measure that follows closely the PSE (producer subsidy equivalent) concept of the OECD (see OECD (1992)) as it accounts for non-product related subsidies and imputes all taxes and subsidies to the product at farm-gate level, using the produced quantities as weights. This PSE-measure considers agricultural production for every commodity. PSE-support can also be expressed as a ratio of the subsidy to the (subsidized) producer price and this is shown in Table A4.6 (multiplied by 100). In ECAM the subsidy includes producer subsidies as well as market and border support. Comparison of the two measures is somewhat hampered by differences in product classification, in levels of processing and in definitions of support. Yet the outcomes indicate an increased protectionism of the EU in the mid-eighties that levels off towards the end of the decade. This increase is above all caused by the important drop in world market prices during this period.

Table 4A.7   FEOGA expenditures

	1982		1986		1990	
	ECAM	FEOGA	ECAM	FEOGA	ECAM	FEOGA
Refunds on exports	4700	4840	9028	6633	8054	6767
Producer subsidies	2024	2536	4119	4156	6506	5872
Consumer subsidies	1108	1024	1139	1075	1448	1377
Input subsidies	2141	1582	3443	2382	2507	1235
Interest and storage	1221	1280	4425	4517	438	394
Stock devaluation	-90	0	-103	0	889	2727
Other EU-9	1025	459	920	1584	1647	2024
New member states	685	685	1690	1690	4285	4285
Total EU-12	12510	12406	24599	22137	25454	26475

Notes:
(a) Computed from the Financial Report on FEOGA (guarantee section, annex 2).
(b) Stock devaluation is given in three-year averages.
(c) Data for 1982 refer to EU-10.

Table 4A.7   FEOGA expenditures, guarantee section.
As already indicated in Chapter 2, the growing discrepancy between production and internal demand in the eighties resulted in increased FEOGA expenditures. Though the bottom row of Table 4A.7 shows this rather clearly, some further remarks are in order. First, as only EU-9 expenditures are computed endogenously, all outlays for Greece, Spain, Portugal and the former GDR are covered under the exogenous item 'new member states', both in ECAM and in the statistical data. Consequently, in all columns items 1) to 7) refer to the EU-9 only. Secondly, in ECAM depreciation of intervention stocks is computed on an annual basis from net stock changes and variations in bookprices, whereas the Commission only records stock devaluations from 1988 onwards. Therefore, FEOGA stock devaluations are zero in 1982 and 1986. In addition, the EU only allows for depreciation if budgetary room permits, otherwise depreciation is postponed and appears in later years. Thirdly, in ECAM only net trade flows are represented; consequently, levies on total imports and refunds on total exports can only be replicated with full accuracy in the base year. Finally, it is not possible to replicate the effect of various policy measures of an incidental nature. For example, the shift of the budget year from calendar year to a budget

year that starts on October 16 has resulted in two bookyears (1987 and 1988) of less than twelve months, which could not adequately be represented in ECAM.[91] To give another example, the large, subsidized sales of butter and skimmed milk-powder in 1987 and 1988, had, in fact, to be paid in advance by the member states and were reimbursed by the Commission in four annual instalments in subsequent years. In ECAM the budgetary implications of this scheme were not taken into account: all costs are incurred in the year the product is exported.

Table 4A.8   Employment, 1982-90

	1000 persons, period average		Annual growth rate	
	ECAM	Eurostat	ECAM	Eurostat
Belgium-Luxembourg	107	110	-1.7	-1.3
Denmark	173	174	-2.6	-2.3
France	1534	1536	-3.2	-3.2
Germany, Fed. Rep.	1328	1271	-1.2	-3.1
Ireland	172	173	-3.1	-1.8
Italy	2235	2233	-3.2	-3.5
Netherlands	263	267	-0.7	-0.6
United Kingdom	602	605	-1.5	-1.4
EU-9	6413	6371	-2.5	-2.9

Note: Eurostat data from *Demographic Statistics, Employment and Unemployment*, and from CEC, *The Agricultural Situation in the Community*.

Table 4A.8   Agricultural labour

In ECAM the size of the agricultural labour force is affected by demographic and by economic forces. The outflow attributable to economic forces is related to the ratio of gross value added per worker (see Section 4.3.5, equation (4.31)). Since the data have been pooled, (see Annex 4B.2.5), the estimated elasticity of the relative inflow in non-agriculture with respect to this ratio is the same for all countries. This explains differences between model outcomes and statistical

---

[91] FEOGA expenditures relating to the period 1 november - 31 december 1987 have been equally allocated to the bookyears 1987 and 1988, while in fact they should have been charged to the 1988 budget. This procedure created two artificial 'bookyears' of about 11 months each.

Table 4A.9   Agricultural value added without transfers, 1982-90

	Mln ecu, average		Annual growth rate	
	ECAM	OECD	ECAM	OECD
Belgium-Luxembourg	2496	2424	3.1	2.9
Denmark	3947	3176	3.6	3.2
France	23204	23562	0.6	1.8
Germany, Fed. Rep.	14831	12844	0.8	0.9
Ireland	2474	2208	3.3	4.5
Italy	22327	24287	2.9	3.1
Netherlands	7886	7215	4.5	5.3
United Kingdom	9365	8533	-1.3	-1.0
EU-9	86530	84249	1.7	2.2

Note: OECD agricultural value added is defined as gross value added by sector of economic activity, see OECD, National Accounts.

data. For West Germany and Ireland the discrepancies are significant. This is mainly due to the erratic pattern in the official statistics for agricultural labour, due to frequent change of definitions.

Table 4A.9   Agricultural value added

For agricultural value added the model outcomes do not fully match the statistics either (Table 4A.9). The size of the differences appears to be rather sensitive to the averaging in the beginning and the end of the series.

Annex 4B

Data and parameters of ECAM: an overview

4B.1   General outline

This annex reports on the estimation and calibration of model parameters. Recall from Section 4.1.4 that though full system estimation of the model coefficients may be desirable, it is not a feasible option. Therefore, the calibration and validation of ECAM was performed in two stages. In the first stage, parameters were estimated by regression methods separately for consumer demand, crop allocation etc. In the second stage the full model was calibrated keeping the more robust parameters of the first stage fixed and adjusting the less reliable ones, as well as the lagged endogenous values. Annex 4A has described the final outcome of the second stage, in this annex we report on the first stage. Table 4B.1 gives an overview of the topics to be discussed, with a reference to the relevant section in the main text.

Table 4B.1   Topics to be discussed

Topic	Section	Refers to section
Agricultural supply:	4B.2	4.3
crop and livestock allocation	4B.2.1	4.3.2, 4.3.3
yield trends	4B.2.2	4.3.2
land outflow	4B.2.3	4.3.5
investments	4B.2.4	4.3.5
labour migration	4B.2.5	4.3.5
Feed demand	4B.3	4.3.3
Consumer demand	4B.4	4.2.4
Exogenous parameters	4B.5	4.1.3, 4.2.3, 4.2.5

The discussion of each topic covers the method used, the motivation for the method, problems in data collection and processing, and data sources. We shall

not try to give a complete presentation of all the parameters that were estimated
and shall refer to background papers for more information.

4B.2   Agricultural supply

4B.2.1   Crop and livestock allocation

In Section 4.2.6, six requirements were formulated to be met by the supply
model: (i) micro economic interpretation, (ii) continuous response to changes in
parameters, (iii) parameter estimation by standard methods, (iv) land and other
balances should be respected, (v) the model should allow for incorporation of
technical information say, on yields and input restrictions and (vi) rigidities in
allocation that are due to unaccounted inputs should be represented. The
decomposability into separate modules makes it easier to meet requirement (ii),
since the submodel for crop and livestock allocation model possesses a structure
such that single-equation econometrics can be used, provided a formulation with
a numéraire is chosen.

The model

The discussion will be in terms of crops but it is similar for the livestock sector.
Recall from Section 4.3.2, footnote 70 that the crop allocation model obeys:

$$\frac{a_h}{a_1} = c_h \left(\frac{\rho_h}{\rho_1} \right)^{\sigma_h}, \quad h = 2, ..., n \tag{4B.1}$$

where a_h, $h = 1, ..., n$ denotes area (or acreage) of crop h, and a_1 the area of the
numéraire crop; ρ_h, $h = 1, ..., n$ denotes net revenue per hectare, c_h is a constant,
and σ_h the (partial) elasticity of substitution between crop h and the numéraire
crop. The constant c_h may include a lagged area term:

$$\left(\frac{a_{h,t-1}}{a_{1,t-1}} \right)^{\beta_h}$$

and possibly also a trend term like t or log(t). The structure of (4B.1) can be represented by a crop 'tree', with the numéraire crop at the root that is connected to the other crops via the elasticity of substitution σ_h (see Figure 4B.1). In fact a more flexible structure was used. By imposing additional separability properties upon the rotation function $g(a_2,...,a_n)$ from which (4B.1) was derived (see Section 4.3.2, Assumption G), additional levels can be introduced in the crop tree. Figure 4B.1 illustrates this for a two-level structure, where crop a_1 is the numéraire for the crops a_4 and a_5.

Figure 4B.1   Structure of crop tree

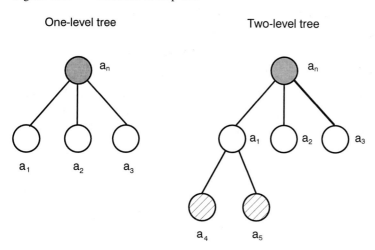

If we denote $\tilde{a}_{h,t} = \log (a_{h,t}/a_{1,t})$, and $\tilde{\rho}_{h,t} = \log (\rho_{h,t}/\rho_{1,t})$, and include the lagged area term in (4B.1), then, with a small abuse of notation, the parameters of (4B.1) can be estimated linearly from:

$$\tilde{a}_{h,t} = c_h + \beta_h\, \tilde{a}_{h,t-1} + \sigma_h\, \tilde{\rho}_{h,t} , \tag{4B.2}$$

where $0 \le \beta_h \le 1$, $\sigma_h > 0$, for $h = 2, ..., n$. The condition on β_h is imposed to ensure that the first-order difference equation (4B.2) is stable; the condition on σ_h ensures that relative areas increase (decrease) when relative net revenues increase (decrease). Equation (4B.2) can be handled with standard econometric techniques once the nature and location of the error terms are decided upon. To this we will now turn.

Because (4B.2) is an auto-regressive model, it is natural to consider an error-in-dependent-variables model, where the endogenous variables are affected by white noise u_t. Dropping the subscript h for convenience, we obtain:

$$\tilde{a}_t - \upsilon_t = c_h + \beta \, (\tilde{a}_{t-1} - \upsilon_{t-1}) + \sigma \, \tilde{\rho}_t \qquad (4B.3)$$

Using a method proposed in Klein (1958), we define the transformation $d_t = \tilde{a}_t - \upsilon_t$. By elimination of d_{t-1} in the right-hand side of (4B.3), the model can then be written in a form linear in β and σ. For a fixed value of β the constant and the elasticity of substitution can then be estimated by Ordinary Least Squares (OLS). If we take the value of β for which the residual sum of squares is a minimum, then this procedure yields maximum likelihood estimates for β and σ. The practical drawbacks of this method are, first, that a scan over β must be performed, and, secondly, that the minimum is not always found. In that case the delayed area term is replaced by a trend term (t or log(t)), or straightforward OLS is applied to the model:

$$\tilde{a}_t = c_h + \beta \tilde{a}_{t-1} + \sigma \tilde{\rho}_t + \upsilon_t \qquad (4B.4)$$

This is a standard error-in-equations model, for which OLS yields consistent, although biased, estimates.

Results

A complete report of the econometric results can be found in Merbis (1995b). Here we summarize the main findings. In ECAM, 17 crops are distinguished, of which three are green fodder crops, and six livestock activities. Not all crops have been represented in a tree and estimated via (4B.2).[92] The substitution elasticity between green fodder crops and the numéraire crop cannot be

---

[92] The six livestock activities have also been represented according to (4B.2).

estimated, because there are no market prices, but only shadow prices for the green fodder crops. Here we have used calibrated coefficients. For several permanent crops (olives, grapes, horticultural crops, fruits) it does not seem reasonable to assume such substitution. Instead a trend equation (either linear or of a satiated form) was estimated.

The econometric results are acceptable, especially in the cases where $\beta_h \neq 0$. The flexibility in the structure of the crop/livestock trees makes it possible to search for statistically significant results which satisfy the bounds on β_h and σ_h, while ruling out implausible structures. Yet the approach did not work well in all cases. One problem was that the tuning of an allocation module becomes rather cumbersome when the numéraire crop is subject to production quota (as for milk and sugar). In general, crops with a large area and with a relatively insensitive net revenue should be chosen as numéraire. This rules out the selection of activities with unstable profitability (like laying hens) as numéraire. These practical considerations limit the choice of the numéraire crops. In a few cases the bounds $\beta < 1$ and $\sigma < 0$ become effective.[93]

Data and data sources

Data on areas and stocks are from the Supply Utilization Accounts of FAO Agrostat, supplemented with data from Eurostat Crop and Animal statistics. Data on net revenues have been constructed with the help of the so-called standard gross margins (sgm) published by the European Commission (in the *Official Journal of the Community, series L*). Standard gross margins are harmonized measures for net revenues which cover only the current costs, namely, feed, fertilizer, pesticides, seeds and fuel for heating.

There are three major problems in the usage of this concept. First, sgm's are not published annually but bi-annually. Secondly, the margins are not compatible with the total national input costs for feed, fertilizer, etc, as published, say, by Eurostat in the Economic Accounts. Thirdly, the sgm's are published for the regions within countries of the Community, and not as national

---

[93] In fact an upper bound of 0.9 was imposed on β_h ; higher β_h-values would place too much weight upon the own dynamics in (4B.2) and too little on the substitution effect.

averages. One could call the incomplete coverage of the inputs (ignoring services and factor inputs) another drawback, although it must be recognised that many of the inputs that were left out cannot be attributed to a single crop.

These drawbacks were overcome by making additional assumptions that lead to time series for the years 1970-85 which fit the classification of ECAM. Essentially, time series of input volumes per crop for each input have been constructed, and valued at observed, annual input prices (from Eurostat Price Statistics) to extend the limited number of years for which sgm's are available.

Experience/conclusion.

The estimation of the allocation model involves time-consuming data processing, especially for the net revenues. The econometrics are relatively easy but the structure used here may be somewhat rigid. A numéraire-free approach deserves further investigation, although it may be problematic to maintain say, concavity properties when a more flexible form is used.

4B.2.2   Yield trends

To estimate yields a simple time trend, based on historical evidence appears to work well:

$$y_{h,t} = \alpha_h + \beta_h\, t$$

where $y_{h,t}$ is the member state specific yield of crop (in ton/ha) or livestock activity h (in kg/head) at time t. Values of α_h and β_h have been estimated using observed data over the period 1970-85 (see Merbis (1994)). These values hold for the period 1982-92. Due to the limited length of this series this simple regression was preferred to more sophisticated formulations which use, for example, data on weather conditions as additional explanatory variables (see e.g. Oskam (1991)). In the policy runs, however, some of the coefficients for cereals, oilseeds and a few minor crops have been adjusted to obtain some degree of convergence among member states. In the long run scenario of Chapter 7, growth rates are adjusted so as to remain below the technological ceilings that agronomists find plausible for the year 2020.

4B.2.3   Land outflow

In Section 4.3.5 several reasons were given for treating agricultural land outflow as an exogenous variable: (a) an endogenous treatment would require an intertemporal optimization framework for various groups of farmers, (b) demand for land by the non-agricultural sector would be more or less exogenous in any case, (c) land outflow is to a large extent controlled by government policies, through licenses, building permits etc.

Table 4B.2   Land availability, 1000 ha

	1983	1993	2006	Annual growth rate 1993-2006
Belgium-Luxembourg	1567.	1502.	1417.	-0.45
Denmark	2850.	2675.	2465.	-0.63
France	31777.	30628.	29134.	-0.38
Germany, Fed. Rep.	12073.	11633.	11061.	-0.39
Ireland	5543.	5676.	5688.	+0.02
Italy	19389.	16740.	15810.	-0.44
The Netherlands	1996.	1969.	1855.	-0.46
United Kingdom	18622.	18116.	17458.	-0.28
EU-9	92932.	88939.	84890.	-0.36

A simple fitted trend actually appears to work well, although there is some problem with respect to the reference period that is being used because the observed trend in the whole period 1960-90 differs from the trend in the eighties. Therefore, the time series were inspected for the latest period over which a constant land outflow could be perceived. This is a feasible procedure for most member states. In the United Kingdom, the data are erratic and in Ireland, there is a long lag in publication. Moreover, we have some doubts about the accuracy of published figures for that country (total acreage is nearly constant over a period and then sudden shifts occur). Results are summarized in Table 4B.2.

In some policy scenarios a different outflow is imposed to reflect the impact of the scenario assumptions on land availability.

4B.2.4   Agricultural investments

The model

Our point of departure is the mathematical program (4.32) of Section 4.3.5:

$$\max P_L Y_L - r(p)K$$
$$K, Y_L \geq 0$$

subject to

$$F(Y_C, Y_L) \leq G(A, K, E)$$

for given Y_C, A and E.

Analytical specifications for F(.) and G(.) are of the Constant Elasticity of Substitution (CES) type (see footnote 84 of Section 4.3.4). Both F and G are assumed to exhibit constant returns to scale; specifying them per unit of land A yields $F(Y_L/A, Y_C/A)$ and $G(1, K/A, E/A)$. Formally, we may write the restriction as follows:

$$F(y_C, y_L) \leq G(1, k, e),$$

or $[\alpha y_C^\rho + (1 - \alpha)y_L^\rho]^{1/\rho} \leq (\beta k^{-\mu} + \gamma e^{-\mu})^{-\lambda/\mu},$

or $y_L \leq \left[\zeta[k^{-\mu} + (\omega e)^{-\mu}]^{-\lambda\rho/\mu} - (\eta y_C)^\rho \right]^{1/\rho}$ (4B.5)

where $\eta^\rho = \alpha/(1 - \alpha)$, $\omega^\mu = \beta/\gamma$, $\zeta^\rho = (\beta)^{\lambda\rho/\mu}/(1 - \alpha)$ and where lower case symbols y, k, and e refer to output, capital and labour per hectare, respectively. To ensure concavity of the iso-output curves of F and convexity of the iso-input curves of G we maintain the restrictions $\rho > 1$ and $\mu > -1$. Moreover, $\lambda < 1$ guarantees decreasing returns to scale of G(1, k, e). Maximization with respect to k yields the first order condition:

$P_L \, \partial y_L / \partial k = r(p)$, or

$$r(p)/P_L = \lambda \, (y_L)^{1-\rho} \, k^{-(\mu+1)} \, [k^{-\mu} + (\omega e)^{-\mu}]^{-\lambda\rho/\mu} \qquad (4B.6)$$

with y_L defined in (4B.5). The elasticities of substitution σ_0 (between y_L and y_C) and σ_1 (between k and e) obey[94] $\sigma_0 = 1 / (\rho - 1)$ and $\sigma_1 = 1 / (1 + \mu)$.

The constant λ in (4B.5) is taken to be time-dependent and is a function of time and a 'weather index' q_t (see Folmer (1989), for more details on its construction):

$$\zeta_t = \zeta_1 \, \exp(\xi_1 t) \, (q_t)^{\xi_2}$$

Full Information Maximum Likelihood is the appropriate technique for estimating (4B.5) and (4B.6) simultaneously, as it allows to take into account the interdependency of y_L and k and the correlation of residuals in both equations. However, FIML estimation was not successful. There were problems in making the estimation algorithm converge (this was in part caused by the calculated value of y_L^ρ, which became negative at times) and the range constraints on the parameters ρ, λ and μ often proved to be binding.

Therefore, it was decided to pool the data (after suitable scaling) and to estimate the following modification of (4B.6):

$$r(p)/P_L = \frac{\lambda \, y_L \, [1 + (\eta y_C/y_L)^\rho]}{k \, [1 + (\omega e/k)^{-\mu}]} \qquad (4B.7)$$

A single equation iterative estimation procedure has been applied: starting from initial parameter values in (4B.7). These values are then adjusted in a successive

---

[94] The elasticity of substitution between A and B is defined as: d log(A/B) / d log(-dA/dB), or as the proportionate change in the ratio A/B as a result of a proportionate change in the marginal rate of substitution between A and B.

relaxation procedure,[95] which appears to yield reasonable parameter values. The three remaining parameters c_1, γ and β (which do not appear in 4B.7)) can be estimated from equation (4B.5) by a similar procedure.[96]

This finally leads to R^2's of 0.61 and 0.55 for equations (4B.7) and (4B.5), respectively. As can be expected, elasticities of substitution of the output side (σ_0) are rather low (between 0.13 and 0.2), and values of σ_1 are high (between 1.6 and 2.0).

The data

All time series, except those for employment and crop area, had to be constructed from raw data. We briefly explain how time series were obtained for (i) output and price indices; (ii) the stock of physical capital and (iii) the user cost of capital.

(i)   Output and price indices

Output indices Y_L and Y_C were constructed using base year net revenues per ton at base year prices as weights (see also footnote 85 of Section 4.3.4). We do not adjust the weights to avoid treating technical progress (say, yield increases) that causes the net revenue to rise as an increase of the price index.

---

[95]   The procedure runs as follows:
(i)   fix initial values: $\alpha = 1.$, $\rho = 6.$, $\lambda = 0.7$, $\mu = -0.4$;
(ii)   estimate ω, conditionally on values obtained in previous step(s);
(iii)   estimate α, conditionally on values obtained in previous steps;
(iv)   return to step (ii) until convergence is obtained for ω and α;
(v)   estimate λ, conditionally on the results of previous steps;
(vi)   repeat steps (ii) to (v) until values for α, ω and λ are mutually consistent;
(vii)   estimate μ conditionally on the results of (vi);
(viii)   estimate ρ conditionally on the results of (vi) and (vii);
(ix)   repeat step (vii) and (viii) until estimated values for μ and ρ are mutually consistent;

[96]   This calculation proceeds as follows:
(i)   fix $\xi_1 = 0$, $\xi_2 = 0$ and other parameters on estimated values;
(ii)   estimate c_1 conditionally on values obtained in previous steps;
(iii)   estimate ξ_1 conditionally on values obtained in previous steps;
(iv)   estimate ξ_2 conditionally on values obtained in previous steps;
(v)   repeat steps (ii) to (iv) until convergence is obtained.

(ii) Stock of capital

Time series for K_t were constructed from gross investment series using the so-called perpetual inventory method. Data from Behrens (1981) and from Economic Accounts for Agriculture have been used. Formally:

$$K_{t+1} = K_t + I_t - D_t$$

$$D_t = \Sigma_i \, g_i \, I_{t-1}$$

(4B.8)

where:

K_t capital stock at the beginning of period t (in constant prices)

I_t gross investment in period t, constant prices

D_t discarded capital stock in period t (constant prices)

g_i fraction of stock of capital installed in t-i that is discarded in t,[97] and where i runs from 1 to m.

Equations (4B.8) can be written as (see Folmer (1989)):

$$K_{t+1} = I_t + \Sigma_i \, I_{t-1} \, (1 - d_i), \text{ with}$$

$$d_i = \Sigma_{j \le i} \, g_j$$

(4B.9)

(iii) The user cost of capital

The user cost of capital is defined as consisting of replacement costs and interest payments. Replacement costs are computed from equations (4B.8) and (4B.9). Data on interest payments are more difficult to obtain because part of the capital stock is financed from equity capital, while reported data on interest paid only refer to outstanding debt and include investment in land and livestock. Two approaches are possible, and have in fact been tried successively. The first is to

---

[97] The parameter g_i is assumed to possess a Γ-distribution with parameters α and Ψ/α. By fixing the average lifetime (Ψ) and the maximum lifetime (ψ) of the stock of capital and using Behrens' (1981) estimate for α (= 9), g_i can be written as a function of Ψ and ψ only (see also Folmer (1989)). Values for these parameters are equal across countries, but different for machinery and buildings: d Ψ = 8, ψ = 12 for machinery and Ψ = 35, ψ = 68 for buildings. The values estimated by Behrens (1981, p. 27), Ψ = 10, ψ = 19 for machinery and Ψ = 50, ψ = 97 for buildings turned out to generate extremely low user costs.

multiply the volume of the stock of capital by an appropriate interest rate but this leads to unacceptable high user costs. The second approach makes the following assumptions: (i) the same interest rate applies to investments in capital stock and land; (ii) the imputed return on equity capital r_t^2 stands in a fixed ratio θ to the interest rate on outstanding debt r_t^1 and (iii) the ratio of debt over total assets (α) is the same for capital goods and other assets. Then, by assumptions (i) and (ii):

$$R_t^k = r_t^1 K_t^1 + r_t^2 K_t^2 = r_t^1 K_t^1 (1 + \theta K_t^2 / K_t^1)$$

where R_t^k equals total interest payments accruing to the stock of capital and the superscripts 1 and 2 refer to debt and equity, respectively. Assumption (iii) enables us to rewrite K_t^2 / K_t^1 in terms of α, the share of total debt in total assets. This finally leads to:

$$R_t^k = \beta_t R_t^d (1 + \theta_t(1 - \alpha_t)/\alpha_t)$$

where β_t is the share of capital stock in total assets and R_t^d the recorded interest payment on total outstanding debt. This relation was used to generate data on R^k, given observations on R^d, β, α and θ. In fact, data were scarce. For some countries only 5 observations on R^d were available (1980 - 1984)[98]. But for a number of countries the OECD (1970) and the Commission of the EU reported useful information.[99] In general α, β, total debt, debt ratios and paid interest could be estimated for some year between 1965 and 1968, depending on the country, as well as α in 1987. This information was used to compute reasonable values for α, β and θ for all countries in all years and to fill the gap in interest paid for years before 1980. Details can be found in Folmer (1989), pp. 6-16.

Experience/conclusion

---

[98] Data for the Netherlands were computed using *Agricultural Statistics (Landbouwcijfers)* published by the Agricultural Economics Research Institute, which reports both total outstanding debt as well as the value of invested own resources. Multiplication by (published) appropriate interest rates yields total paid and imputed interest.

[99] See *The Agricultural Situation in the Community* (1987, p. 59).

Generating the data involves some rather arbitrary choices, and results appear to be sensitive to the specific assumptions made (e.g. on lifetime capital stock and financial structure). Nonetheless, the parameters obtained are plausible.

4B.2.5   Occupational migration

The model

Starting from equation (4.31), the function M_j, specified in multiplicative form, can be written as (dropping the subscript j):

$$m_t = c \; a^{\beta}_{t-1} \; b^{\gamma}_{t-1} \tag{4B.10}$$

where m_t is the ratio of occupational migration to lagged non-agricultural employment $E_{j,t-1}$, a_{t-1} equals $H_{j+1,t-1}/H_{j,t-1}$, the ratio of lagged per capita income, b_{t-1} equals $E_{j,t-1}/E_{j+1,t-1}$, the ratio of lagged employment. Here occupational migration is measured as the net outflow of young farmers (aged 55 years or less) into non-agricultural sectors.

   An equation of this type is not directly based on optimizing behaviour but it can be derived assuming that labour outflow is a substitution process that replaces agricultural by non-agricultural employment, where the speed of the adjustment process is triggered by some variable. Once this variable exceeds a threshold value, the farmer takes the decision to migrate. Here this threshold value is taken to depend on the income parity ratio to $H_{j,t-1}/H_{j+1,t-1}$. It is larger when employment in non-agriculture expands relative to agriculture: the inverse of b_{t-1} can be seen as a measure of the relative absorption capacity of the receiving sector. This leads to a first-order differential equation for the share of agricultural employment in employment outside agriculture. Using equation (4.30) of Section 4.3.5 this differential equation can be transformed in a relation of the form (4B.10). Consequently, the constants c_j depend on current and lagged demographic variables (population growth rates, activity rates, the share of young farmers in agricultural employment). Further details can be found in Folmer (1993).

Data and estimation

For estimation, a complication is that labour outflow is not observed directly, or in terms of equation (4.30), it is impossible to decide whether observed differences between E_{jt} and $E_{j,t-1}$ are due to changes in $g_{j,t-1}$ or in $m_{j,t-1}$. We first observe that 'employment' should be distinguished from 'population', and hence, the corresponding age distributions generally differ. As labour outflow is defined in terms of employment, and the total change in E_{jt} can be obtained from published data, information about the demographic growth rate g_{jt} of agricultural employment by age class is sufficient to compute migration. Although this growth rate is also an unobserved variable, it can be written as the sum of the change in the ratio of age specific employment and population (called the participation ratio or activity rate) and the corresponding growth rate of the population cohort. These two growth rates can be obtained from published data on average national activity rates and population by age classes assuming that: (i) the average participation ratios of agricultural and total population are equal and (ii) the age composition of agricultural population is the same as the one of the total population. Note that (ii) does not hold with respect to employment: in almost all member states the share of old farmers in total agricultural employment is substantially higher than the corresponding portion of old people in total population. Details are provided in Folmer (1993, Annex A)). Demographic data were obtained from Eurostat: Demographic Statistics (populations), Employment and Unemployment (activity rates) and the Commission of the EU (agricultural employment).

For the income per worker the ratio of gross value added at factor cost per worker was used as obtained from the Economic Accounts for Agriculture and OECD, National Accounts, various issues.

Because the computed migration turned out to be negative in some cases, (4B.10) was estimated directly by means of Nonlinear Least Squares, rather than in logarithms and observations were pooled over countries, with a correction for heteroskedasticity among countries. Finally, cross country restrictions were imposed on the parameter β. In equation (4B.10) we estimated $\beta = 0.62$ common to all countries and γ_j in the range (0.62, 0.73). This is more or less in line with results from other studies, quoted in Folmer (1993).

Experience/conclusion

The main problem was to decompose changes in agricultural employment into a demographic and an outflow component. Other difficulties were due to the relatively small variation in the income ratio and the strong trend in the employment ratio.

4B.3   Feed mix

Specification and estimation

We briefly discuss analytical specifications and estimation techniques for (i) compound feeds (ii) green fodder and (iii) feed requirement functions. A more detailed treatment can be found in Folmer et al. (1990) and Keyzer (1989c).

(i)   Compound feeds

We express the L.E.S. per unit of feed intake z_h (cf. footnote 75 of Section 4.3.3):

$$p_{kt}v_{hkt} = p_{kt}\gamma_{hk} + \delta_{hk}(c^1_{ht}(p) - \Sigma_i p_{it}\gamma_{hi}) + u_{hkt} \qquad (4B.11)$$

with $\Sigma_h \delta_{hk} = 1$, $v_{hkt} \geq 0$, $\Sigma_h v_{hkt} = 1$ for all t, and where i runs over the index set M. Indices h and k denote crops and inputs, respectively (see Section 4.3.2).

The vector of disturbances u_{ht} is assumed to be identically and independently distributed with time independent covariance matrix Σ, which does not have full column rank, due to adding up. For every member state, the demand system (4B.11) was estimated by maximum likelihood (ML) for each animal type.[100] The results indicated that the substitution of grains by cereal substitutes could not be explained by price changes alone. Furthermore, in the case of a free covariance matrix ML reduces to minimization of the determinant of Σ, which is equivalent to the product of its nonzero eigenvalues (see Don (1985)). In a number of cases this resulted in a very good fit for some equations but a very bad one for others within the same system. Therefore, two adjustments were made: (i) the committed quantities were specified as functions of a logistic trend:

$$\gamma_{hkt} = \gamma_{hk0} + \gamma_{hk1}/(1 + \zeta_1 e^{-\zeta_2 t}) \tag{4B.12}$$

and (ii) a fixed structure was imposed on the covariance matrix of each system.[101] Since $\Sigma \gamma_{hk1} = 0$, the sum of commitments in the system is constant. This is a reflection of nutritional considerations.

(ii)   Green fodder

Green fodder allocation is specified as (see also assumption W and footnote 71 in Section 4.3.3):

---

[100] As indicated in Table 4.3a, Section 4.2.1, ECAM distinguishes six livestock types: dairy cows, laying hens, non-dairy cattle, pigs, sheep and goats, and poultry. In total, this amounts to $8 \times 6 = 48$ demand systems, with commodity classifications as in footnote 74, including dairy, and with grain substitutes aggregated into one commodity, because an L.E.S. does not allow for full complementarity between commodities.

[101] The structure of the (co)variance matrix was restricted to: $\Sigma = (\text{I} - (1/m)ee')\,\hat{d}\,(\text{I} - (1/m)\,ee')$, with I the unit matrix, e a vector with all elements equal to 1, and $\hat{d}$ a diagonal matrix with positive elements d_i. This implied a fixed weighting matrix for the residuals (i.e. the generalized inverse of Σ). We started with all $d_i = 1$ and in a second round these elements were updated from the estimated (true) variances of the residuals. We also had to impose a normalization rule on the commitments γ_{hkt} to avoid problems of commitments drifting away during estimation ($\gamma_{hk0} \to \infty$ and $\gamma_{hk1} \to -\infty$).

$$w_h = \eta_h \, (w - \Sigma_i \theta_i a_i) + \theta_h a_h, \, h \in L \text{ and } \Sigma_h \, \eta_h < 1$$

where

w_h	green fodder intake for animal of type h
η_h	marginal allocation parameter for type h
w	total green fodder intake (in the country)
a_h	number of animals of type h
θ_h	committed green fodder intake for type h, per head.

The sum constraint on the marginal parameters η reflects decreasing returns due to losses on storage, transport and inefficient allocation. As explained in Section 4.3.3 (footnote 78) the parameters η_h also determine the shadow price of committed green fodder. The value of $\Sigma_h \, \eta_h$ is therefore calibrated in such a way as to yield reasonable net revenues and crop allocations. This results in rather low values, varying from 0.125 to 0.2 depending on the country.

(iii) Feed requirements

Feed requirement functions were specified as in footnote 73 of Section 4.3.3:

$$m_{ht} = \kappa_{ht} + \varepsilon_h \, y_{ht}$$

For dairy cows ε_h was positive and κ_h constant. Straightforward OLS estimation shows that the subsistence requirement κ_h is about 20,000 MJ on average, and the variable intake per kilogram output ε_h is 90 MJ. For all other animal types it was assumed that $\varepsilon_h = 0$ and that κ_{ht} follows a linear trend: $\kappa_{ht} = \kappa_{h0} + \kappa_{h1} t$.

(iv) Data requirements

For the construction of the dataset (volumes and prices) of the feedmix model, the methodology proposed in OECD(1985) has been followed and expanded. Since green fodders play a dominant role in animal feeding, they should be part of the feedmix model, even if the data availability is rather poor. As no prices are available, we use a common volume unit to account for green fodder intake: metabolizable energy (ME, see also Section 4.3.3 and footnote 72 of Chapter 4).

To obtain data on green fodder quantities we have proceeded in four steps: (a) determining total availability of feed (excluding pastures), by member state; (b) computing total feed requirements; (c) confronting availability with requirements and closing the feed balance, assuming that green fodders make up for the difference; (d) allocating green fodder to animal categories.

(a) *Determining feed availability.* Data on quantities of feed are available for 1973-85 for EU-9 with respect to 200 different feed intakes, consisting of both marketable and non-marketable crops. All feed data are expressed in Metabolizable Energy (ME), as well as in Digestible Crude Protein (DCP). Summation yields total annual feed availability by member state, both in ME and DCP.

(b) *Computing total feed requirements.* For every livestock category, the requirements of ME and DCP were computed from technical coefficients, which relate feed intake to animal yield (see OECD (1985)). Detailed information was used to account for the weight distribution and the composition differences within each of the six livestock categories of ECAM. For example, different requirements were used for broilers, ducks, geese, turkeys and rabbits (aggregated into poultry), for pigs under 20 kg, from 20 to 40 kg, etc. (aggregated to pigs), and for 10 subcategories of cattle to aggregate to non-dairy cattle. For pigs and poultry, annual improvements in feed conversion of 0.5 and 0.75 per cent, respectively, were assumed. The feed requirement of dairy cows increases with yield.

(c) *Confronting availability with requirements.* The calculation showed a deficit in terms of ME and a surplus in terms of DCP. This confirms the outcomes in OECD (1986). The balance was closed by adjusting the availability of pasture grass in terms of ME (by adjusting the yield on pastures). The result is a consistent feed data base in energy terms (ME), per year, member state and animal type.

(d) *Allocation to livestock categories.* Data from OECD (1986) were used, which were, however, only available for two years. Data for the other years had to be constructed by interpolation.

Steps (a) to (c) resulted in a consistent database for feed intake volumes. Prices were gathered from Eurostat Price Statistics but not all of the 200 commodities covered in the quantity balances had prices attached to them, and in these cases price series had to be constructed on the basis of price indices of close substitutes. Finally, the prices were aggregated to the ECAM classification (see Merbis et al. (1994) for further details).

Obviously, estimation on the basis of a constructed data-base has its limitations, because some of the restrictions that were implicitly and explicitly imposed upon the dataset will not be maintained by the model specification. For example, one might argue that closing the energy balances at the national level via adjustment of green fodder quantities should imply that green fodders are perfect substitutes for compound feed but we have interpreted it as a linear constraint on a data set. The estimated model has in fact imperfect substitution among compound feeds and does not impose the energy requirements. However, these requirements appeared to hold reasonably well in model simulations.

Experience/conclusion

The most serious problem in formulating the feedmix model was the incomplete coverage and the inaccuracy of the raw data. The information on the allocation of the feed intakes over the livestock categories is especially poor. It may be noted that the methodology for measuring feed requirements is subject to continuous innovation, but not to international standardisation. Each member state has its own approach. At the time of construction of the data no differentiation in requirements over the member states was available and therefore one set of coefficients was applied to all member states.

Estimation results turn out to be surprisingly good: about 70% of all R^2 for individual equations are found to exceed 0.70, and over 90 per cent of the coefficients are significant (full results are reported in Folmer et al. (1990)). The specification of (time) dependent commitments generated a realistic substitution from cereals toward cereal substitutes. However, given the fact that about 50% of compound feed intakes is committed, substitution possibilities within the L.E.S. are rather limited. Moreover, as the shift in commitments is not reversible, some non-estimated price dependent substitution between fixed commitments had to be imposed because the demand system was found to be too rigid for scenario simulations that involved important changes in cereal prices.

4B.4   Consumer demand

In Section 4.2.4 a two-level demand specification was specified. From the corresponding expenditure function, the consumption function can be obtained by application of the chain rule as:

$$x(p, \tilde{h}) = \partial C(P(p), \tilde{u})/\partial P \; \partial P(p)/\partial p + \bar{c} \qquad (4B.13)$$

where

$$\tilde{u} = u^*(P(p), \tilde{h} - p\bar{c})$$

Denote by I an aggregate commodity at the top level and by the index i individual goods within a group I. Then, by Shephard's lemma the first partial derivative in equation (4B.13) can be seen as an aggregate volume index Q_I. Let P_I denote the corresponding aggregate price index of group I, which, according to footnote 64 in Section 4.2.4, is a Cobb-Douglas index of prices of all individual commodities within group I (with weights θ_i). Then the expenditure function yields at the lower level the expenditure of individual commodities within group I as:

$$p_i \, x_i = \theta_i \, P_I \, Q_I + p_i \delta_i \qquad (4B.14)$$

and, at the top level:

$$P_I Q_I / M = \alpha_I + \beta_I \log(M/\wp) + \Sigma_J \gamma_{IJ} \log P_J$$

with

$$\log \wp = \alpha_0 + \Sigma_I \alpha_I \log P_I + (1/2)\Sigma_I\Sigma_J \gamma_{IJ}\log P_I \log P_J \qquad (4B.15)$$
$$M = \tilde{h} - p\bar{\delta}$$

The aggregate cost function has to be nondecreasing and concave in P. Concavity is equivalent to the negative semidefiniteness of the Hessian of C, which is the Slutsky matrix S of compensated price responses. A necessary condition for S to be negative semidefinite is that the diagonal terms are nonpositive, which should also hold for the matrix K:[102]

$$K_{IJ} = \gamma_{IJ} + \beta_I\beta_J \log(M/\wp) + W_I W_J - \Delta_{IJ}W_I \qquad (4B.16)$$

with

W_I the uncommitted expenditure share of group I

Δ_{IJ} the Kronecker delta (= 1 if I = J and 0 otherwise).

A sufficient condition is that the principal minors of the matrix K alternate their signs. In the case of 3 commodities at the upper level, this implies:

$$k_{11} < 0 \text{ and } k_{11} k_{22} - k_{12}^2 > 0 \qquad (4B.17)$$

since the determinant of K is zero due to the homogeneity property of S. So if we (i) scale the price index $\wp$ such that $\log (M/\wp) < 0$, within a relevant range of prices and income, and (ii) assure that $\Gamma = (\gamma_{IJ})$ is negative semidefinite, global concavity of C is guaranteed. But the second requirement is very restrictive, since it implies that all γ_{II} should be negative. In fact, we found statistically significant positive values under free estimation.

Therefore, given the estimates of β and γ, from (4B.16) and (4B.17) analytical bounds on the budget shares W_I have been calculated. If these bounds did not assure concavity of C directly, they have been widened by scaling of the aggregate price index $\wp$ (i.c. via an increase of α_0).

Before discussing the estimation procedure we first present the commodity classification of the consumption module. Table 4B.3 gives an overview.

---

[102] $K_{IJ} = S_{IJ} * P_I P_J /M.$

Table 4B.3   List of consumer commodities

First level	Second level
Food products	Bread and cereals
	Beef and veal
	Lamb
	Poultry meat
	Pig meat
	Fish
	Milk and cheese
	Eggs
	Fats and oils
	Fruits and vegetables
	Potatoes
	Sugar
	Coffee, tea, cocoa
	Other food products
Beverages and tobacco	
Non-food products	

The model was estimated as follows: first, the lower (second) level is estimated, as represented by the derived demand equations (4B.14). As can be seen from the classification, there is only one 'true' L.E.S.-system at this level (food products). For the commodities beverages and tobacco and other non-food products the parameter θ_i equals 1. Yet it is possible to estimate commitments for these goods and even to make these time-dependent. Note that commitments reduce non-committed expenditure M and so promote concavity of the cost function C. For France, Italy and Germany the committed quantities for beverages and tobacco have been estimated as exogenous time trends. This also holds for non-food products in the United Kingdom. Having obtained L.E.S. estimates, aggregate price indices P_I can be calculated.

Secondly, committed expenditures are subtracted from total consumer outlays. At the upper level an Almost Ideal Demand System applies, but simultaneous estimation of the translog price index $\wp$ together with the demand system (4B.15) is troublesome, because they are expressed in the same parameters. In applications an approximation for $\wp$ is often used, for example the Stone index:

$$\log \tilde{\wp} = \Sigma_I W_I \log(P_I)$$

Parameter estimates are likely to be different when $\tilde{\wp}$ is used instead of $\wp$. Therefore, we chose to use an iterative procedure, and to start with $\tilde{\wp}$ as a first proxy, then estimate all parameters, recalculate $\wp$ and so on, until convergence.

The parameter α_0 needs special treatment as it only appears in the price index and not explicitly in the demand system. A shift in $\wp$ through a change in α_0 not only affects the values of other parameters but also the bounds of the aggregate budget shares W_I, and hence the concavity of C. Therefore, we proceeded by adjusting α_0 iteratively. Note that the translog price index merely serves as a notation to write Hicksian demand curves as functions of prices and expenditure only, i.e. to substitute out utility. It cannot be interpreted as the true price index, since for a non-homothetic utility function, the true price index must be utility dependent.

Experience/conclusion

Simulations with the full model indicated that under different economic conditions concavity conditions still hold. However, the derivation of explicit bounds on budget shares at the Almost Ideal Demand System does not easily extend to more commodities. Details about data sources, estimation method, elasticities and relation to the findings of others are given in Michalek and Keyzer (1992).

4B.5 Exogenous variables

The social accounting matrix (SAM) provides estimates for all relevant parameters, exogenous variables and lagged dependent variables in the model. Parameters are coefficients that are kept fixed at their SAM value or at the value that was found after econometric estimation. It is, however, not possible to treat all SAM-based coefficients as constants: to make the model track, some time trends have to be allowed for and estimated. These coefficients then become exogenous variables.

We briefly discuss the exogenous variables related to the following topics: (i) economic developments in the non-agricultural sector, (ii) demographic, (iii) financial variables, (iv) policy variables and (v) central budget items. Details can be found in Folmer (1992).

(i)   Non-agriculture. Price index series for tradeable and nontradeable products were constructed from the manufacturing unit value index and national consumer price indices for transport and communication services. The OECD National Accounts (Detailed Tables) were the source for volume indices for nontradeable production.

(ii)   Realisations and projections of population by age cohort as reported by Eurostat (Demographic Statistics) were used to generate growth rates until 2020 for age cohorts (0-55) and 55+ by country and total population by member state.

(iii)   Financial variables include exchange rates, green rates and MCAs (MCAs are treated as tariffs and subsidies on intra-EU trade, see Section 3.6.3). For all exchange commodities trade prices had to be supplied. Many different sources were used to compute price indices over the period 1982-92. As average EU export prices are not necessarily equal to the 'official' world market prices, this was a time-consuming process. For example, the export price for butter had to be computed from the internal EU price, processing on trade and published refunds per kilogram.

(iv)   Almost all expenditures of the FEOGA guarantee fund (published yearly by the Commission) are represented in the model. All policies are specified exogenously as prices (intervention prices), rates (input subsidies) or as indexed amounts (FEOGA miscellaneous). Some of these are endogenous. The exogenous variables include: subsidies or taxes on production, intermediate use or consumption of agricultural commodities which are expressed as exogenous tax rates per volume unit. For stocks, storage costs per unit of stock volume are expressed via indexed coefficients,[103]

---

[103] Storage costs include losses on sales from stock. These losses are computed endogenously from intervention prices and bookprices, which are both exogenous. See also footnote 59 in Section 4.2.3.

bookprices and intervention prices. Finally, some expenditures are treated exogenously.[104]

(v) ECAM generates community accounts at EU-12 level. Total receipts and expenditures follow the consolidated accounts, published yearly by the Commission (Court of Auditors, various issues). These reports have been used to collect data about non-FEOGA expenditures and miscellaneous receipts.[105]

The collection and construction of appropriate data is a complex process that is greatly facilitated if sources, methods and assumptions are well documented. For ECAM all data processing made use of the SOW-VU Data Management package (see Overbosch (1990)) through which the model input files were created.

---

[104] These include all FEOGA guarantee expenditures not covered by the model, especially for Greece, Spain, Portugal and the former GDR.

[105] Including: exchange rate differences, cancellations of previous years, surplus previous years etc. Community expenditures refer to: public administration, development aid and transfers to member states (linked to: structural, social and regional policy, research, energy etc.) and a number of miscellaneous items, such as current surplus and carry-overs to next year.

Chapter 5

CAP reform in the bureaucratic perspective:
the MacSharry reform and the GATT agreement

Having described the model that we shall use in our scenario simulations, we are now ready to analyze the outcomes from reforms within the different perspectives, starting from the bureaucratic perspective.

Proposals for reform within the bureaucratic perspective consist of corrective actions that reflect the pressures of the day. When there is scarcity on world markets the budgetary cost of the CAP diminishes and there will be less pressure to reduce protection and intervention prices. But that was not the situation in the late eighties and early nineties. At that time world market prices for most agricultural products were low and FEOGA expenditures rocketed. Moreover, the GATT negotiations were dragging on.

So, when in 1991 the Commissioner responsible for agriculture, Mr. Ray MacSharry, launched a plan for a fundamental reform, it fell on fertile soil. With minor adjustments the EU approved the plan in May 1992. This acceptance greatly facilitated the GATT negotiations; as a result, in November 1992 the so-called 'Blair House Agreement' between the United States and the EU was concluded (Anonymous (1992)). And in December 1993 a (marginally) revised version of the US-EU deal was approved as a part of an overall multilateral trade agreement (GATT (1993)). Although both the MacSharry reform and the revised Blair House Agreement contain some radical elements, the two packages must above all be characterized as compromises and they are in most respects of a gradualist nature, and as such, they fit well in the bureaucratic perspective.

The proposed MacSharry reform elicited intensive debate as to its consequences and when the Blair House Agreement was accepted, the issue of compatibility between the two reforms came up. This debate was in fact a discussion on outcomes that were to be expected from scenarios and it is therefore natural to use ECAM in order to investigate them in more detail (see also Loyat (1992) and Keyzer et al. (1994)).

In this chapter we report on this exercise. The presentation will centre around the following three questions:

(i)   How will EU agriculture develop under the MacSharry reform?
(ii) What would have happened if the pre-MacSharry policies had been continued?
(iii) To what extent is the reform compatible with the GATT agreement?

On the basis of outcomes from ECAM, we describe in Section 5.1 the impact which the reform measures can be expected to have on production levels, FEOGA expenditures, international trade, intermediate demand, the size of the labour force, farm income and some other relevant variables. At the end of the section, we assess the reform in the light of the objectives stated in the original discussion document.[106] We then compare the outcomes of the MacSharry scenario with a no-reform scenario that keeps the pre-MacSharry policies unchanged (Section 5.2). The purpose of the no-reform scenario is first, to find out whether the MacSharry reform was unavoidable in the sense that continuation of the existing policy would have led to unsustainable situations (this is the common understanding, and the simulation runs will make us question this view) and secondly, whether the MacSharry reform is a radical departure from prevailing trends. In Chapter 2, Section 2.2.3, it was already emphasized that whatever the merits of the MacSharry reform, the basic principles of protection of the Community against imports from third countries will not change, as the system of variable levies and subsidies at the border remains in place. However, this system will eventually be undermined by the GATT deal and this raises the question whether the GATT agreement is compatible with the MacSharry reform (Section 5.3). Section 5.4 concludes with an overall assessment.

---

[106] The so-called 'reflection paper' submitted to the agricultural ministers of the member states (CEC, 1991a).

5.1   The MacSharry reform package: EU agriculture until 2005

5.1.1   Scenario assumptions

The MacSharry reform package has already been discussed in Section (2.2.3). Its main thrust lies in the significant reduction of the market support for cereals and the elimination of existing deficiency payments for oilseeds. To avoid income losses for the farmers they receive per hectare compensation payments. To reduce subsidized exports of cereals, farmers are required to leave a portion of their land idle, in exchange for the compensation (see CEC (1993)). In (ii) below we shall describe how the various measures have been expressed in scenario terms.

Any specification of a scenario for ECAM proceeds in two stages. First, one must decide on the time horizon of the scenario. Since the MacSharry reform is far-reaching, adjustments will spread over several years. Hence, it seems advisable to choose a medium term horizon. On the other hand in the longer term, external circumstances[107] may compel the EU seriously to adjust its agricultural policies again. Therefore, the medium term horizon should not be too long either. Taking this into account, a simulation period from 1992 until 2005 was chosen. Secondly, assumptions must be made on plausible values of exogenous variables. These fall into three groups (i) world market prices, (ii) agricultural policy variables and (iii) variables relating to the non-agricultural part of the EU economy.

(i) World market prices

World market prices for agricultural products are volatile. A bad harvest in a major producing region in the world can easily result in two-digit rates of price increase. Figure 5.1 illustrates this for sugar, wheat, soybeans and total food. Because the data used for these graphs are annual averages, they omit the stronger actual price volatility throughout the year.

---

[107] For example, the extension of the EU with EFTA and Central and Eastern European countries.

Figure 5.1 Indices of world market prices, 1973=100

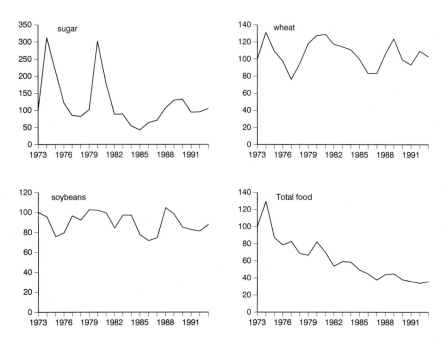

Source: UNCTAD, *Monthly Commodity Price Bulletin.*
Note: Sugar, wheat and soybeans nominal US dollar index; total food deflated with
           Manufacturing Unit Value Index.

As the EU is a major actor on the world market, the Community's budgetary problems and opportunities for exports are very much affected by conditions on the world market. Therefore, it is important to base the assumptions on world prices on careful considerations. At the same time the volatility of world market prices makes it difficult to formulate reliable assumptions.

For the long run price pattern something like a trend can be established. A detailed analysis by Grilli and Yang (1988) reveals a structural tendency for world market prices of agricultural products to fall at a moderate rate.[108] Over the period 1900-86 they estimated average price decreases of 0.3 and 0.8 per cent per year for food and non-food agricultural products, respectively.

In our scenario we take this structural trend as a starting point. Consequently, we assume that the sharp drop of many world market prices (expressed in constant ecu) since the mid-seventies is atypical and due to specific factors.[109] We assume that the current 'imbalance' will be restored somewhat in the coming years and justify this as follows.

First, at the global level, due to demographic trends and economic growth, the potential demand for most agricultural products is very large and fast growing. Of course, many cannot afford to buy food on the world market but the fast growing economies of East and South-East Asia and the fast growing populations of the Middle East will be able to do so. At current (and expected future) prices of major non-farm inputs such as energy, fertilizers and pesticides, it seems rather implausible that global food production will increase at a pace that is sufficient to meet food demand if world market prices continue falling as fast as in the past fifteen or twenty years. In this respect we think that the current situation differs fundamentally from the situation in the mid-seventies.[110]

Secondly, we would contend that a continuation of the price trends of the eighties cannot be established independently from the scenario that is selected. While for several commodities the EU plays a role on world markets that is sufficiently important to affect world prices, ECAM takes these prices as given. Hence it may happen that the model generates a pattern of imports and exports that is incompatible with the price assumptions (for example high exports of dairy together with high world market prices). The scenario formulation has to account for this through an iterative (informal) procedure whereby assumptions

---

[108] These prices are expressed as a ratio to the price of the aggregated internationally traded manufactured product.

[109] To mention a few: changes in the exchange rate between the US dollar and the ecu, agricultural policies in the developed countries, a downward correction for the '73 boom and economic recession in the early eighties.

[110] In Chapter 7 this will be explained in more detail.

on trends in world prices are brought in accordance with the import and export levels. It happens that the MacSharry reform will, according to our results, have effects on the EU's net trade that are significant but very different among commodities.

Table 5.1   Assumptions on world market prices in the MacSharry scenario, ecu/100 kg at 1992 prices

	1992	1993	1996	1999	2005	Annual growth rate 1992-2005
Wheat	9.59	9.87	10.42	10.27	9.96	0.30
Coarse grains	8.70	8.96	9.46	9.32	9.04	0.30
Rice	24.51	24.39	24.03	23.67	22.97	-0.50
Sugar	25.40	25.27	24.90	24.53	23.80	-0.50
Fats and oils	32.70	32.53	32.05	31.57	30.63	-0.50
Protein feed	37.54	36.41	34.09	33.58	32.59	-1.08
Carbohydrates	8.16	7.92	7.41	7.30	7.09	-1.08
Butter	279.00	280.39	281.79	277.58	269.36	-0.27
Other dairy	48.45	48.60	48.65	47.92	46.50	-0.32
Bovine meat	163.48	163.46	160.96	153.82	140.49	-1.16
Ovine meat	158.23	158.71	158.86	156.49	151.85	-0.32
Pork	292.75	291.29	286.94	282.66	274.29	-0.50
Poultry meat and eggs	1042.47	1037.26	1021.78	1006.53	976.71	-0.50
Non-agriculture tradeable	151.20	151.20	151.20	151.20	151.20	0.00

This explains the diverging world market price assumptions in Table 5.1. Global supply and demand developments combined with a reduction in cereal exports by the EU (see Table 5.6) are supposed to result in an increase in world market prices by an average 0.3 per cent per year. On the other hand, since the decrease in internal cereal prices negatively affects internal demand for cereal substitutes, their prices are supposed to decrease more than average. Nonetheless, price decreases of grain substitutes are much less than the thirty per cent price decrease of internally grown feed grains under the MacSharry reform (see Section 2.2.3). We think that it would be unrealistic to assume such a drastic price change, because the prices of protein feed and carbohydrates are not determined by EU feed grain prices only. There are other importers than the EU and the farmers in the exporting countries have alternative options also.

A final remark relates to the prices for bovine meat. The scenario outcomes show a drastic increase in bovine exports (see Table 5.6). World market prices will be affected by this. In the scenario we proceed from an average price decrease of 1.16 per cent annually.

(ii) Agricultural policy

The main elements of the MacSharry reform were described in Section 2.2.3. To represent it, we have tried to express the official EU decisions as parameter values for ECAM to the extent possible but some conversions were required. Under the MacSharry reform farmers receive income compensation linked to their specific production pattern. Because ECAM uses the concept of a national farm and lacks structural and regional detail, the amount of compensation given for the MacSharry commodities had to be computed from other data sources. After the transitional period 1993-95 these amounts have been assumed to be fixed for the remaining period.

Data on farm structure are required to compute how much land will be set aside. From the Farm Accountancy Data Network (FADN) of the EU,[111] we derive how much of the so-called basic area (see Section 2.2.3) is attributable to small and to large farmers. Computations show that in the EU-12 8.9 per cent of the basic area will be set aside, with a minimum of 4.7 per cent for Italy and maximum of 14.7 per cent for the UK (complete results are in Keyzer et al., 1994, Annex B). We have assumed that fodder maize is either eligible for the crop premium, or covers the application for premiums in the beef sector since it cannot be submitted twice for compensation.

The regulations stipulated that fallow land must rotate in the cropping, otherwise a higher set-aside obligation is imposed. It is to be expected that less productive acreage will be taken out of production first, and that crop rotation possibilities will widen. So there is scope for a small increase in yields on non-

---

[111] Thanks are due to Nigel Robson and his group within the Commission for communicating their calculations on the FADN-data to us.

fallow land, the so-called *slippage* effect. This effect is set at a maximum of two per cent.

Compensation of male bovines and suckler cows depends both on herd size and livestock density (see also Section 2.2.3). Using FADN data we have computed the member state specific premium per head of non-dairy cattle, which ranges from 3 green ecu per head in The Netherlands to 54 green ecu in Ireland. The calculation yields an EU-12 average of 33 green ecu per head.

Furthermore, three additional complications had to be dealt with. First, all the official reform measures are specified in nominal terms and there is no provision for adjustment for inflation of prices, or for compensation payments. ECAM operates in real terms, in the sense that it treats the price of non-agricultural commodities as an exogenous variable that is kept constant after 1992. To convert the official measures in such real terms one needs an assumption on nominal ecu-inflation for the period 1993-95 during which the reform will be implemented. We have assumed an inflation rate of three per cent and have deflated all the proposed prices and compensation measures accordingly, to obtain scenario values. This amounts to assuming that, until 1995, all price and compensation measures are implemented in accordance with the official text of the reform, without any adjustment for inflation. For the period beyond 1995 we have assumed that the adjustment will cover half of the inflation, so that there will be a real price reduction of 1.5 per cent annually. It is important to note that this reduction does not require any nominal price cuts, which as mentioned earlier in Section 2.2.2 tend to face strong political resistance. Hence, we assume that the rate of inflation is 'politically sufficient.'

Secondly, the reform does not cover all CAP products. For the products that are not covered, we have assumed that pre-MacSharry policies will continue, with a real price decrease of 1.5 per cent after 1995 as for the other agricultural commodities. The assumptions on intervention prices are summarized in Table 5.2.

Thirdly, the effects of a drastic price fall on yields per hectare and per animal are unknown (recall from the discussion in Section 4.3.2 that yields are practically exogenous in ECAM). Experts agree only with respect to the sign of these effects. For the 'MacSharry'-crops wheat, coarse grains, oilseeds, protein

Table 5.2   Intervention prices in the MacSharry scenario, at 1992 prices, 1992=100

	1992	1993	1996	1999	2005	Annual growth rate 1992-2005
Wheat	100.	80.4	59.8	57.1	52.2	-4.9
Coarse grains	100.	81.2	61.8	59.0	53.9	-4.6
Sugar	100.	99.0	96.1	93.2	87.8	-1.0
Butter	100.	94.1	85.9	83.3	78.5	-1.9
Other dairy	100.	96.9	90.3	87.6	82.5	-1.5
Bovine meat	100.	92.1	77.2	75.4	71.9	-2.5
Ovine meat	100.	95.5	85.1	82.5	77.7	-1.9

crops and fodder maize we have assumed, after elaborate consultations but nonetheless rather arbitrarily, that there is an extensification effect consisting of a once-for-all downward shift in yield per hectare of four per cent in 1993 and, associated with it, a reduction in current inputs of about eight per cent per hectare. For non-dairy cattle we have assumed that the price fall triggers an extensification effect that leads to a similar drop in yield per animal of two per cent and in input requirement per animal of four per cent.

(iii) Economic growth in the non-farm sector

The model treats the growth rate of the tradeable non-agricultural commodity in each member state as an exogenous variable (see Section 4.2.5). For 1993 and 1994 the assumed rate follows OECD forecasts for the member states that were available by the end of 1992. It is assumed that, after a period of recession in 1993 and 1994, growth will pick up to reach an average annual rate of 2.1 per cent. From 1995 onwards this rate has been applied to all member states for all years. The importance of non-agricultural growth for demand of agricultural products must be stressed. Growth rates that lie at a sustained level of, say, 2.5 per cent, cause the model to generate higher consumption and hence higher production, particularly for pork and poultry. Model simulations indicate that this assumption is important indeed and that a period of sluggish growth tends to depress the livestock sector in particular.

5.1.2   Model outcomes for production, demand and external trade

Production

Under the MacSharry reform three instruments are deployed to constrain the (growth of) production: (i) the set-aside obligation for cereals, oilseeds and protein crops, (ii) production quota and quota on the amounts of subsidies payable, and (iii) the reduction in intervention prices.

Table 5.3   Production quantities of selected commodities, EU-9, annual growth rate

	Base 1982-92	MacSharry 1992-2005
Wheat	3.0	0.8
Coarse grains	-0.1	0.4
Sugar beet	0.8	0.2
Oilseeds	11.4	0.6
Consumable potatoes	-0.5	1.3
Dairy cows	-0.3	0.0
Laying hens	0.5	0.5
Non-dairy cattle	0.6	1.4
Sheep and goats	3.6	0.0
Pigs	1.7	1.3
Poultry	3.4	1.8

Table 5.3 summarizes the impact of these instruments over the period 1992-2005. To put the numbers into perspective, growth rates for the same commodities are also listed for the period 1982-92.[112] Not surprisingly, production growth is very modest. For six production activities in the table (wheat, sugar beet, oilseeds, sheep and goats, pigs and poultry) growth is less than in the period 1982-92 and for four activities (viz. coarse grains, consumable potatoes, dairy cows, non-dairy cattle), it is higher. The small acceleration in the coarse grains sector does not mean that the EU can expect mountains of grains to build up. Because the additional coarse grain production is offset by the

---

[112] Outcomes for 1982-90 have been validated in the way described in Annex 4A. Due to a lack of detailed statistics, outcomes for 1991 and 1992 could be validated against few statistics only.

slowing-down in the growth of wheat production, the growth of overall grain production decreases. The growth of consumable potato production is largely caused by a change in relative profitability. The interpretation is that since guaranteed prices are reduced for all CAP crops, farmers must look for alternatives and choose potatoes, a non-CAP crop. Obviously, the scope for such a substitution is limited, due the low price elasticity of demand for potatoes. The calculated increase is considered to be sufficiently small to be realistic.

The quota regulations appear to be effective in stabilizing milk production during the simulation period. However, due to technological developments, milk production per cow increases. The average dairy cow produces 16.5 per cent more milk in 2005 than in 1992. Therefore, less dairy cows are needed to produce the quota. The resulting excess production capacity in the livestock sector is allocated to non-dairy cattle, and this explains the relatively rapid growth of this activity.

Table 5.4   Production quantities for selected commodities by member state, annual growth rate

	Wheat		Oilseeds		Dairy cows		Non-dairy cattle	
	1982-1992	1992-2005	1982-1992	1992-2005	1982-1992	1992-2005	1982-1992	1992-2005
Belgium-Luxembourg	3.2	0.9	3.9	2.3	-0.3	-0.3	1.9	3.0
Denmark	9.1	-0.7	11.3	2.8	-0.7	0.1	-1.4	0.0
France	2.5	1.4	9.9	0.4	-0.4	-0.2	-0.4	0.8
Germany, Fed. Rep.	2.7	2.0	11.0	-0.3	-0.7	0.0	2.0	1.4
Ireland	4.0	-1.0	n.a	n.a	1.6	1.2	0.8	2.7
Italy	-1.4	0.5	23.9	0.7	0.3	0.1	0.9	3.4
The Netherlands	-1.6	0.9	-8.4	1.5	-1.1	0.0	-0.3	0.0
United Kingdom	6.0	-0.6	7.8	0.3	-0.1	-0.2	-0.6	-0.2
EU-9	3.0	0.8	11.4	0.6	-0.3	0.0	0.6	1.4

Growth rates of pig and poultry production range between one and two per cent. As the EU is practically closed to imports from third countries and EU farmers have limited competitiveness on the world market, production can hardly exceed the consumption of these products (see also equations (3.4a-b) of Section 3.1.1).

The overall production pattern is not significantly affected by the reform. This is due to the fact that there is little change in the relative profitability of all the crops that are close substitutes. It also means that the shift toward oilseed production, that was so spectacular in the past, comes to an end.

In Table 5.4 growth figures for selected products are presented by member state. It appears that the member states show rather diverging trends. Partly this can be explained from differences in relative profitability, investment behaviour, migration and the like. It is also a consequence of differences in set-aside obligations and differences in premium per head of non-dairy cattle (see Keyzer et al. (1994)). For dairy cows the differences in growth are mainly attributable to differences in the on-farm use of milk for animal feeding.

Consumption and intermediate demand

In developed countries aggregate consumer demand for agricultural products is usually found to have low price and income elasticities. Estimated price and income elasticities used in ECAM are in almost all cases significantly lower than unity (see Michalek and Keyzer (1992)). In the scenario period three factors specifically affect consumer demand: the decrease in real prices, the moderate increase in *per capita* incomes, and the stagnant population of the EU-9. Together these factors suggest a modest increase in aggregate consumer demand for food and model outcomes confirm this.

Nonetheless, growth rates can differ substantially between products. Consumption of wine is expected to decrease. while demand for fats, vegetable oils and non-bovine meat will increase at more than the average rate. In fact the main dietary trends of the eighties, i.e. the shifts from red meat, wine and animal fats towards white meat, beer and vegetable fats and oils, respectively, are projected to continue at least until 2005. To a large extent this is attributable to assumed drifts in model parameters.

While for intermediate demand (mainly animal feeds) substitution is the consequence of cost minimization by the producers of animal feeds, as the animals themselves have little say in the matter, for final demand, consumer tastes dictate the response to price changes. This explains why price elasticities

Table 5.5   Consumption and intermediate use of selected commodities, EU-9, annual growth rate

	Consumption		Intermediate use	
	1982-92	1992-2005	1982-92	1992-2005
Wheat	1.7	1.2	3.9	1.5
Coarse grains	2.3	1.4	-2.7	1.4
Sugar	0.7	1.0	2.7	2.0
Fats and oils	1.3	2.2	0.7	2.0
Protein feeds	-	-	2.2	-1.4
Carbohydrates	-	-	0.4	-0.2
Butter	-0.5	0.6	-1.9	0.8
Other dairy	1.5	0.3	-1.7	0.3
Bovine meat	0.3	0.8	-	-
Ovine meat	1.4	2.2	-	-
Pork	2.0	1.3	-	-
Poultry meat and eggs	2.1	1.5	-	-

are usually much larger for intermediate demand than for consumer demand.

Table 5.5 shows that the use of cereals in animal feeds increases significantly in the scenario. This is due, first, to the grains price decrease, which causes cassava, soybean meal and other grain substitutes to be replaced, secondly, to the shift in pig and poultry sectors towards regions (member states) where the share of grain in the animal diets is high, and thirdly to an increase in consumer demand for pig and poultry meat because of reduced production costs.

Figure 5.2 summarizes the changes in animal diets in relative terms. At the community level, the share of feed grains in total feeds (excluding green fodder) increases from 53.8 per cent to 61.9 per cent in the period 1992-2005. Although the model outcomes should only be seen as crude indicators, the message is unambiguous. The reduction in protection of cereals rehabilitates their position as an animal feed. The shifts are most pronounced in The Netherlands and Belgium-Luxembourg, where the scope for substitution is largest.

For the EU this 'return to grains' has several attractive consequences. It reduces sales on the world market, hence avoiding export subsidies. This is favourable for the EU budget as well as for its external relations since there will be less ground for accusations of dumping.

Figure 5.2 Composition of metabolizable energy in animal diets, excl. green fodder, EU-9

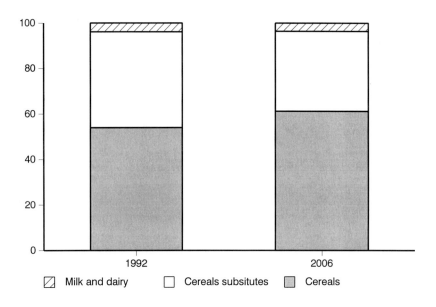

Source: ECAM, MacSharry scenario.

External trade

The reduction in cereal exports is significant. The scenario indicates that exports will fall from nearly 30 million metric tons in 1992 to less than 10 million metric tons in 1996 (Table 5.6). Although exports pick up afterwards, even in 2005 they remain well below the 1992 level. In view of the cereal surplus of the eighties and early nineties and the broadly felt expectation that, in the absence of a reform, this surplus would increase by the year, this certainly is a favourable aspect of the reform (see also Section 5.3). However, for a correct interpretation of these numbers, it must be noted that the external trade positions for the different commodities are balancing items in the model (see again equations (3.4a-b)). A small deviation in production or internal demand can greatly affect the net trade position. The sensitivity of net trade is important in relation to the GATT agreement (Section 5.3 below). Nonetheless, the message from the scenario is clear. If the MacSharry reform is implemented strictly, the problem of a fast growing cereal surplus will virtually be eliminated. The surplus of the EU that would remain in 2005, would be about one per cent of global cereal production (excluding rice) in 1992.

Table 5.6   Net imports of selected commodities, EU-9, mln metric tons

	1982	1992	1996	2005
Wheat	-9.6	-17.0	-9.1	-15.5
Coarse grains	3.2	-11.5	-0.7	-1.4
Sugar	-4.0	-3.5	-3.2	-2.4
Fats and oils	5.1	4.0	4.8	6.2
Protein feeds	11.1	11.8	10.4	9.1
Carbohydrates	21.0	23.3	21.5	21.9
Butter	-0.3	0.0	0.0	0.0
Other dairy	-10.0	-6.8	-7.9	-5.0
Bovine meat	0.1	-0.2	0.1	-0.8

The figures on the imports of grain substitutes show the other side of the story. The import volume of protein feed and carbohydrates are 23 and 6 per cent lower, respectively, in 2005 than in 1992, in spite of the significant increase in numbers of pigs and poultry. As the size of the sugar quota does not change and consumption of sugar increases slightly (mainly for beverages), the sugar surplus falls over time. The reform also affects the trade in fats and oils. Due to the set-aside obligations and the extensification, growth of oilseed production lags behind the EU's internal demand. Consequently, the earlier trend of falling imports comes to an end and in 2005 the level of imports lies above the average level in the eighties. Net exports of butter remain negligible throughout the period but there may be some gross exports, since the EU has an import commitment for butter from New Zealand.[113] Net exports of dairy decrease over time and by 2005 they have fallen by almost 26 per cent of the 1992 level. Because world trade in dairy products is expected to rise in the years to come (World Bank, 1992a), this outcome implies that the EU would gradually lose

---

[113] The size of the commitment is subject to change, and amounts to 52000 metric tons in 1993.

some of its dominant position on the international dairy market, provided other countries are able to meet the demand.

The developments in the trade pattern would imply an alleviation of trade conflicts, but for the growth in exports of bovine meat. Bovine meat production increases by 1.4 per cent annually, exceeding growth in annual consumption by 0.6 per cent. This leads to an annual surplus of more than 800 thousand metric tons in 2005. Since international trade in bovine meat (excluding intra-EU trade) amounted to slightly more than 3.0 million metric tons in the early nineties, this surplus is large indeed.

5.1.3   Protection and the budget

Protection

Community preference, one of the three basic principles of the CAP, can only be realized if the farmers in the EU are protected against outside competitors, who will denounce it as unfair. Therefore, trade conflicts are inherent in the CAP. The MacSharry reform was partly motivated by the wish to alleviate such tensions. We have seen that, to the extent that these conflicts originated from dumping practices, the reform gives reason for optimism.

However, this by itself does not imply that protection will diminish under the reform. It can persist in many other ways. A problem in this connection is that rates of protection can be measured in various ways. In practice this leaves ample room for debates, particularly in the context of negotiations to reduce protection, like the Uruguay Round. In Annex 4A it has already been indicated that we would mainly follow the PSE-concept developed by the OECD, although this choice is open to debate. The PSE measure is a static measure and it does not measure the welfare loss but in the context of negotiations it has the merit of depending only on simple statistical calculations, rather than on model outcomes (which are always controversial).

In relation to the MacSharry reform, there is a special problem as to the treatment of per hectare compensations. Should these be seen as lump sum transfers or as price subsidies? While the GATT has accepted such payments as falling outside the category of protectionist measures, there seems to be a consensus among policy analysts that the payments will in fact affect production decisions significantly.

Table 5.7a   Rate of protection on production, EU-9, percentage

	1992	1996	2005
Wheat	70	62	60
Coarse grains	59	50	45
Sugar	119	117	113
Fats and oils	33	28	27
Butter	39	28	26
Other dairy	38	34	38
Bovine meat	35	17	17
Ovine meat	64	57	54

Note: Protection as ratio of support (producer subsidies plus border support) and production value including support, multiplied by 100.

Table 5.7b   Rate of protection on consumption, EU-9, percentage

	1992	1996	2005
Wheat	11	15	15
Coarse grains	25	24	23
Sugar	29	28	26
Fats and oils	0	0	0
Butter	37	26	24
Other dairy	12	10	10
Bovine meat	21	10	10
Ovine meat	24	19	18

Note: Protection as ratio of CAP-related taxes minus subsidies and consumption value including CAP-related taxes minus subsidies, multiplied by 100.

Similarly, one may argue that border protection on dairy products or sugar on the producer side only leads to transfers, since in this case production quotas and not prices determine the level of output. To this one may respond that the farmer is able to buy livestock and machinery and to service his debt only because of the high prices. Since there is no final answer to these questions, it is not meaningful to base all judgements with respect to protectionism on the PSE-rate alone, we have computed this measure (Table 5.7a) which quantifies protection at farm-gate level, and complemented it with the consumer subsidy rate (Table 5.7b).

It appears that for all products protection on production in 2005 is lower than in 1992. Although for dairy there is an upward trend from the end-nineties onwards,[114] for other products the trend of increasing protection seems definitely broken by the reform. Nonetheless, EU agriculture is still heavily protected in 2005. Moreover, part of the decrease in protection has to be attributed to our assumption on the slower reduction in world market prices.

FEOGA outlays

Reducing protection does not mean that budgetary outlays will fall. The scenario outcomes illustrate that a reduction in protection can go hand in hand with an increase in budgetary outlays (see Table 5.8). Total FEOGA guarantee outlays are projected at 38.3 billion ecu in 2005, a real increase of 6 billion ecu compared to 1992. This increase is mainly attributable to the transition from a regime of market price support to one of compensation payments. Remarkable shifts can be observed. Export refunds decrease on average by nearly five per cent annually, but for producer subsidies there is an annual increase of 5.5 per cent. Interest and storage costs tend to decline. Various mechanisms induce these shifts. First, due to the lowering of guarantee prices, the set-aside measures and the quota on subsidies, the growth in production diminishes. Secondly, the subsidies per unit that are required to bridge the gap between the EU price level and the world market also become less. Hence, the costs of stockholding (which involves an interest charge since stocks are financed through loans) and of export refunds are reduced. The rehabilitation of internally grown cereals in compound feeds has a positive effect on the budget also since less cereals have

---

[114] Although the intervention price for dairy decreases faster than the world market price, the rate of protection increases somewhat during the period 1996-2005. This is due to a development in the denominator of the expression, i.e. to the change in the processing margin between farm-gate and border level, which differs between member states. The drop in this margin causes the farm-gate price to increase.

to be exported. Thirdly, due to the 'decoupled' compensations, there is a significant increase in producer subsidies. Finally, the outlays on the item 'other FEOGA guarantee', an exogenous variable, increase. They refer to FEOGA expenditures concerning southern member states not covered by ECAM. Their increase is mainly caused by the assumed rapid increase in producer subsidies for these countries.

Table 5.8   FEOGA outlays, EU-12, mln ecu[a]

	1982	1987	1992	1996	2005	Annual growth rate	
						1982-1992	1992-2005
Export refunds	4,700	10,666	7,308	4,047	3,854	4.5	-4.8
MCAs	-109	51	0	0	0	-	-
Producer subsidies	2,024	3,956	7,476	15,717	14,995	14.0	5.5
Consumer subsidies	1,108	896	1,499	1,438	1,463	3.1	-0.2
Input subsidies	2,141	1,432	2,927	2,629	2,569	3.2	-1.0
Interest and storage costs[b]	827	3,069	2,521	1,177	1,441	11.8	-4.2
Other FEOGA guarantee	1,819	2,786	10,380	11,676	13,954	19.0	2.3
Total FEOGA guarantee	12,510	22,786	32,111	36,684	38,276	9.9	1.4

Notes: (a) Until 1992 in current prices; thereafter at 1992 prices.
        (b) Including stock devaluation.

Although overall (real) growth in FEOGA outlays may seem rather high, it remains within the spending guideline (see Section 2.2.2). The rate would be higher if compensations were constant in real terms or if world market prices were to fall more steeply. In an earlier ECAM-scenario full indexation of compensation payments was assumed. The additional[115] budgetary costs of the MacSharry reform then amounted to nearly 10 billion ecu (see Keyzer et al. (1994)).

---

[115] Compared to a scenario in which a continuation of pre-MacSharry policies was assumed.

5.1.4   Value added and employment in agriculture

Value added

At aggregate EU-9 level, ECAM forecasts an annual reduction in real value added of 0.7 per cent; here real value added is defined as the difference between the value of total production, including producer subsidies, and the value of intermediate consumption and deflated by an ecu price index. Although this development is less dramatic than during the period 1982-92 (Table 5.9), it is a reduction nonetheless, which means that, for the EU-9, the growth in the production volume and in input productivity is insufficient to compensate for the fall in real prices. The agricultural sectors in Italy and the Netherlands are exceptions to the general pattern. In these countries real value added in agriculture rises somewhat. In the Netherlands this is due to a further expansion of the horticultural sector, while in Italy growth in the livestock sector is above average.

Table 5.9   Real value added of agriculture, annual growth rate at 1992 prices

	Real value added		Real value added per capita	
	1982-92	1992-2005	1982-92	1992-2005
Belgium-Luxembourg	-2.3	-0.6	-0.5	1.6
Denmark	-0.9	-0.2	2.1	3.2
France	-4.0	-1.2	-0.4	2.8
Germany, Fed. Rep.	-2.5	-1.6	-1.2	0.0
Ireland	-1.1	-1.5	3.0	2.3
Italy	-1.5	0.2	2.0	3.0
The Netherlands	0.6	0.4	1.3	1.2
United Kingdom	-3.1	-2.2	-1.5	-0.2
EU-9	-2.3	-0.7	0.5	1.9

Note: Agricultural value added is deflated by the national GDP-deflator in ecu.

It has already been stressed in Section 2.3.5 that value added is not the same as farm income, let alone family income as it includes, among others, depreciation costs, land rent and interests costs. Moreover, many farm families have sources of income outside agriculture. If one is only interested in comparing incomes from agricultural activities between two scenarios, or, as in Table 5.9, between two historical periods, these additional income components do not matter very much. It appears then that due to a reduction in the number of farmers the growth rates of agricultural value added per capita after the reform increases at a somewhat faster rate than during the period 1982-92.

Employment

ECAM projects an average decrease in the agricultural labour force of 2.6 per cent per year. Figure 5.3 summarizes the development for the full period 1982-2005.

Figure 5.3 Agricultural population, EU-9, 1982=100

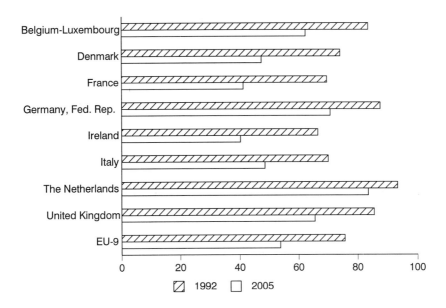

Source: ECAM, MacSharry scenario.

In less than 25 years the agricultural labour force will nearly halve. Labour outflow is especially high in Denmark, France, Ireland and Italy. The figure suggests that a 'revolution' is going on in EU agriculture which, despite the reform, will not come to an end in this century. The fact that demographic factors, more than income differentials between agriculture and non-agriculture, are the driving force behind this process explains the limited effect of the reform on the size of the agricultural labour force (see also Section 5.3.5). This raises the issue of whether in the long run the number of family farmers will remain sufficient to maintain the EU's export position and to what extent the family farm will be replaced by large commercial enterprises. To this we will turn in Chapter 7.

5.1.5   The MacSharry reform: an interim evaluation

From the discussion of the model outcomes so far we may conclude that the MacSharry reform is far-reaching in some respects. Since it is the outcome of a policy discussion that took place within what we have called the 'bureaucratic perspective', the reform should primarily be evaluated according to criteria that are relevant within this perspective. A free trader or an interventionist will, almost by definition, find the reform inadequate. Within the bureaucratic perspective two sets of criteria seem particularly relevant. The first relates to the deficiencies of the CAP as they were perceived by the Commission itself on the eve of the reform and the second to what would have happened in case that the pre-MacSharry policies had been pursued.

The reform started with a discussion paper by the Commission (CEC (1991a)). In this so-called 'reflection' paper the Commission summarized the deficiencies of the CAP as it functioned at the time and revised the original CAP objectives. According to the Commission, a continuation of CAP policies then pursued would lead to growing surpluses, growing international tensions and ever increasing FEOGA outlays. Moreover, it would result in a further intensification of production, with negative effects on the environment. In the reflection paper it is also mentioned that the prevailing CAP was more beneficial to large farmers than to small farmers.

The diagnosis in the reflection paper led to a restatement of the CAP objectives (CEC (1991b)). In this restatement the Commission emphasized that a sufficient number of farmers has to be kept on the land for there is 'no other way to preserve the natural environment, traditional landscapes and a model of agriculture based on the family farm'. In addition, the Commission pointed out that less intensive production techniques should be promoted and that farmers should be stimulated to grow raw materials for non-food uses. The Commission also stressed that markets needed to be brought back into balance and that competitiveness and efficiency of Community agriculture were to be promoted. Support measures should be redirected in favour of those farmers in greatest need.[116]

Although the scenario outcomes are not explicit on all these points, on a number of them they are rather clear.

Environment: The reform may have a positive effect on the environment. One obvious reason is that the land set-aside will not be farmed in an intensive way. Also the compensation payments are expected to lead to a certain extensification of crop production. Then, there is the effect of rebalancing, whereby cereals used as animal feeds become cheaper. This has various consequences. The primary effect is to reduce the volume of trade. Whereas in the pre-MacSharry regime substitutes were imported and cereals exported, after rebalancing, there are less imports and less exports of both. A secondary effect of this change is that it virtually eliminates the competitive edge of specialized livestock farms in areas in the vicinity of the seaports where the substitutes can enter the Community. Hence, the high geographical concentration of pigs and poultry production, that has had devastating effects on the environment, will be reduced somewhat (see also Section 2.4.7 and RIVM (1989)). Of course, little will be gained in the aggregate, as long as the number of animals raised within the Community is not reduced (and in the MacSharry scenario this number even rises). Yet the rebalancing may allow a less concentrated geographical pattern of livestock production, with livestock farms growing their own feed grains, and

---

[116] See CEC (1991b) and CEC (1993) for a further description of the MacSharry Reform.

in this case the reform may be beneficial. Yet negative aspects cannot be ruled out. The numbers of non-dairy cattle rise by nearly 6 million and pig and poultry productions increase as well, due to increased demand. Also, the shift of production may cause damage in areas that were left unspoiled so far and that do not necessarily have sufficient capacity to absorb the pollution.

Market balance and international trade problems: The MacSharry reform will lessen the tensions on the international agricultural markets since exports of traditional surplus products will decrease, with bovine meat as the main exception. Moreover, the policy becomes less vulnerable to charges of dumping, because it operates with lower unit export subsidies.

Efficiency and competitiveness: Due to the fall in consumer prices for food and in the prices for cereals as input in the feed mix industry, there will be efficiency gains and the reduction in feed cost will make the livestock sector more competitive on the international markets. On the other hand, as the system of variable levies will remain in place, there is no danger of foreign imports competing with EU producers. On the contrary, the reform has some autarkic elements as it reduces imports of cereal substitutes. It may also be noted that through the introduction of quota arrangements (set-aside, ceilings on the number of premiums), resource fixities are created that will adversely affect efficiency.

Number of farmers: According to the scenario outcome, the rapid outflow of farmers will in no way be stopped by the reform; in the period 1992-2005 alone the agricultural labour force is expected to decrease by nearly thirty per cent.

Farm incomes and distribution of support: In spite of a sustained rise in FEOGA expenditures, the income gap between agriculture and non-agriculture will not lessen under the reform. However, one may expect that farm incomes of small farmers will improve relative to those of large farmers.

Landscape: Finally, the combination of a continued rapid outflow of labour and an increase of production and yields implies that the transformation process of rural Europe will continue, a process not conducive to the conservation of traditional landscapes. Moreover, the regulation for set-asides requires farmers to leave those areas under fallow crops (lupines etc.) which barely add to the quality of the landscape.

In summary, although a number of problems of EU agriculture may be alleviated by the MacSharry reform, many issues remain unresolved, so that one may expect adjustments in a near future. This makes it all the more relevant to analyze policy alternatives. Yet a critique on the reform is unbalanced unless it takes into consideration that, within the bureaucratic perspective, there is never much room for manoeuvre. The decision process of the CAP, with a council of ministers of twelve countries having to approve every proposal, naturally tends towards patchwork adjustments and gradualism.

5.2 What would have happened in the absence of the reform?

5.2.1 Continuation of pre-MacSharry policies

An assessment of the MacSharry proposal calls for comparison with another scenario that describes what would have happened in the absence of the reform. In this section we consider the hypothetical case that the pre-MacSharry policies had been pursued until the year 2005 and we formulate a scenario accordingly. The main assumptions are the following.

With respect to the future trends in world market prices the general view is the same as under the MacSharry scenario (see Section 5.1.1). However, the MacSharry reform was seen to significantly affect the international market situation of wheat, coarse grains, cereal substitutes, butter, other dairy, bovine meat and ovine meat. Therefore, in the no-reform scenario world market prices differ somewhat: prices are assumed to be higher for protein feeds and carbohydrates, and somewhat lower for cereals, butter, dairy and bovine meat (see Table 5.10).

To represent 'business-as-usual' policies, it is assumed that the policy of reductions in real prices of the years 1982-92 is to be continued until 2005.

Table 5.10   Assumptions on prices of CAP commodities, annual growth rate 1992-2005

	World market prices		Intervention prices	
	MacSharry	Pre-MacSharry	MacSharry	Pre-MacSharry
Wheat	0.3	-0.5	-4.9	-1.5
Coarse grains	0.3	-0.5	-4.6	-1.5
Sugar	-0.5	-0.5	-1.0	-1.0
Protein feeds	-1.1	-0.5	-	-
Carbohydrates	-1.1	-0.5	-	-
Butter	-0.3	-0.5	-1.9	-1.0
Other dairy	-0.3	-0.5	-1.5	-1.0
Bovine meat	-1.2	-1.5	-2.5	-1.5

However, price cuts will be less pronounced than in the earlier period. As a rule intervention prices are assumed to move gradually towards the world market level. The specific assumptions are listed in the last two columns of Table 5.10.

Production quotas on sugar and milk are supposed to be maintained until 2005, but they are loosened whenever the EU tends to come close to self-sufficiency in these products. Producer subsidies on oilseeds, cattle and sheep are adjusted downward so as to maintain producer prices unchanged relative to commodities for which the producer price is controlled through the intervention price. Contrary to the MacSharry scenario no extensification effect is incorporated in the scenario. Other exogenous variables are set as in the MacSharry scenario.

5.2.2   Model outcomes for production, demand and external trade

Production

The model outcomes indicate that continuation of the pre-MacSharry policies would result in a somewhat faster rise in production (Table 5.11). Some differences with the MacSharry scenario may be noted.

If the pre-MacSharry policies were continued, production of cereals (wheat plus coarse grains) would increase by some 1.5 per cent per year. In volume terms, this means that annual production of cereals in the EU-9 would amount to 176.3 million metric tons in 2005, as compared to 158.4 million metric tons under the MacSharry policies. Oilseed production would increase faster as well. Given the policy assumptions, these differences can easily be understood: farm-gate prices for cereals and oilseeds are higher and there are no set-aside obligations.

Table 5.11   Production quantities of selected commodities, EU-9, annual growth rate 1992-2005

	MacSharry	Pre-MacSharry
Wheat	0.8	1.7
Coarse grains	0.4	1.0
Sugar beet	0.2	0.2
Oilseeds	0.6	1.4
Consumable potatoes	1.3	0.8
Dairy cows	0.0	0.0
Laying hens	0.5	0.3
Non-dairy cattle	1.4	2.3
Sheep and goats	0.0	2.1
Pigs	1.3	1.2
Poultry	1.8	1.8

The presence of milk quota effectively stops any expansion of the dairy sector. However, since milk production per cow keeps on rising in this scenario also, less dairy cows are needed to meet the quota. There are no subsidy quotas on sheep production in this scenario and, therefore, the resulting excess production capacity is used for raising additional non-dairy cattle and sheep. The effect of excess capacity in the livestock sector becomes especially manifest after 1996. Until then bovine meat production still hovers around 1992 levels but after 1996 the EU production grows at about 2.5 per cent annually.

Variations in production levels between the two scenarios are reflected in differences in cropping pattern and numbers of animals (see Table 5.12). In the crop sector the results do not vary much. Voluntary set-aside programs are also implemented (exogenously) in the no-reform scenario but on a smaller scale than in the MacSharry scenario. Differences are more pronounced in the livestock sector where an increase by 6 million non-dairy cattle and 20 million sheep is recorded.

Table 5.12   Crop area and livestock numbers, EU-9

	Base	MacSharry		Pre-MacSharry	
Product	1992	1995	2005	1995	2005
Area, mln ha					
Wheat	12.5	11.9	12.4	13.1	13.3
Coarse grains	12.1	10.9	10.6	11.9	11.2
Sugar beet	1.7	1.6	1.4	1.6	1.4
Oilseeds	3.6	3.4	3.5	3.7	3.8
Consumable potatoes	0.8	0.8	0.8	0.8	0.8
Pasture grass and forage	52.1	49.7	46.8	49.4	46.7
Set-aside	2.1	2.9	2.9	1.2	1.2
Total area	89.3	87.6	84.9	87.6	84.9
Livestock, mln heads					
Dairy cows	21.4	20.3	17.9	20.3	18.0
Laying hens	268.9	268.0	268.2	261.0	261.9
Non-dairy cattle	52.5	52.8	58.3	53.9	64.2
Sheep and goats	62.5	61.3	55.6	63.8	74.7
Pigs	83.2	86.5	88.6	84.3	87.3
Poultry	563.1	587.4	634.5	572.4	621.5

Note: Forage includes foddermaize and other roughage.

Consumption and internal demand

Because guarantee prices are higher here than under the MacSharry scenario, one finds less consumption, as would be expected. However, due to the low price elasticities of demand, the differences are modest.

Table 5.13 shows that, had pre-MacSharry policies been continued the shift towards imported cereal substitutes away from grains would have come to an end also. The explanation is that, also in this scenario, cereal prices decrease faster than the prices of cereal substitutes. Moreover, the diffusion process of the cereal substitutes slows down, as it spreads further away from the seaports (in ECAM this is represented through satiation of trends on coefficients in the demand system for animal feed, see also Section 4.3.3). The relative stagnation of the pig and poultry stocks in The Netherlands and Belgium, where the share of substitutes in the feed mix is relatively high, is another explanatory factor. Environmental problems restrict a further growth in the number of animals in these countries (and these have been imposed exogenously on the model). Denmark, Italy, Ireland and France, where the share of substitutes in the feed mix is relatively low, benefit from this.

Table 5.13   Consumption and intermediate use, EU-9, annual growth rate 1992-2005

	Consumption		Intermediate use	
	MacSharry	Pre-MacSharry	MacSharry	Pre-MacSharry
Wheat	1.2	1.1	1.5	1.0
Coarse grains	1.4	1.3	1.4	1.2
Sugar	1.0	1.0	2.0	2.0
Fats and oils	2.2	2.2	2.0	2.0
Protein feeds	-	-	-1.4	-0.5
Carbohydrates	-	-	-0.2	0.7
Butter	0.6	-0.3	0.8	1.2
Other dairy	0.3	0.3	0.3	0.7
Bovine meat	0.8	0.4	-	-
Ovine meat	2.2	2.1	-	-
Pork	1.3	1.2	-	-
Poultry meat and eggs	1.5	1.4	-	-

External trade

A continuation of pre-MacSharry policies would have worsened the international trade problems of the Community. Cereals and bovine meat would in particular have caused increasing strains (see table 5.14). The outcomes show a surplus of cereals that rises from 28.5 in 1992 to 39 million metric tons in 2005; of all member states France has the largest surplus, producing 75.7 million metric tons of cereals with a domestic use of 32.7 million only. Belgium and Luxembourg, Ireland, Italy and The Netherlands would still have a cereal deficit in 2005.

Serious problems would also arise in the bovine meat sector. The significant increase in the number of non-dairy cattle, combined with a very modest growth in bovine meat consumption, would result in an annual surplus of bovine meat of nearly 2.5 million metric tons in 2005, about three times the quantity forecast under the MacSharry scenario. The picture for the other

Table 5.14   Net imports, EU-9, mln metric tons

	Base	MacSharry		Pre-MacSharry	
	1992	1996	2005	1996	2005
Wheat	-17.0	-9.1	-15.5	-25.3	-30.3
Coarse grains	-11.5	-0.7	-1.4	-9.2	-8.7
Sugar	-3.5	-3.2	-2.4	-3.1	-2.3
Fats and oils	4.0	4.8	6.2	4.4	5.7
Protein feeds	11.8	10.4	9.1	11.3	10.2
Carbohydrates	23.3	21.5	21.9	24.0	25.9
Butter	0.0	0.0	0.0	-0.2	-0.2
Other dairy	-6.8	-7.9	-5.0	-7.6	-4.7
Bovine meat	-0.2	0.1	-0.8	-0.8	-2.4

products is less dramatic. The price of butter is slightly higher than in the MacSharry scenario; this leads to a somewhat lower consumer demand and to a slightly larger butter surplus.

5.2.3   Protection rates and the budget

Protection

Trade conflicts start with accusations of unfair competition which are often supported by statistics on rates of protection. We refer to Section 5.1.3 for a discussion of the limitations of such measures. Table 5.15 shows the trends in protection rates in the no-reform scenario. Two points emerge. First, for nearly all products, there is a decrease in protection rates. Secondly, the differences in protection between the MacSharry and the no-reform scenario are relatively modest.

This does not mean that differences in potential trade conflicts are minor also. The fierceness of trade conflicts depends as much on the trade volume as on the level of the protection rates . Especially for cereals and bovine meat these volumes would be much larger had the pre-MacSharry policies been continued.

FEOGA expenditures

Table 5.15   Rate of protection on production, EU-9, percentage

	MacSharry			Pre-MacSharry	
	1992	1996	2005	1996	2005
Wheat	70	62	60	69	68
Coarse grains	59	50	45	58	54
Sugar	119	117	113	117	122
Fats and oils	33	28	27	28	28
Butter	39	28	26	38	36
Other dairy	38	34	38	39	44
Bovine meat	35	17	17	32	28
Ovine meat	64	57	54	62	58

Note: For the definition of protection on production, see Table 5.7.

The outcomes suggest that the budgetary consequences of a continuation of the policies of the late eighties and early nineties are less dramatic than was assumed by the Commission (see CEC(1991a)). Table 5.16 shows an average annual increase in FEOGA outlays of slightly less than one per cent in real terms. This may seem counter intuitive, given the common perception that the excessive growth in budgetary outlays for agriculture was structural. However, given our scenario assumptions, the outcomes can easily be explained. The combination of quota arrangements and increases in demand effectively curbs expenditures in the dairy products and the sugar sectors. For various other crops, like cereals, the budget effect of production growth is largely compensated by the effect of the reductions in the intervention price, which range between 1.0 and 1.5 per cent annually.

The differences between the two scenarios are most pronounced for export refunds and producer subsidies. For export subsidies this is mainly due to the large export surpluses in the pre-MacSharry scenario, for producer subsidies, the difference is a consequence of the change from export subsidies to producer subsidies in the MacSharry reform.

5.2.4   Value added and employment
Real value added decreases by 0.3 per cent annually (Table 5.17). The difference with the MacSharry reform scenario of nearly 0.5 per cent, can be attributed to two factors with a negative effect on value added (less producer

Table 5.16   FEOGA outlays, EU-12, mln ecu and annual growth rate 1992-2005

	Base	MacSharry			Pre-MacSharry		
	1992	1996	2005	Annual growth rate	1996	2005	Annual growth rate
Export refunds	7,308	4,047	3,854	-4.8	8,673	8,732	1.4
Producer subsidies	7,476	15,717	14,995	5.5	6,638	6,932	-0.6
Consumer subsidies	1,499	1,438	1,463	-0.2	1,440	1,465	-0.2
Input subsidies	2,927	2,629	2,569	-1.0	2,765	2,701	-0.6
Interest and storage costs	2,521	1,177	1,441	-4.2	2,550	2,854	1.0
Other FEOGA guarantee	10,380	11,676	13,954	2.3	11,235	13,427	2.0
Total FEOGA guarantee	32,111	36,684	38,276	1.4	33,301	36,113	0.9

Note: Interest and storage costs includes stock devaluation.

subsidies and higher intermediate consumption) and to two factors with a positive effect (higher prices and more production).

Table 5.17   Real value added and employment in agriculture, annual growth rate

	Real value added		Employment	
	MacSharry	Pre-MacSharry	MacSharry	Pre-MacSharry
Belgium-Luxembourg	-0.6	-0.2	-2.2	-2.2
Denmark	-0.2	-0.6	-3.4	-3.4
France	-1.2	-0.7	-4.0	-3.8
Germany, Fed. Rep.	-1.6	-0.4	-1.6	-1.5
Ireland	-1.5	-1.0	-3.8	-3.7
Italy	0.2	0.3	-2.8	-2.8
The Netherlands	0.4	0.8	-0.9	-0.8
United Kingdom	-2.2	-1.4	-2.0	-1.9
EU-9	-0.7	-0.3	-2.6	-2.5

The differences among member states are remarkable. Growth of real value added in Belgium-Luxembourg and Denmark is lower in the no-reform scenario than in the reform scenario. In all other countries a continuation of the old policies would yield higher real value added.

A change in policies also has an effect on agricultural employment. However, as the figures in the table show, the effect is quite modest, as could be expected because farmers receive important compensations. Moreover, as discussed earlier, labour outflow depends on demographic factors, which are the same in both runs, rather than on income differentials.

5.2.5   Consequences for economic welfare

Table 5.18 summarizes the consequences for economic welfare. To compute the economic welfare in 2005, realized consumer utilities have been expressed in expenditures at 1992 prices. The MacSharry reform comes out five billion ecu higher, at EU-9 level. However, against this welfare gain for consumers, there is, in the MacSharry scenario, a reduction in the EU trade surplus. If this reduction is subtracted from the welfare gain for consumers, there remains a welfare gain of about 3.8 billion ecu, which is modest as it amounts to only 0.16 per cent of equivalent consumer expenditure in the EU-9. One reason for this is that this scenario does not attribute any effect on non-agricultural output of the production factors (labour, land, equipment) which are released from agriculture and only considers demand effects. However, calculations show that even under the assumption that the factors could be absorbed in the non-agricultural sectors, the gain is modest.

Table 5.18   Equivalent consumer expenditure in 2005, bln ecu at 1992 prices

	MacSharry	Pre-MacSharry	Difference
Belgium-Luxembourg	91.5	91.2	0.3
Denmark	49.9	49.6	0.3
France	581.8	580.9	0.9
Germany, Fed. Rep.	656.5	656.1	0.4
Ireland	17.8	17.8	0.0
Italy	341.8	340.0	1.8
The Netherlands	129.0	129.0	0.0
United Kingdom	555.9	554.6	1.3
EU-9	2424.1	2419.1	5.0
Surplus EU-9 trade balance	31.8	33.0	-1.2
Welfare gain (MacSharry minus Pre-MacSharry scenario)			3.8

5.2.6   Was the MacSharry reform necessary?

Having compared the no-reform with the reform scenario we may now ask whether no reform would have brought the CAP and EU agriculture into more serious problems than the MacSharry reform. Although we cannot give an unambiguous answer to this question, the scenario simulations suggest that the answer to this question is in general negative. A continuation of the earlier policy would also have resulted in a more balanced development of EU agriculture than was the case in the eighties and early nineties. Differences are only significant with respect to international trade, where the MacSharry reform scenario definitely leads to better results, since less cereal and bovine meat surpluses are dumped on the world markets. But with a slightly more restrictive price policy, these problems could possibly have been reduced as well.

If continuation of the earlier policy would not have caused a crisis, why then, one may ask, was this policy judged so gloomily? How could the budgetary and the international trade problems aggravate so rapidly in the late eighties and early nineties, in spite of the automatic stabilizers? Would the model have been able to predict these problems?

The answer to the last question appears to be affirmative, to a great extent. Running ECAM from the mid-eighties until 1992 and comparing the outcomes with actual realizations taught us that between 1989 and 1992 incidental factors have gravely exacerbated both the budget and trade problems. The unification of Germany as well as the scare due to the 'mad cow disease' created rapidly growing surpluses on the bovine market. In addition, world market prices for many agricultural products dropped to very low levels, especially in ecu terms as the US dollar depreciated with respect to the ecu, reaching a minimum in the early nineties. Together these developments have greatly undermined the effects of the stabilizer policies on the budget and on the international trade relations. Therefore, our claim is that the budget and trade problems in the pre-MacSharry years were less structural than is often assumed.

But even if the incidental character of the developments in the late eighties and early nineties is accepted, one could still reject the conclusion because of the scenario assumptions. One could argue, for example, that, as a consequence of growing cereal and bovine meat surpluses, the world market prices of these products would decrease more than is assumed in the scenario. A sensitivity analysis on this point showed that things would indeed be somewhat worse, but that the overall picture would not be fundamentally different (see Keyzer et al. (1994)).

Coming back to the question whether the MacSharry reform was, in terms of criteria that are relevant within the bureaucratic perspective, economically unavoidable, the answer we arrive at is a qualified no. However, our assessment has been too narrow in at least one respect. The MacSharry reform was proposed and accepted in 1992, at a time when the trade negotiations in the Uruguay Round were in a deadlock. Disagreement between the EU and the US on agricultural policies was a major obstacle for an overall agreement. Due to the MacSharry reform the position of the EU seemed to have changed quite radically, as price guarantees for a number of products decreased significantly. The reform has been an impulse for renewed discussions between the EU and the US. This resulted in a bilateral agreement, the so-called Blair House Agreement and although this agreement has been controversial and heavily criticised, it has definitely removed the last obstacles to a new GATT agreement.

5.3 CAP reform and the revised Blair House Agreement: compatible or not?

5.3.1 Background and main elements of the agreement

The original Blair House Agreement was reached in November 1992. Its revision was part of the final round of the GATT negotiations in December 1993. Initially, the main issue of controversy within the EU was whether the Blair House Agreement was compatible with the MacSharry reform or not. According e.g. to most farmers organizations and (some) food processing industries, this was not the case.

An important element in the Blair House Agreement is that the EU commits itself to reductions in subsidized exports. We have seen that the MacSharry reform can be expected to lead to such a reduction for cereals, sugar, butter and other dairy products. However, the point is that this is a mere expectation, based on model outcomes, not a commitment. Most of the resistance against the Blair House Agreement stemmed from this difference. The basic issue was whether the EU should commit itself to its expectations or find any such commitment an intolerable restriction on its capacity to react and adjust to unforeseen events.

In this section we shall show that, in general, the commitments are indeed compatible with what one may expect to happen in the medium term, now that the MacSharry reform has been adopted. Yet the point remains that, while the expectations may be wrong, the commitments are binding. Further we shall also argue that the GATT agreement imposes important constraints on policy formulation in the long term.

The agreement is to be implemented during the period between 1995-2001. It covers three issues: internal support, market access and commitments on exports (GATT (1993)):

(i)   *Internal support* has to be reduced by twenty per cent in comparison with the base period 1986-88. Internal support is expressed by an Aggregate Measure of Support (AMS). Basically the AMS is calculated as a Producer Subsidy Equivalent (PSE), as discussed in Section 5.1.3 and Annex 4A.

$$AMS \quad = \quad \Sigma_k \, (p_k^q - p_k^w) \, q_k$$

where

q_k Volume of production of product k

p_k^q Internal producer EU price, product k

p_k^w World market price, product k.

(ii) With respect to *market access*, it was agreed, that all non-tariff border protection measures would be converted into customs tariffs, in ecu per volume unit (tariffication), and that all tariffs would be reduced by 36 per cent over a period of six years. This percentage must be calculated as a simple (unweighed) arithmetic average. Each individual tariff must be reduced by at least 15 per cent. The base period for calculating the tariff is 1986-88. In case of excessive downward movements in world market prices, a variable refund (or levy) called 'special safeguard clause' is automatically added to the tariff, so as to prevent a severe drop in intra-EU prices. It was also agreed that import opportunities will be given to foreign exports, up to a level of three per cent of the internal consumption of the reference period. This percentage should reach five per cent in 2001.

(iii) *Export subsidies* must be reduced by 36 per cent and both the US and the EU should reduce the volume of subsidized exports by 21 per cent. This should be implemented within 6 years, starting in 1995 and be applied on a commodity-by-commodity basis. The reference period used for these calculations is 1986-90. In case the average export volume in the years 1991-92 exceeded the level of the years 1986-90, the later period may be chosen as the starting point for the reduction.

These core elements deserve some comment.

(a)   The AMS reduction is a central element in the agreement. Since the AMS is expressed as a sum total, an increase in protection for one commodity can be compensated by a reduction for another.

(b)   Reduction of the AMS can also be obtained by reducing supply. Therefore, reduction of milk or sugar quotas amounts to a reduction in support.

(c)   The tariffication contains a variable element to protect the EU market from excessive fluctuations on world markets. This so-called 'special safeguard clause' may automatically be added to the tariff when the import price for the EU falls by more than ten per cent below the average of 1986-88. Since EU import prices were in the base period much higher than actual world market prices, the clause will become effective very early in practice (see CEC (1992), table 2).

(d)   The average tariff reduction of 36 per cent is an unweighed average. Hence, a large reduction for a product with a small trade weight can be combined with small reductions for trade-wise important products.

(e)   The tariffication and the AMS are expressed in nominal terms without any reference to adjustments for inflation. The original Dunkel Proposal (see GATT (1991)) does contain a suggestion for adjustment in case of excessive inflation rates. The effect of inflation can easily surpass the effect of the reduction rates of the agreement and make it highly restrictive for the EU.

(f)   Compensating payments to producers, like the hectare payment for set-asides or payments per animal, are not subject to any commitment to reduce support; they are (temporarily) excluded from the commitment. The implication is that a fall in farmers' income due to a decrease in border protection can in principle be compensated by these 'decoupled' transfers.

(g)   The regulations should in principle cover processed agricultural products as well as unprocessed commodities. However, the tariffication of processed commodities, like alcoholic beverages and processed meat products, is extremely cumbersome because the tariff must be imposed on every constituent element of the processed product separately. When the world market price of any of the components changes, the aggregate tariff on the processed commodity changes also. This creates heavy administrative tasks, unless the decision were taken to apply the same tariff rate to all components.

(h)   Within the EU there still exist member-state specific green rates. Since the border price is based upon the (green) intervention price for a number of products, it is impossible to define one central border price for the EU unless green rates are fully harmonized over member states. The volatility of the exchange rates makes full harmonization in the near future unlikely. If the MCAs, which have been abolished in 1992, were to be reintroduced, border prices could again become country and product specific. The GATT rules are not explicit with respect to the treatment of the green rates of the EU.

We now turn to the outcomes from model simulations to see whether the GATT agreement appears to require further adjustments in the CAP, beyond those introduced under the MacSharry reform.

5.3.2 The effect of the AMS commitment

The MacSharry reform will, for the products involved, result in price reductions far greater than the expected price fall on the world market. Consequently the ratio of many internal prices to world market prices will decrease significantly (compare Tables 5.1 and 5.2). However, according to the ECAM-simulation, production of most CAP products will increase in the period to come. These two developments have opposite effects on the AMS but on balance, a net decrease in the AMS can be expected. One finds by the year 2001 a fall in the AMS of 69 per cent, relative to the reference period.[117] Since the GATT agreement will probably result in higher world market prices than shown in Table 5.1, this decline may even be on the conservative side.

The AMS should have fallen by twenty per cent in the year 2001, relative to the base period. Because this percentage refers to a nominal amount, a correction should be made for inflation. At an annual ecu-inflation rate of three per cent, the nominal AMS commitment implies a real commitment of 35 per cent.[118] Even then the AMS part of the agreement will not be a problem for the EU. The same conclusion has been reached by Guyomard and Mahé (1992).

The ease with which the AMS commitment can be realised is attributable to (i) the possibility of summation over products, (ii) the fact that all subsidies per hectare and per animal are permitted, and (iii) the very low world market prices in the reference period.

5.3.3 The effect of the import and export commitments

The arrangements with respect to minimum access opportunities and volumes of subsidized exports apply on a commodity by commodity basis. Therefore, an assessment of the effects of the commitments has to proceed in this way also. Our discussion will be limited to the main commodities.

Cereals

---

[117] It is assumed that the producer subsidies for cereals, oilseeds, bovine and ovine meat are in the green box and henceforth are not part of the AMS. Should we assume that the green box is empty, and that these subsidies add to the AMS, it would still fall by 44 per cent.

[118] calculated as $[1- (1.-.02)/(1.03)^7]$.

Average annual cereal exports of the EU-12 amounted to 29.6 million metric tons in 1986-90.[119] This means that, to meet the export commitment the EU should not export more than 23.4 million metric tons in 2001. The ECAM-outcomes show that meeting this requirement will not pose a problem. Lower internal prices combined with the set-aside regulations will result in a drastic reduction of the growth rates for cereals. Moreover, the MacSharry reforms will lead to an increase in the use of cereals by the EU feed sector. Together these developments result in a significant decrease in cereal export (Table 5.6). Although Blom and Hoogeveen (1992) and Roningen (1992) are less optimistic with respect to the increase in internal demand for feed grains, they also conclude that the effect of the MacSharry reform will be sufficient to meet the commitment. It should also be emphasized that the EU is not obliged to improve the access to its cereal markets for imports. Therefore, we conclude that the import commitment will have no serious implications for the EU cereal markets (see also van Berkum (1994)).

Sugar

Table 5.6 shows that sugar exports fall by about one million metric tons, i.e. by more than 25 per cent, over the period 1992-2005. This already suggests that meeting the commitment on market access and export reduction will not be difficult in the case of sugar either. We can reach this conclusion without having to rely on the particular assumptions of ECAM, as follows. The sugar exports of the EU consist partly of production under the C-quota, which is exported without subsidy. Moreover, the EU has committed itself to import 1.8 million metric tons of sugar every year, mainly from the ACP countries. Part of the latter is re-exported. Exports of C-sugar and re-exports of ACP-sugar fall outside the commitment. Therefore, the export reduction has to be less than the base period export statistics suggest. According to the Commission, the export commitment implies a reduction in sugar exports of only 340.000 metric tons in the six year period, relative to the base period. Because sugar consumption

---

[119] Source: CEC, *The Agricultural Situation in the Community.*

in the EU has increased by some 80,000 metric tons annually in recent years, the export requirement can be satisfied even if this trend slows down. This is accentuated when one considers that, because of the imports from ACP-countries, there is no need for further imports from third countries.

Dairy products

For dairy products, the GATT commitments were expressed in terms of four commodity groups, as summarized in Table 5.19. The table shows that import and export commitments amount to 4,254 million metric tons of milk equivalents, or 3.9 per cent of total milk production in the EU-12. Under the MacSharry regulations, it is possible to reduce milk quotas by two per cent. Moreover, due to growing consumer demand, the offtake of most dairy products within the EU increases at a rate around 0.4 per cent annually. Hence, meeting the commitments will, in principle, not cause any serious problems.

Table 5.19   Upper limits of quantity commitments on imports and (subsidized) exports, 2001 relative to 1992, 1000 metric tons milk-equivalents

	Reduction in exports	Increase in imports	Change in trade position
Butter and butter oil	-	179	179
Skimmed milk-powder	524	393	917
Cheese	916	822	1738
Other	1420	-	1420
Total	2860	1394	4254

Source: Van Berkum (1994).

This conclusion is confirmed by the outcomes from the ECAM-simulation of the MacSharry reform, although these suggest that the two per cent quota reduction, which is only a possibility under the MacSharry regulations and which is not implemented in the scenario, may have to be effectuated.

However, other developments, not taken into account in the scenario analysis of Section 5.1, will probably give more room for dairy exports. First, the commitments refer to the EU-12 of 1992. In that year, the Canary Islands and the EFTA countries were considered as third countries. Since January 1993 the Canary Islands were fully integrated in the Community. Consequently, exports to the islands, which are quite substantial,[120] are by definition no longer counted as exports to third countries. A similar, purely cosmetic reduction in exports to third countries that has an even greater effect on statistics, is caused by several EFTA countries joining the EU in 1995.

Secondly, the import commitment is not an obligation to buy but an obligation to offer to third countries the opportunity to sell. As can be seen from Table 5.19, the commitment on imports has consequences primarily for cheese. It is not evident that third countries will be able to utilize the opportunity for additional exports since their internal milk prices are sometimes even higher than those in the EU.[121] Subsidized exports of dairy products would lead them into the same budgetary and trade problems as the EU.

Finally, due to the reduction in subsidized exports, world market prices for dairy products can be expected to increase (we return to this shortly, see also Roningen (1992) and USDA (1992)). Then, it will become more attractive for the EU dairy sector to increase its unsubsidized exports which are not covered by the GATT agreement. Demand for unsubsidized products will certainly increase. In the analysis of Section 5.2, and also in Table 5.19, no distinction was made between subsidized and unsubsidized exports.

Bovine meat

The EU is at the same time a large exporter and a large importer of bovine meat. As long as imports do not fall below the level of the base period, the import commitment will be met. With respect to exports, matters are more complicated. The scenario outcomes foresee a rapid increase in bovine meat production and a relatively slow growth in consumption (see Tables 5.3 and 5.5). By the year 2001 the gross surplus (net exports + imports) amounts to

---

[120] Exports to the Canary Islands amounted to 232,400 tons milk-equivalents in 1990 (Produktschap voor Zuivel (1991)).

[121] See OECD, 'Agricultural Policies, Markets and Trade', various issues.

about 1.2 million metric tons.[122] According to the commitment, the EU is only allowed to export 0.8 million metric tons of bovine meat with subsidies (see van Berkum (1994)). Hence, the scenario outcome suggests that there is a problem here. However, due to a rapid reduction of the intervention price, border prices[123] will by the year 2001 have reached a level close to world market prices (which in case the GATT agreements are implemented will probably lie above the level in the scenario (see Table 5.1 and Section 5.3.5)). Hence, it may occur that all exports will be unsubsidized, so that the commitment is automatically met. Even if this were not the case, the EU could avoid problems by organizing a system of C-quota for exports, as for sugar, or to compensate a reduction in export subsidy by a premium per animal (which is under appropriate conditions not treated by the GATT as a protectionist measure).

5.3.4 The effect of reduced border protection

World market prices

The third main element of the GATT agreement refers to tariffication and the (gradual) reduction of tariffs and export subsidies in (fixed) nominal terms. Despite the safeguard clause, there is no doubt that the system of variable levies will eventually be undermined by this part of the agreement, unless full indexation of the nominal amounts is granted. However, it is difficult to predict the effects for the medium term, since the tariffs are, at present, to a large extent prohibitive. Hence, for several commodities imports are (almost) nonexistent and would remain so after a reduction in the nominal tariff. For the tariff to become binding, the world market price plus the fixed nominal tariff must fall below the intervention price (at border level) that the EU intends to achieve. If the tariffs remain unindexed and inflation continues in the EU and abroad, they will gradually fade away relative to the world price and, become binding. It is hard

---

[122] These are approximated as net exports plus committed imports.

[123] Border prices in ECAM are computed as the supply price at farm-gate level, minus the producer subsidy plus the export processing per unit of the primary output.

to predict when this will happen because so much depends on the world market prices, which themselves are affected the GATT agreement itself. Quantifying the effects of the commitments on world market prices is made difficult because so many countries are involved. Here we make the conservative assumption that, except for bovine meat and dairy, world market prices will not be affected by the GATT agreement.

Because beef exports to Japan and other East Asian countries will probably be stimulated by the agreement, we assume real prices for bovine meat to rise, at an annual rate of 0.5 per cent, relative to the MacSharry scenario. For dairy larger price increases can be expected. Following van Berkum (1994) we proceed for dairy products (except butter) from the assumption that real prices rise by three per cent annually above the rates quoted in Table 5.1.

Tariffication

According to the GATT agreement, the EU farmer may be protected against outside competition in 2001 by nominal tariffs which must lie, on average, at least 36 per cent below the tariff in the base period. Table 5.20 summarizes how this part of the commitment will affects the rates of protection. The first column of the table shows the nominal tariffs allowed in 2001. The second column shows the same tariffs deflated at an annual rate of three per cent. The sum of the world market price and the deflated tariff (from Table 5.1, corrected for GATT price effects of dairy and beef) in column (3) is indicative of the price at the EU border. The last column shows the EU border prices according to our scenario calculations. In all cases the sum of the world market price and the maximum tariff that is allowed exceeds the projected border price. This suggests that there will be no downward pressure on internal prices. This 'optimistic' conclusion rests mainly on the high level of the tariffs in the base year. In the agreement these tariffs are determined as the differences between the EU intervention prices, raised by ten per cent and the world market prices in the base period. EU intervention prices were relatively high in the base period, while world market prices were low for most products.

The special safeguard provision which becomes effective in case the EU import price falls below a prespecified price is also important, in particular because the 'prespecified prices', are significantly higher than the average world market prices in the base period (see CEC (1992)).

Table 5.20   Customs tariffs and border prices in 2001, ecu/metric ton

	Tariff		Import price[b]	Border price[c]
	Nominal[a] (1)	Real (2)	(3)	(4)
Wheat	95	79	181	162
Coarse grains	94	79	172	122
Sugar	419	349	595	553
Butter	1896	1588	4350	3491
Other dairy	187[d]	157	704	573
Bovine meat	1608	1347	2989	1756

Notes:
(a) Nominal tariffs taken from CEC (1992).
(b) World market price + real tariff.
(c) Border prices according to the ECAM-scenario.
(d) Tariff derived from tariff on skimmed milk-powder (1 kg smp = 5.09 units of dairy).

Reduced export subsidies

Although the MacSharry reform will in general result in a reduction of exports, the EU will still be a net exporter for several products. Since, by the year 2001, most internal prices lie well above the world market level, export subsidies will still be needed. Hence, the commitments with respect to maximum subsidy amounts need to be tested also. Here the question is whether the amount of subsidy that is allowed in 2000 will be sufficient to bridge the gap between the internal EU price in the absence of the GATT agreement and the world market prices when the Agreement is implemented. If this question can be answered affirmatively, then the commitment on reducing the export subsidies will have no impact on the internal EU price. Table 5.21 summarizes the results of a simple calculation. The maximum amount $\bar{\zeta}_k$ of subsidy per ton of product k in the year 2001 (column (1)) is obtained as:

$$\overline{\zeta}_k = (1-\alpha)\, S_{k,0} / ((1-\beta)\, e_{k,0})$$

where

$\overline{\zeta}_k$	=	Maximum export-subsidy per ton in 2001
$S_{k,0}$	=	Total export-subsidy in the base period,
$e_{k,0}$	=	Volume of subsidized exports in the base period
α	=	Reduction-factor of total export-subsidy ($\alpha = 0.36$)
β	=	Reduction-factor of volume of subsidized exports ($\beta = 0.21$).

In column (2) of Table 5.21 the deflated subsidy amounts are shown. Column (3) contains the world market price. The minimum supply prices of the EU on the world market are shown in column (4). They have been calculated as the difference between EU border price according to ECAM, in the absence of a GATT agreement and the maximum export subsidy as shown in column (2). A comparison between columns (3) and (4) reveals that the permitted subsidies per ton are easily sufficient to bridge the gap between internal and external prices. For all products, the minimum internal price of the EU lies below the world market price in 2001 incremented by the given tariff. We reiterate that the assumptions underlying the calculations are in general conservative. For example, it has been assumed that volumes of subsidized exports will decrease by 21 per cent only. Our scenario outcomes show larger reductions for some products (see Table 5.5). Consequently, the maximum subsidies per ton that are allowed will probably be higher than the amounts quoted in Table 5.21.

5.3.5   Practical implications of the GATT agreement

The opposition of (French) farmers against the agreement

The discussion on a commodity-by-commodity basis leads to the conclusion that the commitments made in the GATT agreement hardly require adjustments to the current CAP. How then to explain the opposition of EU farmers, the French in particular, against the agreement? We have already suggested an answer to

Table 5.21   Maximum export subsidies and border prices in 2001, ecu per metric ton

	Maximum export subsidy[a]		World market price	Border price[b] minus maximum real export subsidy
	Nominal (1)	Real (2)	(3)	(4)
Wheat	85	69	101	93
Coarse grains	88	71	93	51
Sugar	389	314	244	239
Butter	2317	1872	2762	1619
Other dairy	192[c]	155	547	418
Bovine meat	1542	1245	1642	511

Notes:
(a)   Nominal export subsidies calculated from CEC (1992) (GATT concession list, supporting table 11).
(b)   Border prices according to ECAM.
(c)   Tariff derived from tariff on skimmed milk-powder (1 kg smp = 5.09 units of dairy).

this question. Besides non-economic considerations, the basic issue is, in our judgement, the uncertainty with respect to the impact of the MacSharry reform and world market prices. The discussion in the preceding sections has been in terms of model forecasts and plausible assumptions. In practice there may be unexpected developments. According to public statements by French officials the main uncertainties relate to fluctuations in the exchange rate between the US dollar and the ecu and the future role of imported grain substitutes in the EU feed mix (e.g. Prime Minister Balladur as cited in Schrader (1993)). French cereal growers contend that the GATT deal consolidates US-supremacy by safeguarding the US deficiency payments for cereals (Delorme (1994)). Under the GATT agreement, the EU's capacity to adjust will be severely restricted indeed. A small difference in EU supply or demand can already lead to an important variation in net exports. This is especially so for cereals, where the French interests are at stake. One could object that when such unanticipated developments occur and commitments become binding, the EU still has a wide array of policy instruments at its disposal.

In the short term exports can be restricted through stock adjustments. In the medium term, set-asides of land can be raised and production quotas for dairy can be adjusted. For beef and cheese, where no quotas exist, quota on subsidized exports could be introduced. To compensate for income losses producer subsidies could be raised. However, because of the 'volatility' of net exports, such adjustments would require sophisticated finetuning of policies and the resulting permanent bureaucratic interference would interfere with farmers and the food processing industries. Moreover, since compensations in the income sphere impose an additional burden on the EU budget, unexpected set-backs will probably not be compensated in full. In our view, it is in terms of the resistance against commitments in quantity terms per se that the objections against the GATT agreement should be understood.

A way out for the medium term?

If EU agriculture is caught out by unexpected events and commitments become binding, one may expect pressures to deploy less orthodox strategies. Recall that unsubsidized exports fall outside the committed volumes. Any relabelling of previously subsidized exports as unsubsidized exports reduces subsidized exports, so as to 'meet' the requirements.[124]

Producer's organizations could turn to the use of the practice of market segmentation, producing 'C-crops' and 'C-livestock' like C-sugar. Whenever a significant part of the farmer's costs has the character of setup costs, and this is to a large extent the case for specialized producers like the French cereal growers, an overall reduction in producer prices can, under specified conditions, be compensated by (green-box) payments on a per hectare basis. Moreover, for crops other than cereals and oilseeds, consumer prices will not come close to world market levels in the short term. Hence, domestic demand will remain heavily protected and since most of the production is consumed within the EU, a modest co-responsibility levy would suffice to let the agricultural sector finance such C-exports by its own means.

If such practices become pervasive (and the possibility of exporting unsubsidized production is explicitly granted in the current agreement), the

---

[124] This could, however, have a downward effect on world market prices and hence raise the AMS-measure.

disciplining role of the GATT agreement will seriously be reduced, at least as long as tariffs on imports remain prohibitive and consumer prices remain above world market levels. Whether these loopholes will be effective, depends largely on the GATT's ability (more precisely the ability of its successor, the WTO) to elaborate upon the results of the Uruguay Round.

WTO and the settlement of disputes

The signing of the Final Act of the Uruguay Round in April 1994 in Marrakech marked the start of the transition from the GATT to the World Trade Organization (WTO). The mandate of the WTO specifies that it should (i) facilitate the implementation of the agreements and legal instruments negotiated during the Uruguay Round, (ii) provide a forum for negotiations and (iii) administer rules and procedures for the settlement of disputes and the trade policy review mechanism.[125] Point (ii) means that the negotiations can now proceed in separate committees, and there is no need to wait for a new Round to achieve further progress. Point (iii) is important because the dispute settlement system of GATT has been strengthened and streamlined in the 'Uruguay Round Understanding on Rules and Procedures Governing the Settlement of Disputes' (DSU). The DSU emphasizes the importance in securing dispute resolution. The more reliable the procedures the less incentive there will exist for national governments to recur to the policies of managed trade discussed in Section 3.3.

Technically, the procedure is more or less as follows. A Member must enter into consultations within 30 days of a request for consultations from another Member. If after 60 days from the request for consultations there is no settlement, the complaining party may request the establishment of a panel. Where consultations are denied, the complaining party may move directly to request a panel (three persons from countries not party to the dispute). A panel will normally complete its work within six months or, in case of urgency, within three months. Within 60 days of the issuance of the panel report, it will be

---

[125] Source: 'What is the WTO?', in *GATT Focus*, May 1994, No.107 Special Issue.

adopted, unless the Dispute Settlement Body (DSB) decides by consensus not to adopt the report or one of the parties notifies the DSB of its intention to appeal (appellate review).

The concept of appellate review is an important new feature of the DSU. An Appellate Body will be established, composed of seven members. An appeal will be limited to issues of law covered in the panel report and legal interpretations developed by the panel. The resulting report, to be delivered within 60 days, shall be adopted by the DSB and *unconditionally* accepted by the parties within 30 days following its issuance to Members, unless the DSB decides by consensus against its adoption. The DSB will keep the implementation under regular surveillance until the issues are resolved. The DSU reaffirms that Members shall not themselves make determinations of violations or suspend concessions, but shall make use of the dispute settlement rules and procedures of the DSU. Though these regulations still have to prove their effectiveness in practice (and are in early 1995 yet to be ratified by the national parliaments), many consider the DSU as one of the major achievements of the Uruguay Round because a binding mechanism has been introduced in the sphere of international relations.

Long run implications

The GATT agreement does not only set in place a dispute settlement mechanism. As it stands now, its tariffication has long run implications that should not be overlooked. Since the tariffs are expressed in constant, nominal terms, without any indexation to account for inflation, the tariffication will eventually become binding on the import side. At that point in time, it will eliminate the Community preference and thereby undermine the basic principles of the CAP. Consumers and the feed industry will face prices that follow the developments on world markets. The option of market segmentation will then be ruled out since the import tariffs will become effective and have a visible impact on the EU markets. In our view the GATT agreement is for agriculture only a first step that puts into place the 'machinery' of tariffication. This machinery is probably ineffective in the short to medium term but may become very important in the long run, provided the parties do not adjust the rules in the mean time.

5.4   The future of EU agriculture under the bureaucratic perspective: an assessment

Although the MacSharry reform is radical in a sense, our analysis seems to indicate that after this reform EU agriculture will develop in a rather balanced way in the period until 2005. Our scenario simulations do not suggest that EU agriculture is at a turning point. Overall growth of the sector will decline somewhat, but it remains positive. The same applies to intensification: production growth per hectare and per animal will keep on growing. On a per capita basis, the relative income position of farmers will not deteriorate any further, although many farmers will (have to) leave the sector. Compared with a continuation of the earlier CAP policy, the reform creates a modest welfare gain. Consumers benefit through lower prices. After an initial upward shock in the years when the reform measures are effectuated, FEOGA outlays will increase at a very moderate rate. Moreover, the reform will lead to a reduction of tensions with respect to international trade. The model outcomes also suggest that the 'new CAP' is, in terms of expected outcomes, compatible with the commitments of the GATT agreement.

At the same time it is clear that the reform will not reach all its objectives. The process of intensification will continue: the agricultural labour force will decrease by 30 per cent in the period 1992-2005, bureaucratic interference with agriculture will not be reduced, etc.. Therefore, the MacSharry reform will not stop free traders from criticizing the CAP, even after implementation of the GATT agreement. On the other hand, lower guarantee prices, a continuing intensification of production and prospects of diminished protection in the long term will not please the interventionists either.

Moreover, new problems are already visible on the horizon. Several EFTA countries have obtained full membership in 1995. Agricultural trade relations with Central Europe[126] already take a prominent place on the agenda. The MacSharry reform does not make it easy to integrate the agricultural sector of Central Europe with that of the EU in the foreseeable future (see also Anderson and Tyers (1993), Hamilton and Winters (1992)).

Adherents of the bureaucratic perspective will probably not deny the relevance of these problems but they will point to their limited room of manoeuvre, not only politically but also because more drastic reforms could cause large scale bankruptcy and social unrest. The unpredictability of the end result of a shock therapy justifies their preference for reforms that are conducted as a sequence of corrective actions: the EU's capacity to produce food is too valuable and its farmers are too vulnerable for wild experiments. This means that the 'bureaucrats' are likely to acknowledge that further reforms are still needed, inspired by criticisms from various sides. The next chapter will consider reform alternatives.

---

[126] The Central European countries, which are to be distinguished from the Eastern European countries, refer to Hungary, Poland, the Czech Republic and Slovakia.

Chapter 6

Alternatives: free trade or intervention?

Given the sketch of EU agriculture under a bureaucratic policy regime, we are now ready to consider the alternatives of free trade and intervention. Within the free trade perspective, the competitive market is, as was discussed at length in Section 3.2, the preferred allocation mechanism. If competitive markets can be established, export and producer subsidies should be abolished and distributional objectives should only be pursued through lump sum transfers. On the other hand, the interventionist perspective described in Section 3.3 stresses that, in the real world, market failures do arise. Markets may not exist due to external effects and indivisibilities. They may not achieve efficient allocations because of imperfect competition and, due to negative incentive effects of taxation, the potential for mobilizing lump sum transfers may be limited. It is precisely the role of government to cope with such failures.

The scenarios that we shall present for the two alternatives will be of the gradualist kind. This choice rests on a combination of theoretical arguments, as given in Section 3.4, and the following, more pragmatic considerations. First, under a non-gradualist or shock-therapy scenario, the shock itself causes 'waves', i.e. short term transition dynamics, that are hard to predict in reality and hard to represent in a model. Since ECAM follows the principles of general equilibrium theory, assuming for example that all agents face the same prices on one market, it is by its very nature unable to describe short term dynamics. Secondly, whereas the model largely derives its usefulness from its detailed representation of the CAP and from its elaborate empirical base, the greater the differences between the agricultural policy being analyzed, and the policy that provided this empirical base, the less useful the parameter estimates become. And consequently, the less likely it is that the analysis will benefit from the model's relative strength. Thirdly, a good deal of recent literature on agricultural protectionism has already stressed more radical free trade alternatives (see e.g. Goldin and Knudsen (1990) and Tyers and Anderson (1992)). Our study can contribute little additional insight on this topic. Finally, by expressing our scenarios as variants of the post-MacSharry CAP, it becomes possible to formulate proposals that are sufficiently specific and realistic to be of relevance to the policy debate.

Hence, the scenarios of this chapter take the post-MacSharry CAP as a reference. They are in fact alternatives to this reform and the regulations that would be needed to implement the proposed scenarios can be understood in terms of the present CAP legislation. In order to facilitate a comparison with the MacSharry policy package, the scenarios cover the same time period and are based on the same assumptions for non-agricultural parameters as the MacSharry scenario.

The scenario for the free trade perspective consists of undoing most of the distortions introduced by the MacSharry reform. While diminishing distortions in the markets for cereals, butter, beef and certain other products, the MacSharry reform creates several new distortions. Since the set-aside obligations depend on the particular circumstances of individual farms, each farm is affected differently by the regulations. Large farms suffer more than small farms since the latter are exempted from the obligation. Moreover, according to the MacSharry policies, quotas on premiums payable for cattle, sheep and tobacco are introduced, while the quotas for milk are maintained. The revenues derived from these quotas are pure rents. New farmers have to buy the quotas which to them are nonproductive investments that serve only to increase indebtedness. Also, as the rents are capitalized in property rights, part of the value will leave agriculture through inheritance and migration and thus accrues to the non-agricultural sector.

The free trade scenario, specified in Section 6.1, liberalizes trade faster than the MacSharry scenario. It relaxes quantitative restrictions, including the abolishment of set-asides, and introduces lump sum (or decoupled) transfers as temporary compensation for the income loss that results from lower prices. This scenario will hence be referred to as the 'decoupled MacSharry' scenario. Section 6.2 is devoted to the interventionist perspective. We formulate a scenario with relatively high internal prices, combined with increased border protection measures and quotas on production and set-asides. In this scenario there is no room for lump sum payments, so that the consumer rather than the EU-budget will carry the burden of the protection. Since the combination of supply restrictions and market segmentation with a high price on the domestic market, low prices on the world market is a typical cartel feature, the interventionist scenario will also be referred to as the 'cartel' scenario. The outcomes from various perspectives are compared in Section 6.3 and this leads to conclusions on the desirability and political feasibility of the alternatives. The main program of this chapter will then have been completed, but one further issue needs to be addressed, that will be dealt with in Section 6.4: does implementation of the preferred or most likely alternative require a *common* agricultural policy? The calculations will describe the implications of financial renationalization for the scenarios of the bureaucratic, the free trade and the interventionist perspective.

6.1 More free trade: the decoupled MacSharry scenario

The free trade perspective is analyzed through the decoupled MacSharry scenario, which is characterized by a relaxation of quotas, abolishment of set-asides and by lump sum transfers that compensate farmers for a further reduction in export and producer subsidies. In CAP parlance this is often called decoupling, because subsidies that were previously coupled to production through higher prices, are converted into transfers that are 'decoupled' in the sense that the amount received by a farmer does not depend on his actual production level.

6.1.1   Scenario description

Policy variables

The specification differs from the MacSharry scenario in four respects: (i) all producer, consumer and input subsidies are eliminated; (ii) set-aside obligations are abolished; (iii) quotas on milk and sugar are relaxed at a rate of 0.7 per cent annually; (iv) intervention prices for cereals, sugar, butter and other dairy products decrease by, respectively, an extra 0.5, 1.5, 1.0 and 1.0 per cent annually, again relative to the intervention prices of the MacSharry scenario.

In the mid-nineties the combined sum of producer and input subsidies exceeds 18 billion ecu in the MacSharry scenario. Therefore, if all producer and input subsidies were to be abolished, farm incomes could be expected to suffer heavy losses, at least initially. Compensation in the volume sphere, due to the abolishment of the set-aside obligations and the easing of milk and sugar quotas, would certainly not be enough. Moreover, the net decrease in incomes would lead to a depreciation of farm assets such as land, buildings and quota rights. In order to somewhat ease the negative effects on incomes and asset values, thereby averting social unrest and large-scale bankruptcies, decoupled income compensation is introduced in the scenario. Although it is possible to conceive of many different compensation schemes, we have opted for the following.

Compensation is granted for a limited period only. Rather arbitrarily, the length of the period has been set at 12 years (1993-2005). In the first three years (1993-1995), income losses due to 'free trade' policies will be fully compensated. This means that the total sector income, measured as the total agricultural value added including compensation, will equal the total sector income in the MacSharry scenario for the corresponding years. Hence, for the years 1993-1995, the total amount of decoupled compensation is computed as the difference between agricultural value added in the MacSharry scenario (including all price subsidies to producers) minus the agricultural value added in the decoupled scenario,

From 1996 onwards the total annual amount of compensation received by the individual is kept fixed at its 1995 level. It is also assumed that in order to facilitate a restructuring of the agricultural sector, farmers who retire or migrate to the non-agricultural sector do not lose their rights to compensation. On the other hand, new entrants (young farmers) are not eligible for compensation. The exclusion of young farmers from compensation can be defended on equity grounds, since they need proportionately less investment capital under a decoupled regime. We will return to this point later.

Figure 6.1 Direct income transfers under decoupling

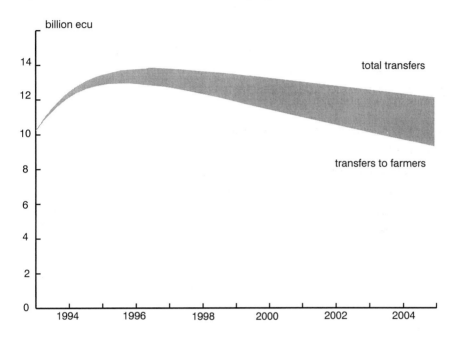

Source: ECAM, decoupled scenario.
Note: Shaded area refers to transfers to migrated farmers.

The proposed scheme implies that an increasing part of the overall compensation will be paid to the non-agricultural sector. Figure 6.1 schematically summarizes the spending pattern of the fund responsible for compensation. Due to mortality, total compensation paid by FEOGA decreases by about 1.6 per cent annually. Since new entrants are not granted compensation, the rate of decrease in the total amount paid is equal to the mortality rate of farmers and ex-farmers over the fifteen years of the scheme.[127]

---

[127] In this scenario the compensation given is country-specific. In the MacSharry regulations compensation is given in a differentiated way according to the farm's production structure and economic size, and the implementation is far more complex.

Exogenous variables

Most exogenous variables are set at the same values as in the MacSharry scenario. For yields, world market prices, land availability and non-agricultural production it seems reasonable to account for the effect of the free trade package itself.

(i)   *Hectare yields.* The yields are assumed to be lower in the decoupled scenario for three reasons. First, since the set-aside obligation is abolished, the less productive areas will remain in cultivation and this will reduce average yields. Secondly, the support is now perceived by the farmer as being completely decoupled from production and this is an incentive for extensification. In all, it is assumed that crop yields per hectare will exhibit a permanent downward shift of 2 per cent in 1993, relative to the yields in the MacSharry scenario.

(ii) *World market prices.* As will be seen hereafter, despite the decrease in hectare yields, overall cereal production as well as net cereal exports increase (in this scenario relative to the MacSharry scenario). As the EU is a major player on the international cereal market, this will have a downward effect on world market prices. It is assumed that a one percent rise in EU-exports leads to a 0.3 per cent fall in world market prices. Due to the relaxation of milk quotas, dairy exports also increase. It is assumed that this entails a downward adjustment of the international dairy price of 0.5 per cent annually.

(iii) *Land availability.* The decoupling will result in a drop in prices of agricultural land. Consequently, there will be an increased demand for land used for non-agricultural purposes such as urbanization, recreation, nature, etc. To avoid being accused of defining away 'the problem of overcapacity in agriculture', we assume that the additional land outflow will be limited to a meagre 0.12 per cent annually.

(iv) *Productivity of farm migrants.* Under the proposed compensation scheme, farmers receive their compensation payment whether or not they stay in agriculture. Since their income, not including compensation, is likely to decrease, an additional outflow of labour can be expected. Some of those migrants will find remunerative jobs outside agriculture, e.g. in the recreation sector or in rural industries. In calculating the medium term effects of the policy package on the standard of living, it has been assumed, rather conservatively, that the extra labour outflow has the same per capita production outside agriculture as it had within the sector. This is about half of the EU average per capita production outside agriculture.

6.1.2   Scenario outcomes

The discussion of scenario outcomes consecutively treats the effects of the proposed policy package on production volumes, external trade, the EU budget, farm incomes and value added before turning to the effect on welfare.

Table 6.1   Production quantities, EU-9, annual growth rate 1992-2005

	MacSharry	Decoupled MacSharry
Wheat	0.8	1.7
Coarse grains	0.4	0.3
Sugar beet	0.2	0.9
Oilseeds	0.6	0.7
Consumable potatoes	1.3	1.4
Dairy cows	0.0	0.6
Laying hens	0.5	-0.1
Non-dairy cattle	1.4	0.3
Sheep and goats	0.0	-0.8
Pigs	1.3	1.2
Poultry	1.8	1.8

Production volumes

Table 6.1 summarizes the effects of the decoupled MacSharry policies on production volumes at the EU level. The abolishment of the set-aside obligations and the easing of sugar quotas open room for expansion in the crop sector. This explains the increase in wheat and sugar beet production relative to the MacSharry scenario. For coarse grains, there is a slowdown in growth. The difference between the outcomes for wheat and coarse grains is due to the slower technical progress in coarse grains. This causes a shift in relative profitabilities in favour of wheat, which is more pronounced in the decoupled scenario than in the MacSharry scenario, because prices are lower.

The outcome suggests that at near world market prices, EU farmers have a competitive advantage in wheat relative to coarse grains and oilseeds. For sugar beets the explanation is more straightforward. In nearly all member states, sugar beet quotas are binding, even at lower prices and relaxing these leads to corresponding increases in production.

Developments are quite divergent among member states. For example, annual wheat production in France grows at a rate of nearly three per cent, whereas in Italy and the United Kingdom there is only a 0.5 per cent increase. These diverging growth patterns are consistent with the calculated changes in the net revenues.

In the livestock sector, milk production expands, which is possible due to the relaxation of the milk quotas. This occurs at the expense of the other land-tied livestock products (non-dairy cattle and sheeps and goats) and suggests that, at near world market prices, it is more profitable for European farmers to produce milk than to raise non-dairy cattle or sheep.

External trade

Decoupling has a significant effect on the agricultural trade balance of the EU. The EU's export position in international markets, in particular for cereals and dairy products, is much more prominent under a decoupled regime than under the MacSharry reform package (see Table 6.2). This can be explained as follows. Since prices do not differ much between the two scenarios, differences in internal demand are modest. Consequently, a large part of the additional production volumes carries over into exports. Decoupling raises the cereal surplus by nearly 15 million metric tons, and the dairy surplus by more than 8 million metric tons in 2005. To put these figures into context: during the 1982-1990 period, annual cereal and dairy exports by the EU amounted to some 20 and 11 million metric tons respectively (see Table 4A.4). Thus these increases are substantial indeed. However, as EU intervention prices decrease at a faster rate than prices on the world market,[128] it is unlikely that these surpluses will cause the same kind of conflicts with trading partners as in the eighties.

Table 6.2   Net imports, EU-9, mln metric tons

	MacSharry		Decoupled MacSharry	
	1996	2005	1996	2005
Wheat	-9.1	-15.5	-18.2	-27.5
Coarse grains	-0.7	-1.4	-4.6	-3.8
Sugar	-3.2	-2.4	-3.5	-3.4
Fats and oils	4.8	6.2	4.7	6.1
Protein feeds	10.4	9.1	10.0	8.1
Carbohydrates	21.5	21.9	21.2	20.5
Butter	0.0	0.0	0.0	0.2
Other dairy	-7.9	-5.0	-8.5	-13.4
Bovine meat	0.1	-0.8	0.2	0.2

Since the production increase in dairy products occurs partially at the expense of non-dairy cattle production, the EU trade position for bovine meat turns from net exports to net imports.

FEOGA outlays

Decoupling appears to be favourable for the EU budget. In real terms, overall FEOGA outlays decrease by 0.3 per cent annually, compared to an average annual increase of 1.4 per cent in the MacSharry scenario (Table 6.3). Such budgetary outlays fall comfortably within the limits set by the spending guideline (see Section 2.2.2).

It is worth noting that there are important shifts in outlays on a per item basis. Not surprisingly, producer and consumer subsidies disappear completely. Remaining input subsidies mainly refer to subsidies for private storage because it is assumed that selling products on the world market will remain as difficult

---

[128] In the decoupled scenario, during the 1993-2005 period real intervention prices for cereals and dairy products are assumed to decrease by 33 per cent and 17 per cent respectively. Whereas real world market prices decrease by only 1 per cent (cereals) and 9 per cent (dairy).

Table 6.3   FEOGA outlays, EU-12

	MacSharry		Decoupled MacSharry	
	2005	Annual growth rate 1992-2005	2005	Annual growth rate 1992-2005
Export refunds	3854	-4.8	4787	-3.2
Producer subsidies	14995	5.5	-14	-
Consumer subsidies	1463	-0.2	0	-
Input subsidies	2569	-1.0	1583	-4.6
Interest and storage	1441	-4.2	1340	-4.8
Other FEOGA outlays	13954	2.3	13954	2.3
Transfers to farmers[a]			9326	-
Transfers to non-farmers[a]			2701	-
Total income transfers[a]			12027	-
FEOGA, incl. transfers	38276	1.4	33677	0.3

Note: (a) Transfers are for EU-9 only. The transfers for other EU members are part of 'other FEOGA outlays'.

as in the MacSharry scenario. Despite lower intervention prices for cereals, sugar, butter and other dairy products, the export refunds decrease less in the decoupled scenario than under the MacSharry policies. The effect of lower internal prices on refunds is more than offset by the combined effect of lower world market prices and increased export volumes. Nonetheless, the model predicts a significant drop in the level of export subsidies relative to the MacSharry policy. Direct income compensation is the main expenditure item in the scenario. The total amounts to 14.1 billion ecu in 1996, and decreases to 12.0 billion ecu in 2005. This is consistent with mortality rates in member states. An increasing part of the overall compensation is paid to ex-farmers. In 2005 this amounts to 2.7 billion ecu.

Value added and farm incomes

Farmers' organizations have often expressed their distrust regarding free trade with decoupled compensation because of its expected effect on farm incomes. They argue that the budgetary cost of full compensation would be too high to find a political majority in favour of it. The scenario outcomes do not corroborate this expectation, provided a gradualist policy is adopted. Overall FEOGA outlays remain well below the spending guideline, and the growth of real value added plus income compensation is scarcely less than under the MacSharry regime (Table 6.4). The figures shown only cover the compensation that is received by those who were farmers at the beginning of the period and continue farming. The new entrants receive no compensation.

Table 6.4   Real value added of agriculture, annual growth rate 1992-2005, at 1992 prices

	Real value added			Real value added per capita		
	(1)	(2)	(3)	(1)	(2)	(3)
Belgium-Luxembourg	-0.6	-1.2	-0.7	1.6	1.1	1.6
Denmark	-0.2	-0.2	0.3	3.2	3.4	3.9
France	-1.2	-3.3	-1.2	2.8	1.5	3.6
Germany, Fed. Rep.	-1.6	-2.9	-1.7	0.0	-1.1	0.1
Ireland	-1.5	-2.1	-0.6	2.3	2.2	3.7
Italy	0.2	-1.0	-0.1	3.0	2.0	2.9
The Netherlands	0.4	0.4	0.5	1.2	1.3	1.4
United Kingdom	-2.2	-4.2	-2.3	-0.2	-1.8	0.1
EU-9	-0.7	-1.9	-0.8	1.9	1.0	2.1

Columns:
(1)   MacSharry
(2)   Decoupled MacSharry, net of transfers
(3)   Decoupled MacSharry, including transfers.
Note: Agricultural value added is deflated by the national GDP-deflator in ecu.

Because the compensation is only based on differences in per capita value added in 1995, the farm incomes are, in the years thereafter, even slightly higher in the decoupled scenario, although some member states are worse off. The average farmer in Ireland 'earns' an extra 22 per cent in 2005, compared with the MacSharry alternative, whereas the average Italian farmer becomes nearly two per cent worse off.

Farm incomes after 2005

As compensation is given for a limited period only, the figures in the table reflect the income situation in the medium term. From 2006 onwards the compensation ceases; it hardly seems realistic to assume a longer period of compensation. Hence, an income shock can be expected in 2006 but its effect must not be exaggerated. Since an estimated 32 per cent of the farmers eligible for compensation at the start of the scheme in the mid-nineties will have died or otherwise left agriculture in 2006, only 68 per cent of the 'original' farmers will suffer from the shock. More importantly, decoupled compensation paid to farmers only accounts for 10 to 11 per cent of the total agricultural value added in 2005. As farm income is in many instances supplemented by earnings from non-agricultural activities (see Section 2.4.3), the share of decoupled income compensation as part of the overall income will be even smaller.

These qualifications apply to those members of the farm population who were already receiving compensation at the start of the scheme. Newcomers on the other hand, are simply confronted with decoupled, lower product prices. Although they do not receive an annual lump sum transfer by way of compensation, even for them the situation is not as bad as the low product prices would indicate. The reason for this is that decoupling will cause a drop in the price of assets that are specific to agriculture like land, farm buildings and quota rights. This means that newcomers need less initial capital to start or to take over a farm. Should there be a total decoupling, quota rights would actually become worthless.

Since the gains of the young farmers in buying a farm will be the same as the losses suffered by the old farmers selling their assets, one could object that agricultural support does not really help the agricultural sector. In a static situation this would indeed be the case but here some dynamic effects play an important role. With every generation, a certain amount of agricultural assets passes into the hands of the non-agricultural sector, mainly through inheritance. Consequently, a significant part of the drop in asset values will be absorbed by the non-agricultural sector. The dampening mechanism that reduces the effect of coupled support on farm incomes (see Tangermann (1989)) is also effective when support is reduced.

Welfare effects

The decoupled policy package results in a welfare improvement for the economy at large. Table 6.5 shows that, compared with the MacSharry outcomes, overall EU welfare rises by some 6.3 billion ecu. Compared to the scenario in which a continuation of the pre-MacSharry policies was simulated, the difference exceeds 10 billion ecu (3.78+6.30). A small part of it is due to a net increase in the trade surplus but the rise is mainly reflected in higher equivalent consumer expenditures;

Table 6.5   Equivalent consumer expenditures in 2005, at 1992 prices

Difference between runs:	MacSharry – pre-MacSharry	Decoupled MacSharry – MacSharry	
	bln ecu	bln ecu	ecu per capita
Belgium-Luxembourg	0.29	0.22	22
Denmark	0.25	0.29	44
France	0.98	1.36	23
Germany, Fed. Rep.	0.45	1.31	22
Ireland	0.00	0.24	69
Italy	1.76	0.22	4
The Netherlands	0.02	0.56	35
United Kingdom	1.25	1.58	27
EU-9	5.00	5.78	21
Trade surplus	-1.22	0.52	2
Total welfare difference	3.78	6.30	23

Consumers benefit to different degrees. On a per capita basis Ireland and Italy are again the extremes. In Ireland, the average consumer gains about sixteen times more than in Italy. However, this does not mean that decoupling is more attractive for Ireland because on the trade balance the gains for Italy exceed those of the other member states.

Origins of welfare improvements

The welfare gain basically originates from three sources. First, there is an expansion in overall agricultural production. This is primarily caused by the abolishment of the set-aside obligations. More land remains available to agriculture, despite the increase in land allocated to non-agricultural uses. The second source of welfare increase is the change in composition of agricultural output. Due to the decoupling measures, including the easing of milk and sugar quotas, signals to farmers become more closely aligned with world market prices. The third and in quantitative terms single most important source is an increase in non-agricultural production. Recall that farmers who move to the non-agricultural sector still receive their decoupled income compensation, which provides them with an extra incentive to leave farming. According to the scenario outcomes, 4.6 per cent more farmers leave agriculture by 2005 compared to the MacSharry scenario. Although these migrants are not assumed to be as productive as the average non-agricultural worker, they do add to the volume of non-agricultural production.

6.1.3   Comparison with other studies

Since the mid-eighties there has been a large number of publications on the (negative) effects of agricultural protectionism. Many of these quantify the economic effects of abolishing agricultural protection, using a partial or general equilibrium model as their tool. It is interesting to compare ECAM outcomes with those from other models, even if these models are different in many respects. We shall only compare the effects of trade liberalization measures on social welfare. Table 6.6 summarizes the outcomes of the IIASA, the RUNS, the Walras and the Tyers and Anderson models.

Like ECAM, these models conclude that a partial and unilateral liberalization will have a clearly positive effect on the overall standard of living in the EU. The extent of this rising prosperity varies widely, however. The WALRAS and the RUNS models project much greater welfare gains than ECAM, while the IIASA model forecasts about equal gains for the EU. There are also striking differences in the sectoral origins of the rising welfare. While the other four models show overall welfare gains as the balance of a net welfare loss in the agricultural sector and a net welfare gain in the non-agricultural sector, in ECAM welfare gains come from both agriculture and non-agriculture, the former contributing about 60 per cent of the overall improvement and the latter accounting for the balance.

Table 6.6   Changes in real income caused by liberalization

Model	Percentage change
WALRAS	1.4
IIASA	0.3
RUNS	
- partial liberalisation	1.3
- full liberalisation	2.4
Tyers and Anderson	0.4
ECAM	0.3

Sources: WALRAS, see Martin et al. (1990); IIASA, see Parikh et al. (1988); RUNS, see Goldin and Knudsen (1990); Tyers and Anderson, see Tyers and Anderson (1992).

A part of the variation in outcomes is due to differences in scenario assumptions. While in ECAM we take the post-MacSharry CAP as reference scenario, the other studies use the pre-MacSharry CAP as their point of departure. They treat quotas on sugar and milk production in terms of tariff equivalents and do not consider set-asides of land. Moreover, they refer to a situation of full liberalization (for agricultural products), whereas the decoupled ECAM-scenario only considers the effects of a policy change in the direction of free trade.

Another part of the differences is attributable to differences in model structure.[129] The RUNS model has a fully endogenous representation of the non-agricultural sector and of factor markets. The IIASA model does not have market clearing wages and interest rates, in the ECAM-model factor inputs into non-agriculture are not explicit, in the Tyers and Anderson model they are completely absent. Hence, after a liberalization the gains in factor productivity do not appear in equal detail in the various models.

The WALRAS, the RUNS and the IIASA models have a similar mechanism by which the EU's rising welfare is generated: following the implementation of free trade measures, there is a drop in internal prices for

---

[129] The WALRAS, the RUNS, the IIASA, and the Tyers and Anderson models are all world models with an aggregated model for the EU. They differentiate between fewer products than ECAM, and do not consider memberstates on an individual basis. Agricultural policies are less explicit, which precludes a detailed comparison. Moreover, their time coverage is different than ECAM's, as is the way in which values have been attached to model parameters. Parameters in the WALRAS, the RUNS and the Tyers and Anderson models have mainly been calibrated according to a benchmark data set.

agricultural products.[130] This basically has two consequences: agriculture becomes less profitable for EU farmers, and EU consumers enjoy lower prices.

As farming becomes less profitable, some farmers react by leaving agriculture for the non-agricultural sector. They find a job, thereby adding to (less protected) non-agricultural production. Since they become more productive when their income is measured at international prices, they also contribute to overall welfare. At the same time, a less profitable agriculture attracts less investment goods and less current inputs and these are employed more productively outside agriculture.

The primary effect of the lower prices for food products is that the consumer's standard of living improves. In the RUNS-model there is also the secondary effect that the wage rate falls relative to the price of non-agricultural products. This improves the profitability of the non-agricultural sector and leads to higher real incomes.

Differences between the predicted welfare gains of, say, the IIASA model and the WALRAS or RUNS models can be related mostly to the rate of the adjustment processes involved, especially for factors. The speed of adjustment in the IIASA model, particularly through labour migration, is much more constrained than in the other models.

In ECAM, the same basic mechanisms are operating. Here also the reduced consumer prices are a major source of welfare gains but there is no wage effect. As in the IIASA model, labour out-migration is modest, in spite of the assumption that farmers do not lose their entitlement for compensation when they leave agriculture. Also, migrated labour is not given a very high productivity. These differences explain the modest gain in non-agricultural production. The gain in agriculture is the main distinction between ECAM and the other models. The abolishment of set-asides and the easing of quotas lead to a rise in agricultural production capacity; farmers utilize the freed capacity despite the drop in prices. Moreover, due to changes in relative prices, production factors are reallocated within agriculture and this appears to improve

---

[130] The Tyers and Anderson model is the only partial equilibrium model. Here standard of living improvements are computed from welfare triangles.

efficiency. Both phenomena add to an expansion of the agricultural sector within the decoupled scenario.

The question remains why the size of the extra migration to non-agriculture is so small in ECAM and why these labourers are assumed to be so unproductive. Although interrelated, the two issues are best discussed separately.

Immobility of agricultural labour. Time series data on agricultural labour reveal that the agricultural labour outflow is predominantly influenced by demographic factors (see Folmer (1993)). Farmers seldom abandon farming because prices decrease. Once a farmer, they only stop farming because they grow old or face bankruptcy. The young can choose between taking over the parents' farm, buying one from a retiring farmer who has no successor, or finding employment outside agriculture. The old (55+) hardly migrate at all. Hence, at every point in time only a small fraction of the population considers leaving.

Low productivity of agricultural labour outside the sector. Farmers who abandon farming for economic reasons will often have to enter the labour market in rural areas as unskilled labourers. In many regions the rural economy is heavily dependent on agriculture. So, if economic conditions compel farmers to shut down, then rural economies will probably be in bad shape. This makes it difficult for the unskilled to find rural jobs. Some of these migrants will remain unemployed, while others will find a minimally productive job at the lower end of the labour market. All in all, it seems reasonable to assume that the average productivity of a migrated labourer falls well below average productivity in the non-agricultural sector.

6.1.4   Unilateral versus multilateral trade liberalization

The scenario description assumes that the shift towards free trade will be a unilateral action on the part of the EU, with limited effects on world market prices. However, it is conceivable that such a policy shift will only take place should other countries follow suit. In this event one would expect the change in world market prices to be more pronounced. The agricultural policy models that were mentioned in Table 6.6 also indicate this. Therefore, to assess the effects of such a 'concerted' action, an alternative scenario has been run which assumes a multilateral (partial) shift towards free trade and associated differences in world market prices. We assume that world market prices for the main product groups will then increase as compared to a situation of unilateral action i.e. to the decoupled MacSharry scenario. The price increases are shown in Table 6.7. They are supposed to result primarily from a reduction in tariffs by net importing countries and are in line with the outcomes of studies in which world market prices are treated as endogenous variables (see e.g. Goldin and Knudsen (1990, p. 91).

Table 6.7   World market prices in case of a multilateral, partial liberalization in agriculture in 2005

Percentage difference between runs:	Multilateral-unilateral decoupling
Wheat	5
Coarse grains	5
Sugar	4
Butter	20
Other dairy	20
Bovine meat	10

Because of the limited changes in the exogenous variables, the differences in scenario outcomes between a unilateral and a multilateral shift towards free trade cannot be very large. Table 6.8 shows the main effects on the FEOGA budget.

Due to the rise in world market prices, internal EU prices approach the world market level at a faster rate. For bovine meat, butter and dairy, the margin between internal and external prices almost vanishes. It is therefore no surprise, that export refunds decrease at a faster rate. Relative to the unilateral shift (decoupled MacSharry scenario), refunds in 2005 will be 1.3 billion ecu less. Since other budget items hardly change at all, the overall FEOGA outlays decrease by approximately the same amount.

A multilateral shift towards free trade appears to increase welfare more than a unilateral shift. ECAM predicts an additional increase of prosperity of nearly 1 billion ecu. The increase in overall welfare arises as the balance of a decrease

Table 6.8   FEOGA outlays, EU-12

	Multilateral decoupled		Unilateral decoupled	
	2005	Annual growth rate 1992-2005	2005	Annual growth rate 1992-2005
Export refunds	3486	-5.6	4787	-3.2
Producer subsidies	-14	-	-14	-
Consumer subsidies	0	-	0	-
Input subsidies	1583	-4.6	1583	-4.6
Interest and storage	1511	-1.2	1340	-4.8
Other FEOGA outlays	13954	2.3	13954	2.3
Transfers to farmers[a]	9326	-	9326	-
Transfers to non-farmers[a]	2701	-	2701	-
Total income transfers[a]	12027	-	12027	-
FEOGA, incl. transfers	32547	0.0	33677	0.3

Note: (a) Transfers are for EU-9 only.

in equivalent consumer expenditure (0.48 billion ecu), and an increase in the net trade surplus (1.4 billion ecu).

6.1.5   The CAP from the free trade perspective: some conclusions

The future of the CAP in the case of a further shift towards free trade can best be described by summarizing the main conclusions of this section's scenario analysis.

(a)   A gradual shift towards free trade need not be disastrous for farm incomes. On the contrary, the simulation reveals that farm incomes can increase not only because of the decoupled support but also because of the cheaper agricultural inputs and the relaxation of quotas.

(b)   Apprehensions concerning rapidly decreasing self-sufficiency ratios do not appear justified. Since restrictions on production volumes and production factors are removed, production capacity increases but, due to the immobility of production factors, only part of the increased potential will in fact be used.

(c) Decoupling, supplemented with full (lump sum) income compensation, does not result in an explosive increase in the FEOGA budget. In the medium term the overall budget picture actually improves in the case of decoupling.

(d) A partial decoupling benefits the standard of living. Depending on the assumptions (unilateral versus multilateral), and the reference scenario (MacSharry scenario versus a continuation of pre-MacSharry policies), one finds overall welfare increases between 6 and 11 billion ecu.

(e) A gradual liberalization say, over a ten or fifteen year period, brings intervention prices very close to world market levels.

We may add that, with respect to the environmental problems of EU agriculture, a shift towards free trade does not necessarily lead to additional environmental damage. A lower output price discourages the use of fertilizer and pesticides. Since the competitive position of internally grown cereals increases relative to imported cereal substitutes, the policy stimulates a shift in the pork and poultry sector towards the parts of the Community where livestock concentrations will be lower because the animal feeds are grown on the livestock farm itself (recall also Section 5.1.5).

The overall conclusion is that a gradual shift towards free trade would be beneficial for the EU. The most pressing problems, i.e. the budget and international trade, would gradually cease, and no new ones would arise. Step by step, the international competitiveness of EU agriculture would improve.

This does not mean that the proposed free trade package is necessarily 'the best there is' for the EU. Both the policy package and the scenario outcomes are subject to further critical assessments, even apart from queries one may like to pose regarding ECAM itself.

First, it may be argued that the policy package contains too many arbitrary elements. If variants of the decoupled scenario were to be analyzed, the conclusions would perhaps be different. Indeed, some degree of arbitrariness must be admitted as there are many gradual roads to free trade. However, with respect to the overall conclusion, this seems to be a minor point. All decoupled policy packages that were analyzed with ECAM led to more or less the same overall conclusions (see e.g. Folmer et al. (1989) and Keyzer et al. (1994)).

Secondly, when a partial liberalization is found to be attractive, it may seem logical to propose full liberalization. Radical free traders probably would prefer to go quite a bit further than is done here. Speedy and radical reforms should in their opinion be given preference over gradualism. They argue that this would save on time-consuming adjustment costs; a 'cold-turkey' strategy would have the immediate result of long run efficiency gains (see e.g. Funke (1993) and Rodrik (1989) for a discussion). We disagree and here we may reiterate the discussion of Section 3.4. A speedy and radical reform would probably result in large-scale bankruptcies. Rigidities in both agriculture and non-agriculture would prevent production factors no longer used in agriculture from becoming productive in the short term. Rather it is more likely that these factors would become idle and produce nothing. The relationship between long term efficiency on the one hand, and rapid, radical adjustments on the other, is less clear-cut than these authors suggest. Consistency and reliability are much more important in this respect.

Thirdly, it could be argued that the scenario's rosy picture is related to the fact that internal gradualism is combined with external gradualism, i.e. due to a gradual change in world market prices. In reality, world market prices often undergo quite drastic fluctuations and if taken into account, this would affect the outcomes. However, in our scenario border protection is only reduced on average, and not completely abolished. The proposed policies allow for countercyclical adjustments of the protection rates whenever world market prices undergo extreme fluctuations. Such adjustments would, in practice, have 'only' short term effects on FEOGA outlays and would not lead to significantly different results in other parts of the model.

Finally, the main conclusions can be dismissed altogether because of a more fundamental difference in perspective. This basically is what adherents of the interventionist perspective do.

6.2　More interventionism: the cartel scenario

Whereas the concept of free trade is relatively straightforward, interventionism is a pluriform concept. It is therefore not surprising that interventionists constitute a very heterogeneous group. Proponents of increased interventionism can be found in farmers' organizations, environmental groups, churches and to a lesser degree, academic circles. They share the conviction that a solution to the problems related to overproduction, budget, international trade and environmental degradation must be found in the effective control of production. In order to prevent farm incomes from dropping to very low levels, quotas must be supplemented with high prices. These prices must adequately reflect the total cost of production, including the 'environmental costs'. Since interventionists form such a heterogeneous group, there are obviously many ways of formulating an interventionist scenario. We shall analyze a gradualist departure from the MacSharry scenario in a direction opposite to free trade, that transforms the CAP into a government supported producers' cartel.

The reasons for choosing the producers' cartel as our point of reference are twofold. First, this gives the opportunity to give a more or less logical explanation for the panoply of policy instruments that are in effect after the MacSharry reform. Secondly, the differences between the current post-MacSharry CAP and a regular government supported producers' cartel also define a coherent change of the current policy into a more interventionist direction.

6.2.1   Scenario description

The CAP as a producers' cartel

In a producers' cartel, producers agree to maintain higher prices for their products, and do so by restricting supply or by segmenting markets. For many products, the pre-MacSharry CAP has the appearance of a cartel that segments agricultural markets into an internal, high-price zone and an external, low-price zone, under a scheme of imperfect competition of the kind discussed in Section 3.3.3. Though the MacSharry reform reduces price differences, it adds supply restrictions in the form of quotas and set-aside schemes.

The main distinction between the CAP and a classical producers' cartel is that the CAP uses government protection to achieve its aims. It is a corporatist arrangement. This is a necessity in the first place in order to protect the domestic market from foreign competition. It is also needed to ensure that the supply restrictions are enforced among the producers. Agriculture is specific in this respect due to the large number of producers and commodities that are involved. Exploitation of the monopoly power of the sector as a whole requires that all close substitutes be brought under the scheme. The farmers' organizations, and to some extent the agricultural ministers themselves, have acted to this effect by gradually extending the coverage of the CAP regulations to virtually all close substitutes. The government involvement in the cartel makes it possible to charge all the expenses to the domestic consumer who faces an artificially high price for his food basket and also pays for the export subsidies, the costs of buffer stocks and the compensation payments.

Towards privatization of the cartel

Compared with the earlier CAP, the MacSharry reform marks a shift towards more direct transfers and lower food prices. As discussed in Section 3.3.1, this makes the support to agriculture more 'visible' to the European consumer and involves deadweight losses because the taxes cannot be mobilized through truly lump sum transfers. Therefore, some interventionists oppose the reform and advocate a move in the opposite direction. Here we consider an interventionist reform in two stages. In the first stage market prices would be raised, producer subsidies reduced, direct transfers abolished and quantity restrictions imposed in order to avoid excessive production. Thereby the budgetary cost of the CAP would be reduced. In the second stage the cartel would become privatized. Then, the outlays for export subsidies, for buffer stock operations and for the remaining subsidies would be covered from direct contributions by producers. A scenario will be formulated for the first stage but we shall point to the implications of the outcomes for the privatization of the cartel, in the second stage.

We may add that, while achieving income support through a price policy is the cartel scenario's main objective, other objectives may be served as well, like coping with pollution, financing rural infrastructure and managing international trade (see Section 3.3). Through its supply controls, the cartel arrangement may indeed contribute to these aims, but more as a side effect that would promote the political support for the arrangement, than as a primary objective.

Policy variables

The policy assumptions of the cartel scenario (stage I) are as follows:

(i)   To improve the competitiveness of domestically produced animal feeds, an eighty per cent import tariff is imposed in 1993 on cereal substitutes (protein feeds and carbohydrates) and fats and oils, from 1993 onwards.

(ii)   For cereals, butter, other dairy, bovine and ovine meat, intervention prices are increased by fifteen per cent in 1993 with respect to 1992.

(iii)   Since measures (i) and (ii) lead to an increase in producer prices, producer subsidies on inputs and outputs become redundant and are abolished for cereals, oilseeds and protein-rich fodder crops.

(iv)   For crops, supply controls are imposed via set-asides. During the years 1993-1995, the set-asides are the same as in the MacSharry scenario but to compensate for the effect of increasing yields per hectare on overall production, from 1995 onwards the set-aside area is increased by six per cent annually, so that, by 2005, some 5.5 million hectares of arable land have to be taken out of production.

(v)   Milk quotas are reduced by four per cent in 1993 with respect to 1992.

(vi)   Livestock production is constrained further through production quotas on bovine meat, for which production levels are frozen at the 1993 level.

(vii)   Other price and quota policies are as in the MacSharry scenario (see Chapter 5).

Exogenous variables

(i) In the MacSharry scenario, intervention prices were diminished drastically during the period 1993-1995. This was assumed to result in a (small) drop in yields per hectare and per animal. In the present cartel scenario, intervention prices do not undergo such a downward shock, so that the need for imposing a yield reduction does not arise.

(ii) Preliminary simulations with the cartel scenario showed, not unexpectedly, an EU agriculture that comes far closer to autarky than under the MacSharry scenario. This led us to deviate from the assumptions on world market prices in the MacSharry scenario as follows: for cereals, where set-asides are tightened, world market prices increase at 0.8 per cent annually from 1993 onwards (as opposed to 0.3 per cent under MacSharry). For carbohydrates, the very high import tariffs that are introduced in the scenario are supposed to have a downward effect on world market prices and lead to a reduction 1.5 per cent annually (as opposed to 1.1 per cent). Finally, for bovine meat the quotas on production prevent the EU from becoming a large exporter and world market prices are assumed to fall at 0.6 per cent annually (as opposed to 1.16 per cent in the MacSharry scenario).

6.2.2   Scenario outcomes

The presentation of the outcomes will focus on export surpluses, output levels, the FEOGA budget, farm incomes and overall welfare. In presenting the results, only overall developments are indicated as well as differences from the MacSharry and the decoupled MacSharry scenarios.

Production volumes and external trade

Table 6.9 summarizes the main results regarding the development of the production volumes at EU-9 level. The most remarkable difference concerns the sharp decline of the cereal production. In the year 2005 this will be reduced by 32.2 million tons (24.5+7.8), as compared to the decoupled scenario. Since, due to higher prices, crop yields are higher in the cartel scenario, this decrease in production volume must be attributed fully to the additional set-aside. The very high levy on imported oilseeds and cereal substitutes pushes up the corresponding internal prices[131] and net revenues. Consequently, it becomes attractive to grow oilseeds. Since the (shadow) price of green fodder is linked to marketable feed prices[132], its net revenue improves also. This explains the expansion of green fodder production.

Table 6.9   Production quantities in the cartel and the decoupled MacSharry scenario, 2005

Comparison of runs:	Cartel – Decoupled (1000 mt)	Cartel/Decoupled (%)
Wheat	-24451	75.1
Coarse grains	-7756	89.0
Sugar beet	-11676	88.8
Oilseeds	1530	112.4
Green fodder	230	118.2
Dairy cows	-14773	87.7
Laying hens	-477	88.5
Non-dairy cattle	-448	93.9
Sheep and goats	79	110.5
Pigs	-541	96.2
Poultry	-246	96.8

The drop in sugar production is induced by both the set-aside obligation and the deterioration of net revenue relative to cereals and oilseeds. Similar changes can be noted in the animal sectors. Apart from sheep and goats, the output in all livestock sectors declines relative to the output level in the decoupled scenario. This decline is especially strong in the cattle sectors where the quotas on milk and bovine meat are constraining. The resulting excess capacity is partly used in the production of sheep and goats but existing quotas on total premiums prevent a further growth.

Moreover, price changes affect the cost of animal feeds. Regions with a high share of cereal substitutes in animal feeds lose their comparative advantage. For example, the jump in feed prices in 1993 raises feed costs by 65 per cent in the Netherlands and only by 37 per cent in Italy. The rise in feed prices reduces the profitability of the livestock sector and this causes a contraction in supply. For pigs, poultry and laying hens, this results in a price increase since

---

[131] Compare equation (3.4c) and footnote 32 in Section 3.1.1.

[132] See footnote 78 in Section 4.3.3.

Table 6.10   Net imports, EU-9 in 2005, mln metric tons

	MacSharry	Decoupled MacSharry	Cartel
Wheat	-15528	-27481	-4679
Coarse grains	-1409	-3815	1598
Sugar	-2429	-3361	-1804
Fats and oils	6171	6070	2919
Protein feeds	9065	8112	5531
Carbohydrates	21929	20543	15602
Butter	77	234	-238
Other dairy	-5033	-13380	-5144
Bovine meat	-818	235	-532

demand has to adjust to the lower supply. It appears that consumer demand is not sufficiently inelastic to eliminate the effect of the higher feed prices.

Given the importance of the effects on total production, one might expect substantial changes in the size of trade flows but Table 6.10 indicates that this does not hold for all products. Higher prices cause a fall in EU demand, mainly in human consumption of fats and oils, bovine meat and all dairy products. The high price level for cereals also prevents a quick rebalancing. Even an import levy of eighty per cent on cereal substitutes cannot prevent all imports.

Budgetary impact

Table 6.11 summarizes the effects of a cartel policy on the agricultural part of the EU-budget.

It may be noted that total FEOGA expenditures are not very much lower in 2005: 4.0 and 8.6 billion ecu compared to decoupled MacSharry and the MacSharry scenario, respectively, but this is because we only performed stage I of the reform: the cartel is not privatized, so that all tariff revenues and FEOGA expenditure still run via the FEOGA budget. The main point is that the net financial contribution from member states is significantly lower, as witnessed by the item 'net difference' in the table. Compared to the decoupled MacSharry scenario a total gain of more than 15 billion ecu will be achieved in 2005. The gain relative to the MacSharry reform is nearly twenty billion ecu.

Table 6.11   FEOGA outlays, EU-9 in 2005, mln ecu at 1992 prices

Difference between runs:	Cartel – Decoupled MacSharry	Cartel – MacSharry
Receipts:		
Levies on agricultural trade	11674	11199
Expenditures:		
Refunds on exports	1815	2748
Producer and input subsidies	4918	-11076
Consumer subsidies	1593	130
Interest and storage	-277	-378
Direct income transfers		0
farmers	-9326	
non-farmers (migrated)	-2701	
Total expenditures	-3978	-8576
Total net difference	-15652	-19775

The sharp increase on the receipts side is above all due to the levies on imported cereal substitutes and oilseeds which are introduced in this scenario. Despite the decline of import volumes total levies will go up by more than eleven billion ecu. A similar effect can be observed on the expenditures side: due to higher internal prices, the dip in the net export volume of cereals and dairy is more than offset by a rise in unit export subsidies.

A further deviation from the MacSharry scenario is the conversion of explicit subsidies (linked to production) into implicit subsidies (via high internal prices): the financial burden is shifted to the European consumer. This is shown in the budget through a sharp decline in producer and input subsidies. The budgetary improvement relative to the decoupled MacSharry scenario occurs because no direct income transfers are given. On the other hand, since, contrary to the MacSharry scenario, the subsidies on production, consumption and inputs are not abolished fully, the total gain is reduced by more than six billion ecu (4918+1593).

Real value added and agricultural income per capita

Obviously, if consumer prices are allowed to rise sufficiently, agricultural income can be brought to levels that are, in the short term, much higher than in

Table 6.12   Real value added of agriculture including transfers, 2005

Country	mln ecu			per capita, 1993=100		
	(1)	(2)	(3)	(1)	(2)	(3)
Belgium-Luxembourg	2631	2621	2347	124	124	112
Denmark	4577	4950	4781	151	166	158
France	18536	18587	22717	143	162	165
Germany, Fed. Rep.	12487	12452	13750	100	102	110
Ireland	2110	2403	2860	136	164	171
Italy	26583	25719	27225	146	146	151
The Netherlands	10201	10471	10173	117	120	117
United Kingdom	8396	8228	8848	98	101	102
EU-9	85521	85430	92702	127	132	136

Columns:
(1)   MacSharry
(2)   Decoupled MacSharry
(3)   Cartel.
Note: Agricultural value added is deflated by the national GDP-deflator in ecu.

the decoupled scenario. Table 6.12 seems to confirm these expectations: the real value added in 2005 is 8.5 per cent higher. Since the intervention prices for cereals are in 2005 about almost twice as high as in the MacSharry scenario, and about thirty per cent higher for other CAP commodities, one might have expected a much stronger increase.

That the gain is not larger can be explained on the basis of Table 6.13 as follows. First, though the increase in the intervention price of CAP commodities is dramatic, all producer subsidies and per hectare compensations are abolished. Secondly, the production quota and set-asides are tighter than in the MacSharry scenario. Thirdly, non-CAP products, like horticultural products and consumable potatoes, do not enjoy the price increase and although they face some reduction in relative profitability under this reform, the substitutability is far from perfect (one could actually argue that the scenario is deficient because these sectors should be included in the cartel, in which case their production would not drop at all). Finally, and most importantly, intensive livestock producers suffer a severe income loss due to higher feed prices. While net revenue from production of CAP commodities is about eleven per cent higher in 2005, the net revenue from pig and poultry activities falls by thirty per cent.

Table 6.13   Production value and net revenues compared over scenarios, EU-9

	Cartel/MacSharry	
	1993	2005
Ratio of production values at farm-gate level		
CAP commodities	1.23	1.22
Intensive livestock products[a]	0.92	1.06
Ratio of net revenues		
CAP commodities	1.20	1.11
Intensive livestock products[a]	0.56	0.70

Note: (a) Pig meat, poultry meat and eggs.

This points to the major weakness of any cartel, that the interests of the various farm groups are divergent. The livestock farmers would benefit from a lower price of cereals and cereal substitutes and only those who raise cattle and sheep can be compensated via higher CAP prices for their own products. Of course, one may be tempted to conclude that bringing pork and poultry meat and eggs under the standard CAP regime would overcome this problem but in view of the limited possibilities for exports and the modest price elasticities on the demand side, this hardly is a viable proposition: since foreign trade cannot adjust, a high stabilization would have to be realized via production quota but due to the low demand elasticity, this would lead to important price instability (see also Section 2.2.1).

The outcomes from the cartel scenario need to be qualified further. First, it is to be noted that this general increase does not apply to all member states. In Denmark value added falls due to the high set-aside obligation. In Belgium-Luxembourg and The Netherlands there also is a reduction because of the large share of cereal substitutes in the feed mix. The high levy on these imported feedstuffs reduces the profitability of the livestock sector. The rise in value added is largest in France and Ireland. France benefits from the jump in cereal prices, while the positive results for Ireland originate from the increase in the intervention price for livestock products, the large share of green fodder in animal feeding and the small area under set-aside.

Secondly, the positive effect on real value added is partly offset by a smaller outflow of agricultural labour. This reduction in migration is the result of a 'push' and a 'pull' factor. Due to the rise in agricultural value added, the financial stimulus to move out of agriculture is waning. The pull factor is due to the inefficiency of a cartel policy, to which we return below where we discuss welfare effects. At EU-9 level, agricultural value added per capita in 2005 is only three per cent higher in the cartel scenario than in the decoupled MacSharry run, while agricultural employment is 6 per cent higher.

Finally, since supply constraints and high prices will tend to push up the value of the agricultural assets, it will become more difficult for new entrants to acquire a farm, whereas old farmers who retire and heirs who move out will receive more.

Welfare effects

So far, we have seen that the cartel scenario has as clear advantages that subsidized exports decline and that the income position of the European farmer improves.[133] Obviously, incomes would be lower than is indicated in Table 6.12 once the cartel was privatized, since in that case the farmers would have to bear the full cost. At any rate, these are only secondary criteria which cannot replace the calculation of welfare gains as a yardstick. As can be seen from Table 6.14, there is a substantial welfare loss compared to the other two scenarios.

The total loss relative to the decoupled scenario is the balance of a fall in consumer welfare of 34 billion ecu and an improvement of the trade balance of sixteen billion ecu. The loss of consumer welfare is due to higher consumer prices and higher costs of animal feeds. As animal feeds have a relatively high

---

[133] On the other hand, it is highly unlikely that trade partners of the EU agree with the introduction of high import levies on oilseeds and grain substitutes.

degree of substitution, interventionist policies can be expected to cause significant distortions in this sphere. The lower trade deficit is mainly due to the reduced budget deficits of the member states (as a result of lower VAT transfers).

The total loss is unequally distributed across member states. Large agricultural net importers like Germany, Italy and the United Kingdom, as well as countries that suffer most from the import levies on cereal substitutes (Belgium-Luxembourg and the Netherlands) lose most. Losses for net exporters like France and Denmark are relatively small. Welfare in Ireland even improves slightly.

Table 6.14   Equivalent consumer expenditures in 2005, bln ecu at 1992 prices

Difference between runs:	MacSharry − Cartel	Decoupled MacSharry − Cartel
Belgium-Luxembourg	1.9	2.1
Denmark	0.3	0.6
France	3.3	4.6
Germany, Fed. Rep.	7.4	8.7
Ireland	-0.3	-0.1
Italy	6.3	6.5
The Netherlands	2.1	2.7
United Kingdom	7.4	8.9
EU-9	28.4	34.2
Total welfare gain	11.7	17.9
EU-9 trade surplus		
- on agriculture	0.3	3.3
- other	-17.0	-19.6

The financial gains from the transition to the (non-privatized) cartel accrue to national governments via a substantial reduction in total VAT transfers to the EU: fifteen and twenty billion ecu, compared to the decoupled and the MacSharry scenario, respectively. Although these savings could be transferred to the consumer, e.g. via a general reduction of tax rates, this has not been assumed. In the model they now lead to a reduction of foreign savings. The model does not allow the consumer to compensate his loss from higher food prices through higher wages. If he were able to do so, his direct loss would be reduced but the comparative advantage of the tradeable sector on the world market would deteriorate. It also appears that an overall increase in food prices affects the consumer demand for non-agricultural commodities more than the demand for food itself.

Possible consequences for the environment

Although the effects of changes in agricultural policies on the environment are not explicit in ECAM, some tentative conclusions may be drawn. It seems that a general tendency towards autarky, reduces the (large) net flows of minerals and this will be welcomed by environmentalists, who emphasize the importance of the loss of soil fertility when a country exports more minerals than it imports and, conversely, the problem of pollution, usually through an excess of manure, when there is an import surplus (see e.g. Daly (1993)). The simulation results suggest other environmental benefits as well. In the crop sector, the set-asides may alleviate environmental pressures, although production is intensified on non-fallow land, due to the high prices. In the livestock sector, restrictions on animal stocks cause an extensification of production.

6.2.3   The CAP from the interventionist perspective: some conclusions

Though significant, the welfare losses that occur in the interventionist scenario are only a minor fraction of total consumer expenditure. Even the difference between the most extreme scenarios only amounts to 0.7 per cent of equivalent consumer expenditures in 2005. Given the difficulties associated with direct transfers that were discussed in Chapter 3 and the advantages that the cartel scenario may bring for the environment, the interventionist scenario cannot be dismissed as totally nonviable. Moreover, due to the imposition of production quotas for livestock and set-asides on land, exports are being reduced, so that the EU would not be accused of dumping practices. However, this completely neglects the welfare loss inflicted on others who would gain from exporting to the EU.

So far, we only considered stage I of the reform. We now briefly discuss the implications of the scenario outcomes for stage II, i.e. for privatization of the cartel. As mentioned earlier, privatization would mean that all FEOGA outlays have to be covered from direct contributions by the farmers themselves. The cartel scenario leaves about fourteen billion ecu to be paid from the central budget in 2005.[134] If this cost were fully shifted to the farmers their income would come out 15.0 per cent below the level in the MacSharry scenario. If only the export refunds and the producer subsidies are being charged, there is a fall by 11.1 per cent.

This percentage is, as such, not very dramatic provided the privatization is implemented in a gradual way, so that the outmigration and other adjustments can play their role. We have seen (Table 6.4) that while the real value added drops by 0.7 per cent annually under the MacSharry reform, per capita real value added rises at a rate of 1.9 per cent. Therefore, it seems that the sector would be able to absorb the shock, although more pronounced price increases would be required to avoid losses in the aggregate and, again, these price increases would harm the intensive livestock sector.

6.3 The CAP until 2005

6.3.1   A summary of alternatives

We shall now take stock of the main conclusions of this chapter but first, for ease of comparison, we very briefly summarize the main findings from the three alternatives that were treated in the previous chapter, namely, continuation of pre-MacSharry policies, the MacSharry scenario and the GATT agreement.

Continuation of pre-MacSharry policies

A continuation of the earlier policy would have resulted in a more balanced development of EU agriculture than was the case in the eighties and early nineties. It would not have led to extreme FEOGA outlays but the rise in

---

[134] This amount consists of 6.6 billion ecu export refunds, 3.7 billion ecu producer subsidies, 2.8 billion ecu input subsidies and 1.0 billion ecu for interest and storage costs.

subsidized exports, especially in cereals and bovine meat would have created increasing tensions with other exporters.

MacSharry scenario

The MacSharry scenario changes the trading pattern of the EU. Through its rebalancing of the prices of animal feeds it reduces cereal exports and through the quotas on the premia in the bovine sector, the meat surpluses to be dumped on the world market are less. The scenario leads to welfare gains for the consumer due to lower prices but this effect is mitigated by the increase in the budgetary expenditures and the efficiency loss caused by the set-asides of land.

The GATT agreement

The GATT agreement is to a great extent compatible with the MacSharry reform, with the qualification that, since it does not account for inflation, the tariffication will eventually become binding on the import side.

Decoupled MacSharry

The outcome from the decoupled MacSharry scenario seems promising. The main weak point is, however, that the payment of compensation to farmers over a period of twelve years may not be acceptable politically. In many member states the welfare payments are being reduced already and minimum wages are being relaxed. This will create strong political resistance against transfer payments to farmers. Also, it is questionable whether the international markets would be able to absorb the impressive increase in output of wheat and dairy that is due to abolishment of set-asides and to the relaxation of quotas. Even if they were, competing exporters might object. Moreover, environmental problems may call for supply controls.

Cartel

The cartel scenario reduces FEOGA outlays and it seems to have favourable effects on the environment. Though the income position of the European farmer improves on average, the intensive livestock sector suffers a loss due to increased feed costs. Also, to make the cartel fully self-financed, stronger price increases are needed and this sharpens even further the divergence of interests between cereal growers and cereal users.

6.3.2   An assessment

Besides the problem that it would be difficult to maintain cohesion within the cartel, we do not expect the CAP to shift in the interventionist direction for several other reasons.

First, the GATT Agreement, with all its qualifications, definitely points in a free trade direction, especially in the long run, when inflation will have led to the erosion of many of the protective barriers that are currently in place. This was discussed at some length in the previous chapter. The new constraints on imports of oilseeds and cereal substitutes and the rise in protection for cereals and animal products would meet serious resistance from the traditional exporters to the EU.

Secondly, as the farm population becomes an ever smaller part of the overall population in the EU, its capability of maintaining political support for a high price policy seems doubtful.

Thirdly, this political support also becomes less, as there is increasing awareness that farm households earn a significant part of their income outside agriculture and that in many countries the income distribution has turned significantly in favour of farmers (recall Table 2.18 in Chapter 2).

Fourthly, in many member states welfare payments are being reduced and minimum wages are made more flexible. Consequently, more people will find themselves in a situation where expenditures on food become a significant part of total income. These groups will resist any increase in food prices and will call for price liberalization since they are not being helped by high prices (i.e. minimum wages) themselves. Incidentally, this can also be expected to create a stronger political resistance to the decoupled payments to farmers.

Finally, the joining of member states from Central Europe, scheduled to occur in the beginning of the next century, would make it virtually impossible to maintain high and common internal prices in all countries. The consumers of these countries would be unable to afford these high prices unless wage rates would rise (in ecu terms) but this would threaten the competitiveness of the non-farm sector, while for the farmers the high prices would lead to a bonanza that cannot be justified politically.

6.4   Implementation: financial renationalization of the CAP

Although complete renationalization is not a serious option on any member state's current policy agenda, in many countries the financial consequences of the CAP do provide points of contention from time to time. Debates centre around the net contribution to the EU, with members wanting to receive at least as much as they pay. Therefore, it is of interest to investigate the consequences of a CAP whereby the principle of 'common financial responsibility' is replaced by a financial renationalization whereby every member state will bear its own financial costs incurred under an otherwise common agricultural policy.

Financial renationalization can be welfare improving, since it eliminates the problem of member states free-riding at the expense of the common budget: the governments no longer have an incentive to stimulate domestic production of commodities for which there is a surplus. It could also be argued that the 'solidarity' that is needed to maintain political support for lump sum transfers between farmers and non-farmers is easier to effectuate on a national level than on a Community level and that the development of a broader rural policy is also easier at national level. In the applications that we shall consider this renationalization does not by itself provide the appropriate price incentives to producers and consumers within the countries. They are still faced with high prices for agricultural products but since the previously implicit transfers from the foreign consumers are now outlays for the own national government, they become more visible and this may strengthen the political support for a free trade orientation.

Financial renationalization is more than a theoretical issue, it is to a certain extent a reality already. In 1988-1990 the member states provided on average around eight per cent of gross agricultural value added as national support to agriculture, and in Germany more than twenty per cent (Kjeldahl and Tracy (1994)). The principle is also perfectly in tune with the 'subsidiarity principle' of the Treaty of Maastricht, whereby all EU regulation should take place with a maximum degree of decentralization.[135] Of course, renationalization does not necessarily end with financial settlements. In Kjeldahl and Tracy (1994) various forms are discussed that go further. From the viewpoint of the Community and the Treaty of Maastricht, the main restriction on renationalization should be that the principle of market unity and fair competition between member states is to be safeguarded: there should be no impediments to trade and no member state should subsidize its farmers in a non-decoupled way. Although it may not be easy to monitor this, since the line between coupled and decoupled support is extremely fine, fair competition is a general principle that applies to all sectors alike and, over the years, the EU has gained considerable experience in effectively enforcing such a competition policy in other sectors. Financial renationalization is also the main suggestion in the report by the EU-expert group on CAP-reform (CEC(1994)), that used ECAM-calculations of the MacSharry and decoupled MacSharry scenarios (Keyzer et al. (1994)).

In the longer term, a certain degree of CAP renationalization seems inescapable. In the previous section we already mentioned that, when the Central European countries join, it will be impossible to maintain a cartel policy. It will also be difficult to pursue the lavish payment of direct compensations of a decoupled policy.[136] The list of problems that this would create is long. First, the present CAP would boost supply in these countries and distort factor allocations. The reform process has given a plot of land to a very large number of people and thus created many small farms. Under the conditions of the CAP,

---

[135] For a discussion of the origins of this concept, see Van Kersbergen and Verbeek (1994).

[136] The enlargement in 1995 with some of the EFTA countries does not pose serious problems: whereas, the FEOGA budget is predicted to rise by 4.4 billion ecu, the VAT contributions amount to about 6 billion ecu (Agra Europe, 18 february 1994, this calculation included Norway).

these undersized farms would nonetheless be able to attract all the equipment, fertilizer and fuel they want, at the expense of the other sectors in the economy. The high prices would also cause a 'bubble' in land prices, the adverse consequences of which are difficult to foresee. Secondly, the food prices would place a heavy burden on the relatively poor consumers who cannot be expected to tolerate farmers receiving compensation payments that bear no relation to the average income in the country. Thirdly, it would be difficult to explain the payment of 'compensations' to farmers who actually gain from joining the EU. Finally, under the MacSharry regime as it will prevail in 1996, an EU enlargement to the East would be rather costly in FEOGA terms. Even if one disregards all expansion in production it would, under conservative assumptions, lead to an increase of about nine billion ecu, which is around one fourth of the expected FEOGA outlays for the EU-12 in 1996,[137] and this for countries that will not contribute much to the budget revenue. Therefore, after the EU enlargement, support to the Central European members should be given via infrastructural investments, not via per hectare payments, and consumer prices should be lower than in the current CAP, which calls for a CAP that is differentiated by country.

We conclude that financial renationalization of the CAP is a serious, and, to some extent, unavoidable option.[138] This section will consider the effect of financial renationalization for the main scenarios of the three perspectives: MacSharry, the decoupled MacSharry and the cartel scenarios. Since the settlement of the accounts is assumed to affect only the government budget deficit and the balance of payments, without any feedback to the behaviour of the agents, the calculations can be performed 'ex post' on the basis of the model

---

[137] The amount is computed on the basis of the 1995 level of CAP support (the first year in which the MacSharry reform is in full effect) and 1993 production levels, as follows: Guarantee: 6.7 billion ecu consisting of cereals 2.8, oilseeds, 0.4, bovine meat 0.5, milk 0.9, ovine meat 0.1, other products 2 billion ecu; Structural funds: 1 billion ecu. This yields a total of 7.7 billion, which could rise up to 9 billion ecu due to change in product mix and output expansion. This calculation is, of course, conservative because it assumes only a modest expansion in output and because the outlays from the structural funds do not follow from any logic of the CAP itself. The experience in the German unification has taught, that, depending on the political circumstances, much higher amounts can also be envisaged.

[138] A precursor of ECAM was already used in 1987 to test this option, (see Folmer et al. (1987)).

outcomes that were reported on already, and only the budgetary consequences have to be considered here.

6.4.1   Implicit transfers

The issue of the 'fairness' of the rules for sharing the costs between member states has played a role in discussions on the CAP ever since its conception. This was perhaps most apparent during the early eighties when the United Kingdom wanted to renegotiate its budgetary contribution. In practice the discussion on costs and benefits is often narrowed down to the question, 'how much do we pay to Brussels and how much do we receive?'. The reason for such a narrow focus is rather obvious: transfers to and from Brussels are the most visible part of CAP costs and CAP benefits. Moreover, since the CAP has resulted in structural changes within the agricultural sectors of the member states, it is impossible to draw up a final full account of costs and benefits. However, it is misleading to restrict attention to explicit transfers because this disregards say, the implicit export subsidies which the German consumer of Dutch dairy products pay to The Netherlands via the CAP price-support. It is indeed possible to go one step further than just drawing up accounts for the net explicit transfers to Brussels. Implicit transfers between member countries can also be calculated.

For example, suppose that wheat is exported from France to Italy say, at the intervention price p^d, which is higher than the export price on the world market p^e. Then, if the export price p^e is equal to the import price p^m, the implicit subsidy per volume unit from an Italian consumer to the French farmer is equal to $(p^d - p^e)$.

If explicit and implicit transfers were fully settled, by which we mean that member states would pay the explicit and implicit subsidy bills of their farmers themselves and compensate foreign consumers for the implicit subsidies received from them, the budgetary side of the CAP would become renationalized. It would be as if the member states were only coordinating their policies, maintaining a common intervention price and common subsidy rates on production, allowing for free trade among themselves, with a joint financing of the buffer stocks, but without a common budget. Nothing would prevent member states from granting transfers to those who need them, as long as competitive conditions are being maintained.

The amounts for settlement can be very large, especially if internal prices are high relative to prices on the world market, individual member countries have diverging self-sufficiency ratios and direct payments to Brussels have no strong relationship with the size of the farm sector. Therefore, renationalization is possibly more relevant in an interventionist perspective than under free trade. Under free trade oriented policies, it would be practical to limit the financial renationalization to the compensation payments, since this avoids the cumbersome calculation of the implicit transfers, which are vanishing at any rate.

6.4.2   Financial consequences of renationalization

The calculation proceeds in three steps. In the first step, the EU border protection is expressed in terms of protection at the national level. The implicit levies on imports and refunds on exports between member states are calculated and added to the explicit ones. For this, we calculate the implicit net tariffs based on (unchanged) national clearing prices and world market prices. In the second step, the consequences of transferring EU subsidy payments on production, consumption and intermediate inputs to national governments are considered. Finally, in the third step, we compute the net financial effect by member state.

Since the price and subsidy levels remain unchanged, the net effect by member state is the sum of the renationalization effects on trade (step 1) and subsidies (step 2), corrected for changes in VAT (and GDP) contributions:

the net change in a national budget

=

implicit and explicit subsidy payment due to EU protection on trade

+

explicit (net) subsidy payment to farmers and consumers

+

net change in the VAT (and GDP) contribution

Tariff receipts and export refunds

Table 6.15 summarizes the results of a financial renationalization of the EU's trade policy for the year 2005. As noted above, protection on external trade has now been shifted to national borders. Levies on imports accrue to member states and, on the other hand, each country has to finance its own export refunds. The distinction between internal and external EU trade is no longer a useful one: all trade flows between member states are subject to levies and refunds. Of course, at EU-9 level the net tariff receipts on internal trade add up to zero. Therefore, the total in the table equals net tariff receipts of the EU before renationalization.[139]

As in all scenarios levies on imports exceed export refunds in 2005, net receipts are positive in all three cases. Due to both the sharp rise in the import levy on oilseeds and cereal substitutes as well as the relatively small export volume, the net receipts in the cartel scenario are by far the largest (10.1 billion ecu).

Table 6.15   Net tariff receipts under financial renationalization in 2005, mln ecu at 1992 prices

	Cartel	MacSharry	Decoupled MacSharry
Belgium-Luxembourg	1224	-55	87
Denmark	78	-228	-94
France	-5618	-1709	-1093
Germany, Fed. Rep.	3240	832	1039
Ireland	-770	-191	-135
Italy	5741	2167	1695
The Netherlands	843	-845	-372
United Kingdom	5400	1720	1591
EU-9	10138	1692	2719

As can be expected, the effects on member states differ widely. *Belgium-Luxembourg* would lose from a financial renationalization of trade support in the

---

[139] Levies and refunds on pork, poultry and eggs, and fish have not been taken into account.

MacSharry scenario but gain otherwise. The loss under the MacSharry scenario is mainly linked to refunds on the exports of sugar and bovine meat which now have to be paid by the national government. The positive outcome in the cartel scenario is the result of large levies on the imports of oilseeds and cereal substitutes.

Budgetary changes are modest for *Denmark*. This country is a small exporter of most of the agricultural commodities. For cereals, however, the trade flow will reverse in all scenarios towards the end of the century. In the cartel scenario, grain imports will rise to 2.5 million tons in 2005 and, as in this scenario cereals prices are relatively high, the resulting levy on imports is sufficient to generate a small gain on trade. Export refunds per volume unit are substantially lower under both the MacSharry and the decoupled MacSharry scenarios but as the same holds with respect to import tariffs, a larger net export will result in a budgetary loss.

France and *Ireland* will always lose from a financial renationalization of CAP-support through trade. This seems reasonable as they are both large net exporters of agricultural commodities. Although net export volumes under the cartel scenario are lower than in the other scenarios, the net loss in this case is largest. The decline in export volumes is insufficient to compensate the budgetary effect of the rise in refunds per unit.

The consequences for the large agricultural importers *West Germany, Italy* and the *United Kingdom* are just the opposite of those for France and Ireland. Import levies will generate substantial receipts, notably in the cartel regime, where prices are high and domestic supply is relatively small.

Finally, it depends on the scenario whether *The Netherlands* gain or lose. In the second and third variant, simulation outcomes are dominated by the net export position, mainly for sugar, dairy and meat. In the cartel scenario the large receipts from import levies on cereal substitutes and oilseeds more than compensate the rise in export refunds. On balance, there will be an increase in net receipts of 800 million ecu.

Subsidies and income transfers

The second step in our calculation shifts the income transfers and the subsidies on production, inputs and consumption from the EU budget to national governments.[140] Results by member state are shown in Table 6.16. Here also the differences between scenarios and countries are striking. The total shift in financial burden is smallest in the cartel scenario (about 6.5 billion ecu). This is in line with expectations, as the conversion from explicit subsidies into implicit subsidies through higher consumer prices is one of the main elements of the cartel policy. In the decoupled MacSharry scenario subsidies on production, consumption and inputs vanish almost. Hence, the payments in the fourth column of the table only relate to income compensations, to be paid by the national governments.

Table 6.16   Subsidies[a] paid by national governments under financial renationalization in 2005, mln ecu at 1992 prices

	Cartel	MacSharry	Decoupled MacSharry[b]
Belgium-Luxembourg	25	362	651
Denmark	137	762	287
France	1336	6501	4017
Germany, Fed. Rep.	319	2111	1859
Ireland	351	631	424
Italy	2812	3987	2679
The Netherlands	453	594	190
United Kingdom	1122	2605	1890
EU-9	6554	17553	11996

Notes:
a) Subsidies on production, consumption and inputs, net of sugar and input levies.
b) Direct income transfers included in the decoupled MacSharry scenario.

The size of the losses incurred by *France* under the MacSharry and decoupled scenarios is remarkable, but not surprising. In both scenarios the national government would need to pay large amounts to producers in the crop sector, whereas under cartelization these payments would be made by means of export refunds (see Table 6.16). The result for *Italy* in the cartel run also stands

---

[140] Levies on sugar and input use have been subtracted.

out. As this country would receive the largest amount of producer subsidies, budgetary consequences of renationalization are also substantial. *Belgium-Luxembourg* would hardly lose under the cartel arrangement, mainly because ewe premiums are so low in this scenario.

6.4.3   Overall consequences

We assume that after financial renationalization, the VAT (and GDP) contributions are as before distributed according the prevailing shares (i.e. more or less in proportion to the national GDP).[141] The figures listed in Table 6.17 were computed according to this procedure: the total amounts from Tables 6.15 and 6.16 were added and the VAT (and GDP) contributions subtracted. Since the CAP itself is left unchanged the net losses necessarily add up to zero.

Table 6.17   Net gains under financial renationalization in 2005, mln ecu at 1992 prices

	Cartel	MacSharry	Decoupled
Belgium-Luxembourg	1071	157	-229
Denmark	-146	-607	-156
France	-7783	-4558	-2975
Germany, Fed. Rep.	1922	3146	1767
Ireland	-1148	-706	-491
Italy	2360	709	498
The Netherlands	186	-532	-31
United Kingdom	3539	2391	1616
EU-9	0	0	0

Note: The calculation accounts for changes in national VAT transfers to the EU.

The results suggest a classification of member states into three groups: countries which always gain from a renationalization, countries that always lose and countries that lose or gain depending on the scenario.

The winners are *West Germany*, *Italy* and the *United Kingdom*, the net importers of typical CAP commodities. Since the EU prices lie above the world market level, tariff receipts are positive for these countries. As to Italy and the

---

[141] Compare the stylized model outlined in Section 3.1.1 where the EU budget equation (3.4.f) also balances through adjustment of the tax rate τ (defined in 3.4.e).

United Kingdom, the total gains increase from decoupled to MacSharry and from MacSharry to cartel: the higher the internal prices, the higher the gain. Germany also gains from renationalization but its gains are lowest under the cartel scenario. This is because Germany has a relatively high share in VAT contributions to the EU budget and FEOGA expenditures are lower under the cartel scenario.

Countries in the second group will always lose. The agricultural net exporters *Denmark, France* and *Ireland* lose the benefit of cost sharing of export refunds. The total losses for Ireland and France increase when the scenario is more interventionist. In Denmark, however, a renationalization has hardly any net budgetary effect in the cartel scenario. This is because the increase in export subsidies on livestock products balances against the rise in import levies on cereals.

Belgium-Luxembourg and *The Netherlands* belong to the third category. One would expect that a small net importer like Belgium-Luxembourg always benefits from renationalization. However, it incurs a small loss under decoupling. This is due to the relatively high income compensations that have to be paid from the national budget and to the small gains on tariffs. Since The Netherlands is a net exporter of sugar and animal products, one may have expected a net loss under the cartel scenario. The net gain results from the high levies on imported cereals and cereal substitutes.

Finally, although Table 6.17 gives an indication of the net gains of member states under the CAP, one should keep in mind that all computations refer to a static situation. In practice it will be hard to leave the CAP unchanged after financial renationalization. Countries would tend to make their own arrangements. Yet, one could argue that this is precisely how it should be in a European economic union. While it is a task of the European Commission to ensure that intra-union trade is free from tariff and non-tariff barriers and that there is fair competition between member states, this does not mean that national governments should abstain from pursuing a redistributive policy of their own, nor that they should withdraw from targeted programs like agricultural research, environmental conservation or rural development.

6.4.4   The need for financial renationalization

As was explained in Chapter 2, agriculture was one of the first sectors into which the EU had an active involvement. After more than thirty years the national authorities are now used to the fact that all major decisions on agricultural policy are made in Brussels by a lengthy process of negotiation. This setup has served the agricultural interest groups well because it has met their claim that agriculture needs special treatment. Even those who felt that agriculture is an economic activity like any other had to concede that the sector was different because of the decision process in Brussels. No national government or parliament was in a position to make its own decisions on agriculture and the complexity of the regulations made it impossible for the public at large to understand the details. Moreover, the CAP made a large part of the transfers to agriculture implicit through its price policy. Due to the importance of the food processing sector in the EU the consumer has little idea of the size of the implicit transfer within the country, let alone between member states. Hence, the CAP has successfully created a bureaucratic apparatus that disguises and protects the subsidization of agriculture. It is doubtful whether such a system could have survived for so long had the policies been organized in the renationalized way.

Our calculations show that the implicit transfers are quite large and because they are unevenly spread over member states, abolishing them would eliminate the incentives of net exporting countries to free ride on the budget of net importers. Hence, the financial renationalization would probably promote political support for trade liberalization. It would also facilitate the monitoring as well as the administration of the CAP-implementation. For example, the new measures (set-asides, quotas, compensation payments) that were instituted by the MacSharry reform are to a large extent to be monitored and administered at the national level. It would be natural to conceive of these as part of regionalized rural development programmes which could be supplemented with payments from the EU's structural fund as well as from national sources. The logic of such a decentralization is even more clear after decoupling (when a compensation payment is given to agriculture).

6.5 The CAP in the long term

Any discussion of alternatives is academic to some extent. The EU did adopt the MacSharry reform (with some amendments made after the subsequent GATT agreement). Legislation is in place for many years to come and, as has been the case in recent years, it will take substantial time to reach consensus on a revision. Moreover, farmers want clear signals. A perpetual reassessment of current policies creates uncertainty and a poor climate for investment.

Nonetheless, policies will have to adapt eventually. When the Central European countries join, some form of CAP renationalization will become a necessity. Therefore, it may be interesting to extend the horizon of investigation and inquire what may happen after 2005. This is the subject of the next chapter, where we develop a long term scenario until 2020. This scenario will be characterized by an evolution of the CAP towards more free trade but without the compensation payments of the MacSharry policy.

Chapter 7

EU agriculture in the long term:
a future as an exporter?

Since the MacSharry reform and the GATT agreement contain commitments for many years to come, the main outlines of the policies for the late nineties are already drawn. Further CAP reform is now a matter for the medium and the long term. Chapter 6 led us to conclude that such reform would probably be in the direction of more liberalization, probably with a renationalization on the financial side. This is the type of long term scenario to be analyzed in the present chapter.

7.1 Background for a long term scenario

If one conclusion were to be drawn from the analysis in Chapter 5, then it should be that both the budget and the international trade problems of EU agriculture are manageable in the medium term. This conclusion was reinforced in Chapter 6, where it was shown that, also under quite different policy regimes, the trade, budget and income problems did not really get out of control. So the worries of the late eighties and early nineties about exploding budgets, dramatically decreasing farm incomes and negative consequences of integrating EU agricultural policies in the GATT, seem to have been exaggerated. With hindsight this finding should not be surprising as it was already evident in the trends of the 'fundamentals'. The continuous outflow of labour implies that every year fewer farmers experience income problems. The annual increase in agricultural productivity creates room for a gradual decrease in real product prices without posing a threat to farm incomes. As discussed in sections 2.2.2 and 5.1.1, it is difficult to gain political support for such price cuts in periods with low inflation, when they require reductions in nominal prices but in the

ECAM scenarios the assumed rate of inflation was sufficient to allow for real price reductions and nominal price increases. Moreover, since the MacSharry regime (or a decoupled variant thereof) has internal prices of most products steadily moving towards the world market level, and volume growth of other products is constrained by quota regulations, there will be increasingly less reason to accuse the EU of dumping.

Thus, the prospects outlined by ECAM seem to be moderately positive. Yet even the reform in the free trade scenario was so gradual that it did not require EU agriculture to maintain itself without protection and income support. On the other hand, the scenario outcomes also suggest that the long term future of EU agriculture may be even less problematic. If the relative price trends of the MacSharry scenario and its decoupled variant continue, internal EU prices will eventually reach the world market level. If, at the same time, the rising trends in yields and productivity continue, the growth in production will certainly exceed the growth in consumption. Consequently, EU exports will expand but they will be sold without subsidy. The agricultural sector of the EU will have been transformed into a competitive producer of cheap, unsubsidized food. Rather than being an economic burden to the European taxpayer, the agricultural production capacity of the Community will have become a valuable economic asset.

Such a scenario rests on the four following assumptions. It presupposes that, due to international supply and demand trends, real world market prices will only decrease moderately, if at all. It also assumes that the agronomic and technological potential of EU agriculture is sufficient to allow for a continuation of productivity trends and production growth. At the same time, farms in the EU will restructure sufficiently to develop into efficient economic enterprises, so that agronomic and technological potentials can be exploited. Finally, it presupposes that food demand by EU consumers will hardly increase. Below we shall try to justify such assumptions and base a long term scenario on them, which starts in 2005 at the end of the MacSharry scenario and runs until 2020.

However attractive such a scenario may be, it is certainly not the only avenue along which EU agriculture may develop. In addition to being competitive with other agricultural sectors throughout the world, EU agriculture must also compete internally for production factors that can also be used outside agriculture and in this respect we see two potential threats for the sector.

The first is the increased demand for land for non-agricultural use. A continuous relative decrease in agricultural prices would go hand in hand with ever lower land prices. Consequently, it would become increasingly profitable for non-agriculture to develop land-intensive activities such as recreation, forestry, nature and urbanization. Needless to say, such a development would cause a reduction in agricultural production but the income of the farm household need not suffer, because its members may find employment on the same land as before, in new activities.

The second threat concerns agriculture's lack of attractiveness as a way of life. It has already been evident for many years that EU farmers are ageing and that the countryside is becoming depopulated. This process may be amplified in the future, due to demographic factors, rather than income differentials, since thirty per cent of the farmers are above the age of 55 (see Folmer (1993)). It is conceivable that in the long run, there will not be enough farmers to exploit the potential competitive advantage of EU agriculture (see also Frohberg (1994)). This would happen if a career as farmer was considered so unattractive in itself that only a high labour income could induce a farmer's child to succeed his parents, so that successors would decide to use the land for other purposes, like real estate development or tourism.

The chapter is organized as follows. In Sections 7.2-7.4 we develop a long term view that serves as the basis for the long term scenario that is presented in Section 7.5. In Section 7.6 we consider an alternative scenario which assumes that land availability drops at a faster rate. Section 7.7 concludes. At this point a word of caution is in order. ECAM was built for medium term analysis, not for the long term. Its long term dynamics are not well developed and it does not generate intertemporally efficient or even time-consistent paths of resource accumulation. Moreover, the fifteen to twenty years of data that were available to calibrate the model, hardly allow for such long term explorations and, more generally, the type of variables in the data base is too restricted for long run forecasting, although this shortcoming can be cured to some extent by complementing the data used so far with agronomic information and long term assessments from other studies. Yet in view of the limitations, we shall, in the sections that deal with scenario simulations, restrict ourselves to a general and aggregate interpretation of the results.

7.2 Long term prospects for world food supply and demand

What we have called potential threats to EU agriculture are more like innocuous tendencies in the face of the problems that the world food supply will have to address in the coming decades. A world population that is expected to rise from 5 billion in the early nineties to 8.3 billion in 2025, limited perspectives for land reclamation and a slowing down of the rate of growth in crop yields, seem to indicate that the current surpluses on the world food markets will soon disappear. Of course, food shortages do not by themselves imply a shortage on the food market. While per caput food supplies are now eighteen per cent above their level thirty years ago, a large number of people have been bypassed, particularly in Sub-Saharan Africa. FAO (1993) estimates that in the early nineties over 800 million people were still undernourished, mainly due to lack of purchasing power.

An assessment of the long term future of EU agriculture must take this into account and start from the supply and demand prospects for the world at large. Will food be scarce due to overpopulation and resource constraints or will the international market conditions of last decades persist in which international food surpluses and lack of purchasing power coexist?

A rapidly increasing global demand for food

According to Table 7.1 which presents the so-called medium variant of the UN population projections, the world population will increase by about 1.6 per cent annually in the period 1990-2020. Over this period, the world population will increase by almost 100 million people annually, of which 94 million will live in what is commonly referred to as the developing world. In absolute terms, such an increase over such a long period is unprecedented in the history of mankind. Clearly, such a projection can only materialize if there is sufficient

Table 7.1   Population by region, million people

	1990	2025	Annual growth rate 1990-2025
Industrial countries	1207	1345	0.5
EU-12	327	350	0.2
East Europe and CIS	413	454	0.4
Other industrial countries	467	541	0.4
Developing countries	4076	6958	1.9
China	1139	1609	1.3
Other Asia and North Africa	1969	3372	2.0
Sub-Saharan Africa	526	1246	2.7
Latin America	442	731	1.8
World	5283	8303	1.6

Source: World Bank (1992b) and UNDP (1992).

food.

Actual food demand is expected to grow at very different rates in the various parts of the world. In very poor countries total demand may stagnate and per capita demand may fall as population increases, due to supply constraints. In moderately poor countries, the rate of increase of population is the main determinant. In fast growing developing countries the demand for staple foods barely follows the growth in population and may even fall, but the demand for meat and hence the demand for animal feeds is booming (since three to ten kg of feed grains are needed to produce one kg of meat). Finally, in developed countries food demand is almost stagnant due to low population growth, ageing of the population and satiated consumer needs. Table 7.2 shows the demand prospects by, among others, the FAO, which are based on World Bank assumptions of an annual growth in per capita income of 2.1 per cent in the developed countries and 3.4 per cent in the developing world (World Bank (1993)).

The combined effects of population growth and per capita income growth result in an increase in total food demand of about 1.8 per cent annually. For the full 1992-2020 period this implies that global food demand will increase by nearly 65 per cent. As can be seen from Table 7.2, there are significant differences between commodities: in developing countries, demand for cereals

Table 7.2   Prospects for agriculture as found in the literature, annual growth rate

Source:	FAO(1993)	Crosson and Anderson (1992)		Alexandratos (1990)	
Region:	92 Developing countries	Developing countries		EU-12	
Period:	1990-2010	1985-2005	2005-2030	1970-1985	1985-2000
Demand					
all cereals	2.2	2.5	2.3	-0.4	-0.4[a]
wheat	-	3.0	2.3	-	-
coarse grains	-	2.2	3.2	-	-
rice	-	2.4	1.3	-	-
meat	3.9	-	-	1.3	0.4
tropical beverages	2.7	-	-	0.1	0.3
Agricultural land	0.6	0.6	0.6	-0.3	-
Yields					
wheat	1.6	2.3	1.5	3.9[c]	1.9
maize	1.5	2.0	2.0	3.9	1.7
other coarse grains	1.2	≤1.0	≤1.0[b]	3.3	1.3[d]
rice	1.5	2.4	1.3	-	-
cattle	1.1	-	-	-	-
sheep and goats	1.3	-	-	-	-
pigs	1.0	-	-	-	-
poultry	1.5	-	-	-	-

Notes: (a) including root crops
         (b) mainly barley
         (c) yield data for EU-8 (Italy has been excluded)
         (d) sorghum, millet.

follows more or less population growth but meat demand follows and even exceeds income growth. In absolute terms, the increase in food demand due to population growth will be greatest on the Asian and African continents. The increase in demand due to per capita income growth will probably be greatest in East and Southeast Asia and to a lesser extent, in South America also (Table 7.1). Of course, such estimates are very crude. Over these long time periods outcomes are very sensitive to small changes in the assumptions. In particular, small changes in growth assumptions concerning large and densely populated countries can have major effects on estimates of the direction and magnitude of food trade.

Constraints on food production

An increase in global demand does not automatically entail an increase in demand for EU agricultural products. In practice, most food is produced in the country where it is consumed. Figure 7.1 shows that this is even the case for non-perishable products such as wheat or refined sugar. Moreover, international trade is to a large extent intra-regional. The EU is illustrative in this respect: in the early nineties the EU countries sold over 75 per cent of their food and agricultural exports to other EU members or to EFTA countries.

Figure 7.1 World trade in 1992 as a share of total production, percentage

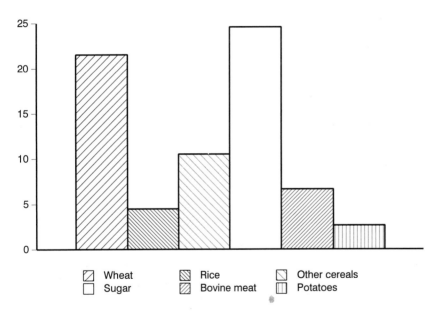

Source: FAO (1993), *Trade Yearbook* and *Production Yearbook.*

The high rates of regional food self-sufficiency throughout the world can be attributed to a number of factors. In many developing countries the dependence of a majority of the population on agriculture plays a dominant role. Government policies, high transportation costs, the costs and problems involved in food preservation, regional taste differences, etc. also provide elements for an explanation. Most of these 'natural' trade barriers are not expected to lose their relevance in the foreseeable future, irrespective whether and at what speed international trade in agricultural products becomes liberalized. This suggests that a permanently higher food demand can only be sustained through a structural increase in domestic food production.

Of course, this does not mean that international trade will stagnate. If trade liberalization continues in the direction set by the Uruguay Round agreement, many new opportunities for exports may arise not only because markets are being opened up but also because new demand will arise due to the increased prosperity and to further specialization. The opportunities for food exports by the EU will improve significantly in the future if several regions in the world face supply constraints. Since this aspect is rarely taken into account in the policy debates on the future of the CAP it deserves some further comment.

World food production has risen at the rate of 2.1 per cent over the period 1973-92. In Asia food production grew even faster and, although in Africa per capita food supplies have fallen during this period, even here total food supply grew significantly, despite the huge economic and political problems which this continent had to cope with.

For the world as a whole, but for Asia in particular, events of the past decades concerning food production growth can only be described as unprecedented in history. Yet, if our demand projections are accepted and if self-sufficiency ratios are to be maintained, production should in the coming decades increase at rates that are not much lower than in the recent past and this raises questions as to the feasibility of such a development.

The underlying factors behind the high production growth rates in the developing countries operated mainly through improved yields per hectare. About a quarter of the overall increase is attributable to an expansion of the agricultural land base and increase in cropping intensity (see FAO (1993, Table 4.2)). A rise in hectare yields was possible due to the application of new technologies. High-yielding varieties, combined with fertilizer, pesticides and irrigation, have played a crucial role in this process, not only by improving the output per harvest but also by making growing periods of crops and the fallow periods shorter and by allowing multiple cropping.

Figures 7.2a

Index of food production

1972/74=100

Figure 7.2b

Index of food production per capita

1972/74=100

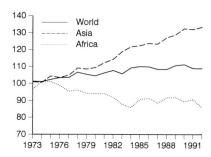

Source: FAO (1993), *Production Yearbook.*

Even in the most densely populated areas where yields are already high, the agronomic possibilities of increasing production beyond current levels have certainly not been exhausted (see Smil (1994) and for a calculation of potentials, see Linnemann et al. (1979)). Moreover, there is still much scope for a reduction in losses both on the fields and along the processing chain from producer to consumer (see Dowler and Seo (1985) and Bender (1994)), for improving technology, say, of irrigation systems (see van Tuijl (1993) and Critchley (1991)), and in developed countries large areas are lying idle under set-aside arrangements. With respect to primary production, FAO (1993) expects on the basis of an analysis of production possibilities, that, for crop production, an average annual growth rate of 2.4 per cent can be realized in developing countries, much less than the 3.3 per cent recorded over the past twenty years. Of this growth 1.5 per cent would originate from yield increase, 0.6 per cent from expansion in the land base and 0.3 per cent from increase in the cropping intensity. Nonetheless, for a number of reasons it will not be easy to achieve this 2.4 per cent growth rate.

(i)   Ecologists and agronomists (see e.g. Stiles and Brennan (1986), Brown (1989), Brown and Young (1990), Crosson and Anderson (1992), Pinstrup-Andersen (1994)) increasingly doubt the long term sustainability of a large share of currently available production capacity. Erosion, salinity and other forms of land degradation are manifesting themselves on an increasingly large scale. A significant part of the existing agricultural land base can only be maintained through large investments and adjustment of agronomic practices. The negative effects of unsustainable production practices are already being felt in a number of regions; undoubtedly these problems will become more acute in the future.

(ii) The contribution of land reclamation to production growth will diminish in the years to come, because the opportunities for reclaiming new lands have almost been exhausted and because the lands that are available are of a lesser quality (see Crook (1988), USDA (1989) and FAO (1993)).

(iii) Irrigation has made a significant contribution to the growth of food production since the mid-sixties. In many areas double cropping and high-yielding varieties would not have been possible without irrigation. The scope for further increases in irrigated areas is much less now compared to twenty or thirty years ago. Lack of water is one reason. But even in countries where water availability is less of a constraint, problems arise because the construction of new waterworks is more expensive since in many cases the cheapest investments were made first. Another financial constraint arises because maintenance costs of existing irrigation works claim a growing share of government budgets (see Markish and Gray (1989), Postel (1990), USDA (1990), Yunlong (1990) and FAO (1993)).

(iv) Urbanization and industrialization usually compete for the same land as agriculture. Cities and industry tend to develop in areas where the population density is already high and these are often fertile plains. This means that claims for land for non-agricultural use often concern the soils that are best suited for agricultural production. These claims will probably rise significantly in the coming decades not only because of growth in population but also because the share of the age cohort between eighteen and sixty years, which requires more room for living than children or elderly people, will also rise. Moreover, industrialization will also be demanding more land in the near future (see Brown (1989), Crosson and Rosenberg (1989), Yunlong (1990) and Stolwijk (1991)).

(v) Unlike 25 years ago, there are presently no new yield-increasing technologies which can be applied on a large scale. Developments within biotechnology will probably, for some time to come, have a relatively minor effect on the growth of world food production (see Crosson and Rosenberg (1989) and Ruttan (1991)).

(vi) High-yielding production systems require such inputs as fertilizer and power say, for pumping irrigation water. The price of these inputs depends heavily on the price of energy. In the second half of the eighties and the early nineties energy prices were relatively low. Price projections point to substantial real increases as from the beginning of the next century (see for example CPB (1992) and World Bank (1993)). This will make it less profitable to cultivate high-yielding varieties.

(vii) Finally, should the consequences of 'global warming' become tangible, they will probably not have a positive effect on agricultural production in most developing countries (see IPCC (1990), Rosenzweig et al. (1992)). In any case, since the water systems of many agricultural areas will be affected by a rise in temperature, agriculture will have to deal with higher adjustment costs (see Postel (1990), Parry et al. (1988), Melillo et al. (1993)).

Consequences for EU policies

Although the EU will also face many of the problems that the developing countries will have to address, it has entered the nineties with the containment of its surpluses as its main problem. The MacSharry reform lays significant surfaces of arable land idle and the environmental policies seek to limit application of current inputs and growth in yields.

Hence, the scarcity of food in the world does not figure high on the EU's policy agenda. Any reference to possible scarcity of food in the future has in fact become somewhat suspect, because it has served too often as a phrase in the farm lobby's rhetoric to protect EU agriculture. Moreover, it is by now widely accepted that an increase in food production by the EU does not contribute much to the reduction of world hunger, basically because the poor do not have sufficient income to buy this food and because the drop in food prices caused by the increase in EU surpluses would hurt farmers in the developing world. EU surpluses are mainly useful as food aid in emergency situations and may possibly act as a stimulus for industrialization in the developing world, because they keep the prices of wage goods low. It is not a solution to the hunger problem. Nonetheless, the trends in world food supplies that were sketched in this section have, if they materialize, important implications for the course that the CAP should take.

One conclusion is that world prices will fall less in the period between 2005 and 2020 than they did in the past two decades. There may be an opportunity then for the EU to sell on the world market at reasonable prices. Whether European farmers will be able to make use of this opportunity will depend on their capability to produce at these prices.

Another conclusion is that, even if the EU does not intend to be a major food exporter, it should not rely on the world market to satisfy its food needs under every emergency (like war, droughts, nuclear and other environmental catastrophes in any part of the world). While the EU may be sufficiently rich and powerful to procure the food it would require for itself under such circumstances, this would shift the burden of adjustment to others and could lead to famine in poorer countries. The EU should preserve at least its capacity to produce food, even when it chooses temporarily to allocate its arable land to other uses. Unless specific restrictions are imposed, it will hardly be possible to ever reconvert agricultural land back to food production once it has had a non-agricultural use. 'Asphalt is the land's last crop', as they say. Therefore, the safeguarding of the productive capacity of land should become a major preoccupation of European agricultural policy in the future.

We shall return to these two points when we specify our scenarios (Sections 7.5 and 7.6) but for now we narrow our focus to a discussion of the EU's capability to produce more at lower prices: its agronomic potential (Section 7.3) and its international competitiveness (Section 7.4).

7.3 The agronomic and technological ceilings for EU agriculture

Technological change has undoubtedly been a major driving force behind past changes in EU agriculture. The main indicators for this progress are the steady increase in yields per hectare and per animal, the decrease in input per production unit and the rise in labour productivity. In ECAM, these developments are exogenous for yields and largely endogenous for labour productivity. Over the full 1993-2005 period, wheat yields per harvested hectare rise by seventeen per cent in the MacSharry scenario, or 1040 kg per hectare, milk production per cow increases by eighteen per cent and labour productivity is projected to improve by thirty per cent.[142]

In the short to medium term, the scope for productivity improvement depends on the adoption by farmers of already available technology. This type of technological progress may be predicted from data on the difference between best practices and data on adoption behaviour. However, over the longer term inventions and biological as well as physical limits dominate; yields and input efficiency rates cannot rise indefinitely. Since actual yields and input efficiency in (parts of) the EU are already quite high, and ECAM projects them to be much higher in the year 2005, the possibility cannot be ruled out that some of these ceilings will be hit before 2020, the final year of our long term scenario. Should the growth in yields and improvements in input efficiency rates come to a gradual halt during the initial decades of the next century, then this could have consequences for the dynamics of EU agriculture, and consequently, for the potential role EU agriculture might play in the international agricultural market. Therefore, a meaningful long term scenario requires the model assumptions on technological progress, relative to the agronomic and technical potential of EU agriculture to be reconsidered.

Potential for yield improvement

---

[142] Recall from Section 5.1 that the MacSharry scenario introduces an extensification effect that results in a downward shift in yields per hectare and per animal.

The yield projections that we shall assume in the long run scenario will be based on extrapolations from past rates that are adjusted to account for agronomic ceilings. For crops we start from an assessment of yield potentials by De Koning and Van Diepen (1992), which is based on a land evaluation procedure for grass, cereals, oilseeds, potatoes and sugar beets. For soils classified as suitable, potential yields are estimated using a crop growth simulation model. Potential yields are determined according to crop properties, solar radiation and temperature.

For the majority of crops, the yields in the MacSharry scenario for 2005 come nowhere near these agronomic potentials. Thus, from an agronomic point of view, there is considerable room for further yield increases per hectare. It should be noted that the study by De Koning and Van Diepen refers to a limited number of crops only.

Figure 7.3 Yields of selected crops in four member states, potential yield = 100

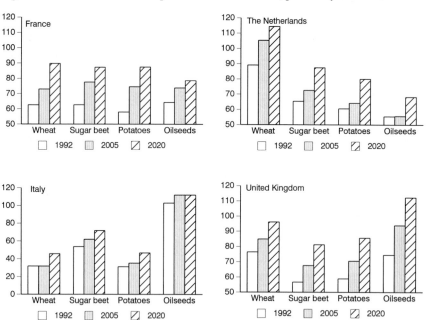

Source: De Koning and van Diepen (1992) and ECAM results.

As all ECAM crops are by and large in the same 'technological trajectory', we have extrapolated the selected findings to all of the crops distinguished in ECAM.

Figure 7.3 compares actual, projected and potential yields for wheat, sugar beet, oilseeds and potatoes. In most countries there is a large scope for increasing hectare yields after 2005.[143] The difference between actual and potential yields is largest in Italy and Ireland.

It seems reasonable to assume that in the long run, there will be some convergence in relative yields among countries. In terms of the scenario this means that growth rates of hectare yields should be adjusted slightly upwards in countries were yields are relatively low, and downwards in countries where yields are already close to agronomic potentials.

For livestock, a similarly comprehensive study of the potential yields was not available to us. This did not pose a serious problem, however, for two reasons. First, there is no clear absolute ceiling to the total number of livestock that can be kept in the EU, and consequently there is no agronomic upper limit to total livestock production. Secondly, since the average yields per animal that are projected for 2005 remain well below the actual yields already realized on high yielding dairy farms in The Netherlands (LEI-DLO (1993)), there is in 2005 considerable scope for further productivity increase.

Figure 7.4 illustrates this for milk yield per dairy cow. In 2005 average annual milk yield varies between 4598 kg in Italy and 7279 kg in Denmark. The figure shows that even in Denmark there still is a significant gap between yields attained on high-yielding farms and those in the MacSharry scenario. This means that a further yield increase per cow in the years following 2005 can be expected. It can also reasonably be assumed that average yields within the EU

---

[143] Relative wheat yield in Italy appears very low, because of the large share of (low-yielding) durum wheat in Italy's total wheat production. On the other hand, oilseed and wheat production in Italy and The Netherlands, respectively, have already surpassed their yield potentials by 2005. With respect to oilseeds in Italy, this implausibility must be attributed to the fact that rapeseed (used in the study by De Koning and Van Diepen) is not a good 'proxy' for oilseeds in Italy. With regard to the figure for wheat production in The Netherlands, it should be noted that even by 1992, actual production per hectare on some farms in The Netherlands had already surpassed the theoretical potential.

will eventually converge, since it is possible to transfer technologies in the livestock sector to all member states.

Figure 7.4   Yield in high-yielding dairy farms in The Netherlands (1993) and yields per cow in 2005

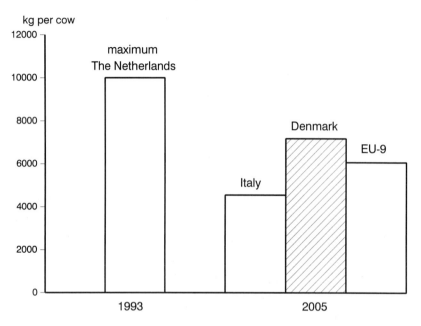

Source: ECAM resuls and LEI-DLO (1993).

Efficiency of input use

In financial terms, animal feed is the main category of intermediate inputs in EU agriculture. Feed input efficiency (expressed as kg of meat per kg of feed) has improved in the past, at the rate of around 1.5 per cent annually. It seems unlikely that such a rate can be maintained in the longer term, because of limitations in animal physiology (see e.g. Scheele and Frankenhuis (1989) and Luiting (1991)). At high yield levels, livestock has to function within very narrow limits and its adaptive capacity to variations in external circumstances is greatly reduced. Hence, there is a greater risk of metabolic disorders and premature mortality (see Dijkstra and Makkink (1993) and Vos (1993)). In the MacSharry scenario, feed conversion rates increase by 0.1 to 1.3 per cent per year. Although conversion rates in 2005 still remain well below the levels attained at experimental stations during the early nineties, the long run scenario assumes these trends to continue. For pigs and poultry this implies a reduction by 50-60 per cent compared to the 1982-level.

An overall assessment

Linear programming calculations in WRR (1992), that evaluate the potential for crop production and (input) efficiency improvement within EU agriculture, come to the conclusion that EU agriculture can achieve considerably higher yields with lesser use of fertilizer, pesticides and labour. Input use per hectare can be reduced to a fraction of current usage (down to thirty and even to twenty per cent). Since the 'best technical means' on which the study is based are theoretically available (certainly in the longer run) to all farmers in the EU, the study concludes that EU agriculture can eventually expect a structural and significant increase of input efficiency. This suggests that the agronomic and technological potential of EU agriculture allows for a continuation, or even an intensification, of productivity trends and production growth for quite a number of years. Only with respect to the further improvement of feed conversion rates a gradual slowdown should be foreseen. Hence, given the opportunities for EU exports that were described in the previous section, there appear to be no serious agronomic or technological constraints preventing EU agriculture from playing a more substantive economic role in the international food market in the long term.

7.4 Restructuring of the farm sector

Whether the growing demand for food on the world market and the large technological potentials will actually transform the EU into a competitive exporter, will also depend on the adjustments within the agricultural sector. At present only few farms within the EU would be able to compete at international prices. In this section we want to describe in some detail the type of restructuring that the sector would undergo after a gradual fall in prices and when land-tied compensation payments are no longer given.

In the short run and in the absence of major policy changes, the farm structure is relatively rigid. Purchases and sales of land are rare, most farmers continue their operations until retirement and many of them find a successor who continues the same enterprise. In the medium term downward price trends may play a role in the restructuring of the agricultural sector, although in the MacSharry reform the effect of price reductions will be cushioned by compensating payments. In the longer term these payments will be terminated. Then, many farms will be unable to survive and the size distribution of farms will adjust. This has to be taken into account in this chapter when we explore possible long run tendencies in the structure of EU agriculture.

A sector model like ECAM suffers from the limitation that it does not represent the size distribution explicitly. As the changes in this distribution are slow, this shortcoming may not have too serious consequences for short and medium term investigations. On the other hand, analyses with a time horizon of more than, say fifteen years, have so many limitations in any case, that introduction of scenario assumptions that reflect expectations on structural developments may in fact lead to more reliable conclusions than an endogenous representation of a size distribution of farms. In this section we review empirical evidence and theoretical considerations that will guide the design of such a scenario.

Average cost falling with farm size

In a study at the farm level, Upton and Haworth (1987) report, for a sample of farms in the United Kingdom, that growth rates of individual farms are independent of the size of the farm but strongly and positively associated with measures of managerial ability and family size, and negatively with off-farm income. This suggests that short term constraints keep the farm-size distribution away from its optimal level, as confirmed by Zachariasse (1990) who studies the relation between unit costs and farm size for several farm types in the

Netherlands. The author concludes that many farms operate at a level where unit costs are falling with scale, so that they operate at a scale that is inefficient. The empirical literature also indicates that the unit costs vary greatly between the regions within a country. It also illustrates how much the capacity of coping with price reductions differs among farms. Econometric studies of cost functions often reach similar conclusions (see e.g. Fernandez-Cornejo et al. (1992) for the German dairy sector and Perrigne and Simioni (1993) for the French cereal sector). The premise that European farms tend to be too small can already be found in the Mansholt Plan (CEC (1969)). The agricultural policy makers of the EU seem to accept as an economic necessity that the size of the average farm should be increased (see CEC (1994)).

Traditionally, agricultural economists and development economists have tended to emphasize decreasing rather than increasing returns to scale in agriculture, due to the short term fixity of inputs. In their view the long run production function exhibits constant returns, at best. One may indeed try to maintain such a position in the face of the empirical evidence by arguing that the findings mentioned above are questionable because the accounting of costs and returns is inadequate or incomplete. A literature survey by Binswanger et al. (1995) reaches the conclusion that while farm operations often have increasing returns to scale due to lumpy physical inputs, supervision costs of labour do impose decreasing returns, and on balance the optimal size of the farm is restricted and lies well below the optimum level as determined by cost minimization at the market wage rate. To maintain the decreasing returns view, one may also argue that costs and returns should be measured as present values discounted over an indefinite future and not as values of a particular year. Production for self-consumption should be valued at consumer prices. Non-insurable risks and liquidity constraints should be accounted for as well (Johnson and Ruttan (1994)). A further point that may be stressed is that if some markets say, for environmental resources, are missing, then scale inefficiency may be socially desirable, because the large farms are only more efficient in appearance, i.e. for as long as they enjoy free use of environmental resources, that affects them like a price subsidy, of which they receive more than small farms, due to their size.

Usually, scale inefficiency is viewed as a temporary phenomenon that is due to indivisibilities. Constant returns is thought to prevail in the long run production function in which all production factors adjust freely. For EU agriculture this short to medium term friction can be given various explanations.

First, there is the obvious fixity of nontradeable quotas on dairy and sugar. The MacSharry reform adds new quantitative restrictions to these; the new ones specifically favour small farms and restrict expansion (see Section 5.1). Secondly, no land may be available for expansion of a particular farm. In general little land is offered for sale. Since farmers need land as collateral for loans, selling land restricts the capacity to borrow; in turn, this restricts the sector's capacity to adjust. Thirdly, scale inefficiency makes farmers who sell or lease land (i.e. reduce their production capacity) more vulnerable, so that farms which suffer from scale inefficiency may not be willing to lease. Finally, farmers are, for obvious reasons, not willing to rent land that lies far away from their holding.

Hence, various factors limit the farmer's possibility of reducing scale inefficiency by extending the area of the holding and/or by investing in additional equipment. Over time, scale inefficiency may increase if farms are split by inheritance. Technical progress and price changes may also shift the average cost curve to the right, making more firms scale-inefficient. However, this should not too quickly be interpreted as a causal relation. Weersink and Tauer (1991) perform Granger causality tests for dairy farms in selected regions of the United States and find that large farms need high milk yields per cow, rather than yield increases forcing farmers to extend their herd sizes.

Scale inefficiency in a static framework

So far, we have defined scale inefficiency as indicating that a farm is 'too small' because the unit cost of a larger farm is lower. To make this definition more precise and to illustrate the consequences of scale inefficiency we choose a single-output, cost-minimization framework.

Figure 7.5 The cost function

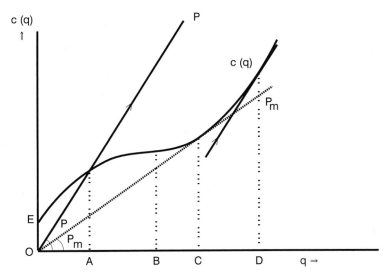

Figure 7.6 The average (AC) and marginal (MC) cost functions

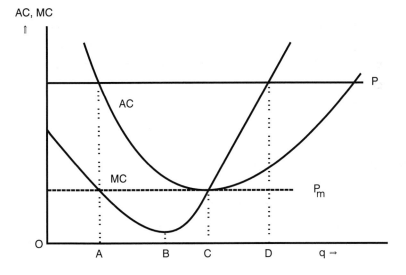

Assume that, at given input prices the cost function c(q) of the firms - the minimum cost incurred, at given input prices, in the production of an output level q - starts with setup costs, the intercept OE in fig. 7.5, then has an increasing returns to scale segment OB, which is followed by a decreasing returns part on the right of B. Average cost is at its minimum at C. Profit maximization implies that production is zero when the output price falls below average cost, because at such a price any farm in the sector makes losses. For a price p that exceeds this level, and in the absence of further constraints, D is the optimal output. Figure 7.6 gives the associated schedules for average cost (AC) and for marginal cost (MC).

In order to represent the short run rigidity, we introduce an upper bound $\bar{q}$ on output (a quota). The profit maximizing decision will now lead to a choice $q = \bar{q}$ for $\bar{q} \geq q_A$, where the subscript A of q_A refers to the point A in Figures 7.5 and 7.6, where the price is equal to the average cost.

To explain the basic principle, we abstract from differences in management practices and suppose that all farms have access to the same technology and hence have the same cost function. We assume that the upper bound $\bar{q}$ has a given density function $f(\bar{q})$ defined on the interval $[q_A, q_D]$. Now the unit profit for a farm with the bound $\bar{q}$ is the distance between the price line P and the AC curve in Figure 7.6.[144]

Note that in the absence of setup costs and increasing returns, point A coincides with the origin. The segment CD in Figure 7.6 separates firms on the decreasing part of their average cost function from the unconstrained optimum

---

[144] The discussion in terms of cost functions may seem restrictive because it assumes that farms produce a single output for which they face a constraint on sales. However, the cost function is only used in order to facilitate exposition and it is now easy to see that the reasoning applies more generally. The restricted profit function of this model is defined as $\Pi(p, q) = pq - c(q)$. Obviously, we can repeat the above discussion in terms of this profit function: profit is zero at A, rises until D and falls beyond this point; marginal profit reaches its maximum at B and intersects with average profit at point C, where average profit is maximal and becomes zero at D; finally, average profit is zero at A, rises until C and falls from there onwards. Note, however, that this profit function is convex in p and concave in q so that it is an ordinary restricted profit function that treats q as a fixed factor. This profit function is easily generalized into a multiple output, multiple factor function, similar to the one in section 3.3.1, by defining p and q as vectors and the prices of inputs can be represented explicitly. Hence the earlier discussion applies, in theory, to the multiple output farm with quota on outputs and with fixed factors.

D. The distance of the actual output q from the point D measures the scale inefficiency.[145] This describes the initial distribution.

A price reduction leads to a change in the density $f(\bar{q})$ that can be understood as follows. Consider a price reduction from p to p'. This would shift points A and D to A' and D', respectively. Whereas farms on the interval $[q_A, q_{A'}]$ are now making losses and forced to either increase their size or cease their operations, those on the interval $[q_{D'}, q_D]$ choose to reduce their farm size. This frees resources and facilitates restructuring towards the level $q_{D'}$. Therefore, while this framework suggests that price reductions facilitate the restructuring of the agricultural sector, it also indicates that restructuring may be a difficult and painful process when a large proportion of the farms operates on the downward sloping part of the AC-curve.

However, this conclusion needs qualification because the holdings of part-time farmers may survive many shocks and eventually become more like a garden around a house, producing recreational services. Moreover, the balance sheets of technically identical farms may be very different. Farms with high debt-to-equity ratios are obviously more vulnerable. For example, a sole heir will have to carry less debt than a farmer who has to reimburse his brothers and sisters for their share in the farm.

Scale inefficiency and long run developments

Despite these qualifications, the general point remains that, since they are more vulnerable, many of the farms with scale inefficiency will have to close down when faced with a large price reduction, thus facilitating the creation of larger units and causing a change in the density function f(q). Therefore, the fact that so many farms appear to operate on the downward-sloping part seems to indicate that there is scope for reducing the scale inefficiency in the sector.

---

[145] Point observations on farm production can also lie above the cost function (pure technical efficiency) and the input mix chosen may not be cost minimizing (allocational inefficiency). Finally, the production frontier approach to estimation of the cost function treats observations below the cost curve as measurement error (see Aigner et al. (1977) and Grabowski et al. (1990) for further discussion).

After a full restructuring farms would produce at a uniform scale q^* such that marginal cost is equal to marginal revenue $(p - \rho)$, where ρ is the rental price of the production factor q. If this factor is unbinding, then ρ will be zero but otherwise it is the rental cost which a farm wanting to expand has to pay for additional capacity.

This full restructuring can be achieved only if three conditions hold. First, there is the assumption that farms can be treated as infinitesimally small units, so that there are no indivisibility problems. It was already mentioned in Section 3.3.2, that land always creates local indivisibilities. Therefore, such a full restructuring is an unattainable goal. Secondly, full restructuring presupposes that all farms with scale inefficiencies disappear because they cannot compete at the lower prices but, as mentioned earlier, such farms are not necessarily vulnerable. One may think of old farmers who have paid off all debt and who largely produce for own consumption or of part-time farmers who earn a good living elsewhere and use the farm as a country house. Finally, after restructuring, the larger enterprises can only survive under fluctuating market conditions if they are not too heavily indebted. Therefore, larger farms should have some access to venture capital for their expansion. An expansion that is only financed through bank loans is not a viable option.

This suggests that if the future of the EU is one of a liberalized agriculture, the sector will consist of larger enterprises, whose scale is mainly constrained by the venture capital they can attract, and of small farms, whose owner operators produce at low cost and receive income from non-agricultural sources (pensions, non-farm employment). It is against this background that we will formulate our scenario.

7.5 A competitive EU entering the world market

In Section 7.2 we concluded that for many countries, notably in Asia and Africa, it will be difficult to maintain high agricultural growth rates during the next decades. This could lead to a pauperization of the population, in which case there will be no additional, commercial demand on the world market and hence no outlet for the commercial exports by the EU (though there may be a need for additional food aid). However, we have argued that some of the countries concerned will be in a position to cover their production deficit through imports and this will make food more expensive. To reflect this, we made the assumption that real world market prices will fall less in the long run than they did in the seventies and the eighties.

If one also agrees with the view, expressed in Sections 7.3 and 7.4, that within the EU there is ample room for efficiency gains by technological progress and by restructuring of the farm sector, and taking into account the slow demographic growth in Europe and the satiation in consumer demand, then it becomes plausible that the EU has the prospect of meeting part of the food needs of the rest of the world and becoming a competitive exporter, that will be able to face the competition by traditional exporters such as the United States, Argentina, Brazil and Australia and newcomers in Eastern Europe and in republics of the former Soviet Union. As long as the future of EU agriculture is one of efficient, large commercial farms, it may be expected that the European Union will manage to gain its share in a fast-growing world market, provided of course that it does not find it preferable to allocate its production factors to non-agricultural uses.

We shall now report on the use of ECAM to analyze the chances that European agriculture grows into a competitive seller on the world market. For this we formulate a long run scenario and one variant which assumes that more land is used outside agriculture. We have already pointed to the limitations that we face when using ECAM for this long run investigation. That we nonetheless find this exercise useful is because we use the scenario to draw a picture of the combined effect of various exogenous trends, that we have assessed on their own merits, rather than to reveal to us surprising endogenous developments.

7.5.1   European agriculture towards 2020: scenario specification

The point of departure is the situation to be obtained under the MacSharry reform scenario in the year 2005. The long run simulation extends this scenario until 2020, introducing a gradual liberalization without compensation payments. A motivation for this type of reform was already given in Section 6.4. During the period 2005-20 all remaining price support is further reduced in real terms.

It is assumed that set-aside obligations for cereals and oilseeds as well as production quotas in animal sectors (milk and sheep) will be abolished.

Figure 7.7 World market prices, 1992=100

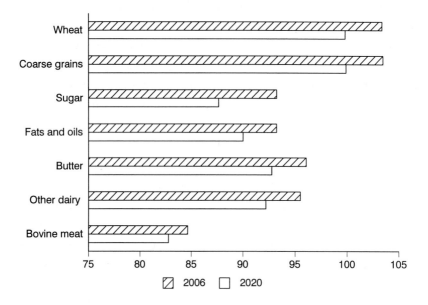

Moreover, producer subsidies linked to these quotas are also reduced at a rate of ten percent annually. For sugar, intervention prices are cut down by one per cent annually, until they reach the world market level.

To express the food scarcity on the international market, world market prices are assumed to fall at the rate of 0.25 per cent only after 2005, which seems moderate in view of anticipated scarcities. We want to avoid a scenario with world prices that increase, because this would unavoidably make the EU competitive whatever the other assumptions. Figure 7.7 shows the assumed trends in world prices for the main ECAM commodities.

Physical yields per hectare and per animal are assumed to grow on average at current rates until a given technical maximum is reached. In case this maximum is not known from technical studies, current growth rates are maintained. With respect to yields and feed conversion rates, it is assumed that, due to the process of technology diffusion, yield differences across countries in the EU will gradually diminish.

Production in non-agricultural sectors is assumed to rise at the rate of two per cent annually in all member countries and income from these sectors is to grow at the same rate. Because the parameters of the consumer demand system are based on data until 1985 and thirty-five years later, income is so much higher, it can be expected that some consumption levels become unrealistically high. This problem has been addressed by imposing an upper bound on annual per capita meat consumption. This bound was set at about the current level of meat consumption in the USA, i.e. at 120 kilogram per capita per year.

Finally, the area available for cultivation is assumed to fall at a rate of 0.35 per cent annually.

7.5.2   Scenario outcomes: production and trade

In Section 7.3 it was argued that agronomic ceilings on production were unlikely to be reached in 2020. Accordingly, the scenario outcomes reflect steady production increases. Despite the persistent decline of agricultural prices, the reduction of producer subsidies and the reduction of the area under cultivation, the growth rates remain significant, as can be seen in Table 7.3.

Table 7.3   Production quantities, EU-9, annual growth rate

	1982–92	1992–2005	2005–21
Wheat	3.0	1.7	2.3
Coarse grains	-0.1	1.1	1.0
Sugarbeet	0.8	0.2	0.2
Oilseeds	11.4	1.9	1.8
Consumable potatoes	-0.5	1.2	1.4
Dairy cows	-1.8	0.1	1.9
Laying hens	-0.3	0.5	0.1
Cattle	-0.3	1.6	1.9
Sheep and goats	2.3	-0.0	0.3
Pigs	0.8	1.2	-0.1
Poultry	1.8	1.8	0.4

Cereals

Total cereal production (wheat and coarse grains together) of the EU-9 exceeds 205 million metric tons in 2020. By comparison, the model generates a cereal production of 130 million metric tons in 1993, the first year of the MacSharry reform, rising to an estimated level of 159 metric million tons in 2005. This sharp increase in production is mainly the consequence of two distinct developments. The first is the abolishment of the set-aside obligations. This causes a jump in the total area cultivated of nearly three million hectares. An important part of this extra acreage is planted to cereals. The second development, with an even larger impact on volumes, is the sustained rise in yields per hectare. This is illustrated in Figure 7.8 below.

Figure 7.8 Cereal yields per hectare, EU-9, 1982=100

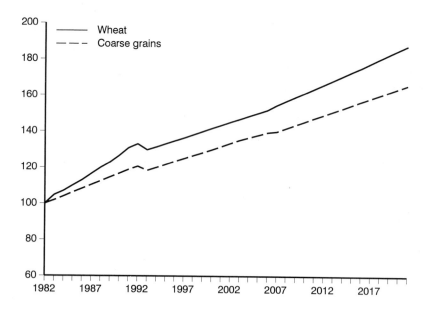

Source: ECAM, MacSharry and long run scenarios.

The average yield for wheat will rise from 4.78 in 1982 to 8.75 metric tons per hectare in 2020. This average includes the relatively low yield increase for durum wheat which slows down this expansion. The yield of coarse grains lags somewhat behind that of wheat and reaches about 7.9 metric tons per hectare in 2020.

The simulation shows that increase in cereal production does not necessarily lead to rapid growth of exportable surpluses (see Table 7.4). There is a rise in human consumption of about five million metric tons, but particularly intermediate demand for cereals picks up sharply due to continued substitution back to grains in animal feeds. This creates an additional demand of about 28 million metric tons. As discussed earlier, this follows logically from the drastic price cut as part of the MacSharry reform and the further reduction of support in the years thereafter. Nonetheless, the rise in domestic uses does not fully absorb the additional production: the cereal surplus will increase by about fourteen million metric tons, i.e. by one million metric tons annually. Against an expected increase of cereal demand by developing countries of 27 million metric tons annually (FAO (1993, Table 3.5)), this will probably have only a marginal effect on international market conditions. Moreover, the scenario assumes that export refunds will be close to zero by the year 2020 and this precludes complaints of dumping.

Table 7.4   Net imports, EU-9, mln metric tons

	2005	2020
Wheat	-15.5	-35.2
Coarse grains	-1.0	4.4
Fats and oils	6.3	6.4
Butter	0.0	-0.7
Other dairy	-4.6	-26.5
Bovine meat	-1.0	-4.1

Other crops

The total arable area in 2020 amounts to 80.5 million hectares, a loss of nine million hectares compared to 1992. The largest area (43.5 mln ha) is used for pasture and feed crops. The remaining 37 million hectares is planted to cereals (24.5 mln ha) and other non-feed crops, see Figure 7.9. For most of the non-cereal crops, production appears to grow at approximately the same rate as demand.

Oilseeds and sugar beets are affected most directly by the liberalization policy specified in this scenario. Therefore, we limit the discussion to these crops. Recall that the MacSharry reform did not change the existing quotas regulations for sugar and that, in the long run scenario, sugar quotas are maintained and intervention prices are reduced by one per cent annually. It appears that, by 2020, the EU is still subsidizing its sugar exports to the world market.

Figure 7.9 Cropping pattern in 2020, EU-9, excluding cereals and fodder crops

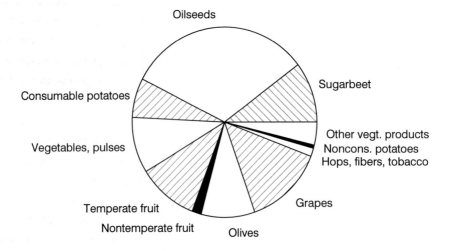

Source: ECAM, long run scenario.

Although the termination of the set-aside scheme somewhat speeds up the growth in oilseed production, most of its effect is dampened by the continuous fall of producer subsidies. The eventual increase in oilseed production is mainly attributable to yield improvements and the area under this crop hardly changes.

The scenario outcomes suggest that net revenues per hectare are too low relative to those of cereals to generate growth figures that come in any way close to those of the eighties. Therefore, imports of fats and oils stabilize at a high level even though the self-sufficiency ratio increases from 47 per cent in 2005 to 53 per cent in 2020.

Dairy products

The development of the dairy sector is more pronounced. The long period of quantitative production restrictions comes to an end with consequently more room for expansion. Table 7.3 already indicated that substantial growth is achieved: milk production in 2020 lies about thirty per cent above its 2005 level. Slightly more than half of this increase in production is due to an increase in the yield per cow. The remainder is caused by an expansion of the herd size.

The average yield per cow will rise from 5100 kilogram in 1992 to about 7300 kilogram per year in 2020. In spite of the assumed convergence of yields across countries, yields per cow still diverge substantially across member states. While Italian cows are at the lower end of the scale with 5100 kg per animal per year, dairy cattle in Denmark and the Netherlands produce about 8500 kilograms per year.

The removal of quotas has a strong impact on the position of the EU on the world markets for dairy products. For butter, a significant rise in supply, together with a modest decrease in internal demand leads to a spectacular enlargement of the export surplus. From a situation of near autarky in 2005 the EU turns into a large exporter of butter. Exports will rise to 0.75 million metric tons in 2020, which begins to approach the order of magnitude of total world exports in 1992 (1.2 million metric tons). Export refunds are still needed in the beginning of the projection period, but are projected to vanish from 2010 onwards.

Exports of other dairy products basically follow the same pattern. Quotas on production limit exports in 2005 to 5 million metric tons of milk equivalents, but in 2020 total exports are over four times higher. Internal demand increases only marginally (from 76 to 81 million metric tons of milk equivalent). Since there is hardly any protection on exports left in 2020, these exports may be called competitive. We consider such exports feasible because several studies have indicated that markets prospects are indeed relatively favourable for dairy products, especially in South Asia (with almost one billion vegetarians by the year 2020) and the Middle East (see Parikh et al. (1988))

Other animal products

The recovery in the supply of bovine meat is partly linked to the changes in the milk sector. A rise in the number of dairy cows appears to stimulate non-dairy cattle production. Non dairy-cattle also becomes more profitable relative to sheep. This has two causes. First, as the internal price for bovine meat already reaches the world market level in 2005, the fall in internal prices for bovine meat is less pronounced than for sheep. Secondly, the assumed reduction in producer subsidies has a greater effect on the sheep sector than on cattle production. Since consumption of bovine meat falls slightly during the period of simulation, all additional supplies must eventually be exported. Consequently, total net exports show a rapid rise to 4 million metric tons in 2020. To put this figure into perspective, this is about eight per cent of world bovine meat production in 1992, which amounted to 52 million metric tons; yet it is over 80 per cent of total world trade in 1992 (FAO, *Trade yearbook*) and this seems rather large.

Expansion of the pork and poultry meat sectors is discouraged by insufficient opportunities to sell on the world market. Exports of pork and poultry meat to third countries are restricted by assumption. This assumption reflects the character of production in these sectors: production is not tied to land, it is based on feedstuffs that are easily stored and more easily transported than live animals and meat. Exports require a reliable certification of product quality, in particular with respect to veterinary and sanitary conditions. Therefore, one may expect that production will continue to take place rather close to the consumer, in spite of the environmental problems this may pose.

The pig and poultry sectors are also constrained by satiated domestic demand. Hence, while the supply of poultry meat increases slightly during the projection period, pork production in 2020 in fact lies below the 2005 level. We conclude that the EU becomes a relatively modest exporter of cereals and a large exporter of dairy products and bovine meat.

7.5.3 Producer subsidies and export refunds

The EU is not only able to remain an agricultural exporter, in the scenario simulation it also becomes a competitive one. Section 5.1.3 indicated that by 2005 the European farmer is mainly protected from external competition through producer subsidies and, to a lesser extent, export refunds[146]. Total outlays on these two items amounted to 15.0 and 3.9 billion ecu respectively in that year. Table 7.5 lists the protection for selected commodities in 2020.

Commodities affected by the MacSharry reforms will be virtually without protection by 2020.[147] More than half of the remaining subsidies are linked to cereals. Despite reductions at a rate of ten per cent annually, there still is a subsidy of about 77 ecu per hectare by way of compensation payments in 2020.[148] Border protection will have disappeared almost completely for cereals though a small net import levy remains related to imported coarse grains.

For sugar 329 million ecu of export subsidies are needed in 2020. These outlays are largely covered from production levies. Oilseeds and protein crops still receive a subsidy per hectare. The sheep sector appears to be self-financing: existing producer subsidies will be more than covered by levies on imports.

The table presents only part of the budgetary implications of the scenario. However, the effects on the other budget items are negligible. In 2020 the overall reduction in FEOGA expenditures for the EU-9 amounts to fourteen billion ecu, as compared to 2005. All in all, we may note that due to productivity gains, the exports of the EU hardly need any financial support, notwithstanding the ongoing fall in world prices.

---

[146] Recall that expenditures related to Greece, Spain, Portugal and the former GDR are contained in the item 'FEOGA-miscellaneous'.

[147] For some products, there are still subsidies on inputs or on consumption but since only very small amounts are involved these subsidies do not appear in the table.

[148] Due to changes in the area shares of countries, the reduction in producer subsidies at EU-9 level comes out below 10 per cent.

Table 7.5   Producer subsidies and net subsidies on trade, EU-9 in 2020, mln ecu at 1992 prices

	Producer subsidies	Net subsidies on trade	Total
Wheat	1231	39	1270
Coarse grains	678	-77	601
Sugar	-254	329	75
Fats and oils	465	-44	421
Protein feed, excl. dairy	462	-182	280
Wine	88	91	179
Butter	0	20	20
Other dairy	0	69	69
Bovine meat	511	0	511
Ovine meat	167	-345	-178
Total	3348	-100	3428

7.5.4   Real value added in the member states

The reduction of intervention prices and production subsidies causes farm prices to fall. Therefore, despite the volume increase of agricultural production, real valued added in agriculture declines in almost all member states, as shown in Table 7.6.

Table 7.6   Real value added of agriculture, including transfers, annual growth rate 2005-2020, at 1992 prices

	Total	Per capita	Per farm worker
Belgium-Luxembourg	0.2	2.4	2.3
Denmark	-2.8	1.2	0.5
France	-1.2	1.8	1.6
Germany, Fed. Rep.	-0.1	2.4	1.9
Ireland	0.0	3.8	2.5
Italy	-0.6	2.2	1.9
The Netherlands	2.3	3.3	3.0
United Kingdom	-1.4	1.0	1.0
Farmers EU-9	-0.4	2.3	1.9
Non-farmers EU-9	2.0	2.2	2.2

Note: Agricultural value added is deflated by the national GDP-deflator in ecu.

Growth rates range from -2.8 per cent in Denmark to 2.3 per cent in The Netherlands. The reasons for the wide differences can be summarized as follows.

Belgium-Luxembourg will, due to its relatively small cereals- and oilseeds production, not suffer very much from reductions in producer subsidies. The small positive growth rate is a consequence of the expansion of the dairy sector and horticulture. In *Denmark* the crop sector is relatively important, with an emphasis on cereals. Value added growth is depressed by the reduction in subsidies. The positive developments in the dairy sector are insufficient to compensate for this. As animal yields are already very high in 2005, there is less scope for further improvement of yields as compared to most other member states. Moreover, Danish farmers face a satiated EU demand for pork and poultry meat. In *France,* there are also negative effects in the crop sector as well as a declining demand for wine. These dominate the positive effect of the substantial increase in output volumes for dairy and bovine meat. Developments in *West Germany* are rather stable. Output growth nearly compensates for the drop in prices, the reductions in subsidy payments are of limited importance to the crop sector and the animal sectors benefit from lower feed costs due to reduced cereal prices. In *Ireland* real value added does not decline, mainly because the crop sector is small compared to the livestock sector and the relaxation of the quota regulation in the dairy sector is very favourable here. The crop sector in *Italy* is rather insensitive to the abolishment of the MacSharry regulations because of the relatively small acreage under fallow in the MacSharry reform. Moreover, falling prices for cereals and a shrinking demand for wine, tobacco and olives take their toll. An average growth rate of 2.3 per cent places *The Netherlands* in a very favourable position. The (assumed) ongoing expansion of horticulture combined with the rise in dairy production has a positive impact on value added, whereas cereal production will almost vanish. The decline in the *United Kingdom* is also due to the crop sector, which has a large share in value added. Also, crop yields per hectare are already relatively high at the beginning of the simulation period, leaving little room for further increases.

Table 7.6 also indicates that developments at sector level do not coincide with the evolution of income per capita or per worker. Demographic change and migration reduce the agriculturally active populations and allow real value added per capita to improve at rates that vary from one per cent in the United

Kingdom to 3.8 per cent in Ireland. Note, however, that the increases per head are everywhere larger than the growth per worker, except in the United Kingdom. This reflects changes in the age structure of total farm population: as the share of the age cohort 55+ becomes larger, the average activity rate rises.[149] In Chapter 2 we have emphasized that 'real value added' and 'real income' are two different concepts altogether.

Nonetheless, the similarity in the development of value added per capita in agriculture and other sectors suggests that in the long run labour outflows will almost eliminate income differentials. We also note that, in this scenario, the opportunities for further mechanization of agriculture are apparently sufficient for a successful development of exports at virtually unsubsidized prices.

7.5.5   Agricultural production capacity

The projected output levels suggest an increase of total production capacity in agriculture. In this section this point is examined in more detail. The model distinguishes three types of resources: labour, land and physical capital. Through the transformation function,[150] these inputs generate production capacities for crops and livestock. Table 7.7 shows the average yearly growth rates of resources and production capacities.

As both total acreage and employment fall during the projection period, one would expect capital stocks to rise, but the table indicates only a marginal increase at EU-9 level. In some countries capital inputs even decrease. However, growth of production capacity is achieved through disembodied technological progress: labour and capital requirements do not increase proportionally with yields per hectare and per animal. The numbers in the table can be understood on the basis of the earlier discussion on production, value added and labour migration. Labour outflow in *The Netherlands* is rather small due to relatively high incomes in horticulture. The growth of crop capacity in *Ireland* also stands out. It arises because the net outflow of land is zero and because there is a shift in the cropping pattern from grass to other crops, mainly potatoes and cereals.

---

[149] In all countries (except the UK) the activity rate of elderly workers exceeds the rate of the younger workers (less of farm employment).

[150] See program (4.29) in Section 4.3.4.

Table 7.7   Factor inputs and production capacity in agriculture, annual growth rates 2005-2020

Country	Labour	Land	Capital	Production capacity	
				Crops	Livestock
Belgium-Luxembourg	-2.2	-0.5	1.1	1.2	1.6
Denmark	-3.3	-0.5	-0.5	1.4	0.5
France	-2.8	-0.4	-1.2	1.2	1.8
Germany, Fed. Rep.	-2.0	-0.4	1.0	1.0	1.4
Ireland	-2.5	0.0	2.2	3.1	1.8
Italy	-2.5	-0.4	1.0	1.0	0.9
The Netherlands	-0.9	-0.5	-0.8	2.4	1.2
United Kingdom	-2.4	-0.3	-0.5	0.6	1.9
EU-9	-2.3	-0.4	0.2	1.2	1.4

Even so, the crop sector remains relatively small in Ireland.

7.5.6   The position of agriculture in the national economy

Share in total value added

Ever since World War II the importance of agriculture in the European economies has been in decline. Despite the persistent growth in the quantities produced, the share in total value added has dropped, as real price increases lagged persistently behind inflation. In the simulation this trend continues: the contribution of agriculture to national value added drops from 2.4 per cent in 1992 to 1.2 per cent in 2020, see Table 7.8. Of course, agriculture is still of more economic importance than this figure would suggest. Various food processing industries, such as sugar refineries or the dairy industry would not be able to survive without inputs from local agriculture. Also, the contribution of agriculture to food security, rural development and preservation of the landscape are not to be belittled.

The two columns on the right-hand side of the table demonstrate deviations in the relative position of agriculture among member states and differences in the rate of decline. In all member states the speed of reduction has been largest in the years before 1992. A closer look at the model results shows that the relatively favourable position of agriculture in *The Netherlands* and *Ireland* is linked to the dominant positions of horticulture and of the dairy sector, respectively. In *West Germany* and the *United Kingdom* shares were already small in 1982; in 2005 they are even below one per cent.

Table 7.8   Share of agriculture in real GDP, percentage

Country	1982	1992	2005	2020	Annual growth rate 1982-2020
Belgium-Luxembourg	3.2	2.0	1.5	1.1	-2.6
Denmark	7.8	5.0	3.8	1.9	-3.6
France	4.7	2.4	1.6	1.0	-3.9
Germany, Fed. Rep.	2.4	1.4	0.9	0.7	-3.2
Ireland	12.7	8.9	5.8	4.4	-2.7
Italy	6.5	4.2	3.3	2.3	-2.6
The Netherlands	5.3	4.3	3.6	3.7	-0.9
United Kingdom	2.6	1.4	0.8	0.5	-4.2
EU-9	4.0	2.4	1.7	1.2	-3.0

Agricultural population

The declining macro-economic importance of agriculture also finds expression in the evolution of agricultural employment. Figure 7.10 shows the developments by member states over the period 1982-2020. The figure shows that the decline of the agricultural population (including part-time farmers) continues at a rapid pace. In 2020 only 2.3 per cent of total population is 'agricultural', in contrast with the five per cent share in 1982. In *Denmark* and *Ireland*, within a time-span of forty years, a reduction of 75 per cent is expected, mainly due to demographic trends. The fall in The Netherlands is smallest due to the favourable income position in horticulture.

When interpreting the projections of agricultural employment and populations one should keep in mind that agricultural migrants are assumed to obtain employment in other sectors. This may not be unrealistic, provided an average growth rate of two per cent outside agriculture is realized.

Figure 7.10   Share of agricultural population in total, 1982 and 2020, percentage

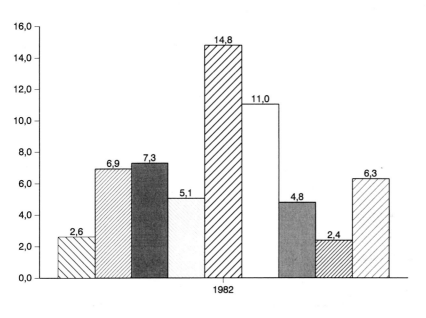

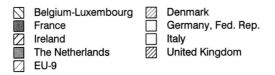

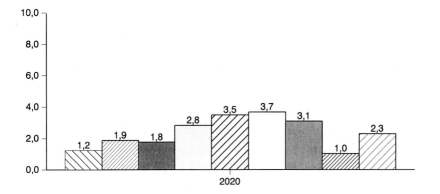

7.6   More land used outside agriculture

7.6.1   Scenario specification

The scenario simulation of the previous section suggests that European agriculture, in the long run, appears able to compete on international markets.

Of course, one may argue that the assumed modest decrease in world market prices combined with the relatively sharp decline in internal support, eventually has to lead to an agricultural sector that is competitive in the sense that world prices come close to internal prices. We must also repeat our earlier warning that in these long run simulations the distinction between assumptions and conclusions is necessarily vague.

Nonetheless, in the introduction of this chapter we have indicated that it is by no means evident that European agriculture will become a net exporter. A steady decline in agricultural prices within the EU would have an impact on factor rewards in agriculture and this could lead to a rapid 'outflow' of land and labour.

It is difficult to anticipate how attractive such non-agricultural use of land would become. There is little experience with such a situation since land prices have been kept at artificially high level for such a long time and the prevailing laws on the use of land constrain the conversion of agricultural land into non-agricultural land and vice versa (see also sections 4.3 and 4.4). Therefore, the scenario simulation treats the land outflow exogenously. The preceding scenario assumed that the reduction of total cultivated area would continue at the same pace as in the eighties. The demand for non-agricultural uses (recreation, urbanization) would lead to a reduction of 0.35 per cent annually. This leads to a reduction of 9 million hectares over the period 1992-2020, which is significant and amounts to a surface that is more or less as large as the current agricultural area of Belgium-Luxembourg, the Netherlands and Ireland taken together.

Since the speed of land outflow is so uncertain, we now specify a variant on the earlier scenario, in which land outflow is more important. The persistent decrease of prices (and per hectare compensations) for land-tied products and the steady improvement of the standard of living outside agriculture are assumed to push up the rate of land outflow. One could imagine that it will become increasingly profitable for the European farmer to respond to the growing demand for land from outside agriculture. It will be assumed that in the period 2005-20 the demand for land for non-agricultural uses causes an additional annual outflow of one per cent. This implies that the total cultivated area in 2020 will be about seventy million hectares, a reduction of 11.5 million hectares compared to the earlier scenario. To sharpen the contrast with the other scenario and because most of the non-agricultural use can be expected to occur in the neighbourhood of urban areas, it is assumed that this reduction takes place disproportionately at the expense of the areas under cereals, oilseeds, sugar and potatoes (a reduction in marginal pasture land would have a smaller effect).

Since land outflow occurs only if non-agricultural use is more profitable than farming, we also assume that a hectare of land that leaves agriculture, as part of the additional outflow of this scenario, generates a value added in non-agriculture which lies ten per cent above the average value added of agricultural land of the country concerned. This value added is supposed to accrue to farm households in their capacity as managers and operators of golf-courses, natural parks, camping sites etc.

7.6.2   Scenario outcomes

We only discuss outcomes that differ significantly from those of the earlier long run scenario.

Production volumes

The impact of the extra outflow of land on the acreage used for grass and feed crops is much smaller (by assumption) than on the part used for other crops (Table 7.9). The acreage under cereals is most seriously affected. This is an immediate consequence of the scenario specification, because only the part of pastures that is suited for growing other crops is adjusted.

Cereal production is reduced substantially by about 54 million metric tons. This is assumed to cause a modest recovery of internal cereal prices. The reduction in the area under cultivation could be expected to cause a substitution towards animal products, since less production capacity is needed for crops.

Table 7.9   Cropping pattern, EU-9 in 2020, mln ha

	Long run	Landout
Wheat	14.3	10.4
Coarse grains	10.3	7.7
Oilseeds	4.0	3.3
Pasture and other forage crops	43.4	40.2
Other crops (incl. perennial crops)	8.5	7.4
Total crops	80.5	69.0

However, the reduction at the same time lowers the marginal productivity of investments in livestock and this second effect appears to dominate in the long run. This explains, together with a minor increase in feed costs, the decline in non-dairy cattle. For pig and poultry production the decline is more modest because here the demand side dominates. The effects on production are summarized in Table 7.10. The export volumes of the two simulation runs are compared in Table 7.11.

Table 7.10   Production quantities, EU-9 in 2020, mln metric tons

	Long run	Landout
Wheat	125.1	91.9
Coarse grains	81.7	60.7
Oilseeds	16.0	13.0
Dairy cows	148.3	148.1
Laying hens	4.5	4.4
Non-dairy cattle	11.2	10.4
Pigs	14.0	13.8
Poultry	8.1	8.1

Differences are, as expected, largest for cereals and bovine meat. The EU-9 is again a net importer of cereals, while net exports of bovine meat are lower in 2020, due to the fall in production. Not listed in the table are fruits and vegetables, for which imports double between 2005 and 2020. However, these imports are still less than 9 per cent of internal demand in 2020. The results confirm that in the long run the difference between a net import and a net export position can already be generated by minor changes in production levels.

Table 7.11   Net imports, EU-9 in 2020, mln metric tons

	Long run	Landout
Wheat	-35.2	-7.5
Coarse grains	4.4	21.2
Fats and oils	6.4	7.2
Butter	-0.7	-0.7
Other dairy	-26.5	-26.9
Bovine meat	-4.1	-3.4

Total receipts and expenditures

The additional land outflow reduces the outlays of the EU because it diminishes the area under subsidized crops in 2020. The sharp fall of cereal exports leads to a drop of export refunds of almost 400 million ecu. The decrease in total acreage under cereals and oilseeds will reduce producer subsidies by some 650 million ecu and storage costs by nearly 400 million ecu. Total savings on the FEOGA budget amount to 1.4 billion ecu in 2020, see Table 7.12. In addition, higher imports will push up levies by more than 500 million ecu, of which 400 million can be attributed to fruit and vegetables and the remaining part to cereals. Total budgetary gains are transferred to member states via reduction of the VAT and GDP contributions.

Table 7.12   FEOGA outlays, EU-9 in 2020, mln ecu at 1992 prices

Difference between scenario's	Long run – Landout Savings
Total FEOGA	1441
of which	
Refunds on exports	378
Producer subsidies	647
Interest and storage	388

Total agricultural income

Recall that the additional acreage taken out of agricultural production is assumed to yield a net revenue which is ten per cent higher than the average on agricultural land. This leads to the agricultural income account in the year 2020 of Table 7.13.

Table 7.13   Agricultural value added, EU-9, mln ecu at 1992 prices

	Long run	Landout
Total real value added	81,214	75,245
Extra income through land outflow		12,462
Total income	81,214	87,707

An additional demand for land from the non-agricultural sector will, given the assumptions on productivity and management, push up agricultural income. The impact is quite sizeable: one would expect an additional outflow of land of 13 per cent to generate an income increase of 1.3 per cent only. The realized increase (eight per cent) is larger because the production on the remaining acreage will shift to activities that are more profitable in terms of value added.

7.7 Long run perspectives for agriculture in the EU-9: some tentative conclusions

We stress again that, due to the ad hoc nature of the assumptions, the calculations should be interpreted with caution. Nonetheless, a few points stand out.

(a) In the long run, agriculture in the EU-9 has the potential to develop into a fully productive sector that is able to compete with other exporting countries on the world market.
(b) If protection is reduced gradually, the EU is able to export surpluses of cereals, dairy and bovine meat without subsidy.
(c) The EU remains a large importer of oilseeds and of sheep meat.
(d) Export refunds for sugar are necessary to dispose of the surplus on the world market (assuming that the present regulation is maintained).

(e) The relative contribution of the agricultural sector to total value added continues its decline.

(f) The role of agriculture as an employer also diminishes.

(g) The production capacity of agriculture can be maintained in spite of a reduction in the labour force and the area under cultivation.

These are the conclusions that we draw from the long run scenario. The variant with less land adds the following two, more general points.

(h) A persistent decrease in the price of land-tied products will stimulate alternative uses of land. Even if yields rise continuously, real value added per hectare will decrease over time. Moreover, land substitution also has the advantage of leading to an increase in the marginal productivity of land used in agriculture. Our calculations for real value added and acreage suggest that the average net revenue per hectare of discarded land would have been less than 500 ecu per hectare had it remained in agriculture. We therefore conclude that if yields continue to improve, the EU will have the comfortable choice between becoming a competitive exporter or enjoying non-agricultural activities like recreation and natural parks.

(i) Finally, the variant shows how much the trade patterns of the EU can vary under alternative assumptions with respect to factor availability. This is of course not very surprising but it makes the point that the EU should anticipate the possibility of important changes in conditions on the world market and be prepared to reconvert non-agricultural land back into arable land if the need arises, perhaps not so much to ensure food security within the EU, as the EU may be sufficiently rich to buy its food abroad, but to avoid extreme shortages in the rest of the world in the wake of wars and other calamities. Therefore, the EU should always keep open the option of reconverting land to agricultural use and act, even under the most liberal scenario, so as to preserve the productive capacity of this land.

Chapter 8

Summary and conclusions

In this study we investigated the consequences of the MacSharry reform and the GATT agreement, situated these on the axis free trade - interventionism and analyzed policy alternatives along this axis. We started from a welfare theoretical angle and concluded that though this theory basically advocates free trade, its advice is subject to major qualifications. Even under first-best conditions, there may be a case for specific interventions say, to regulate land markets or to subsidize regional development programs. When markets are imperfect (managed trade) or missing (environmental resources), the first-best conditions do not hold and this gives further ground for intervention. Also, the theory does not permit any judgement on reforms that reduce support without any compensation to the losers.

Hence, two approaches are possible. One is to elevate the principle of free trade to a moral status. All deviations are then obstacles to be removed by policy. This simplifies the policy discussion, since it permits to proceed in small steps but it may, until the final aim is reached, lead through highly undesirable states. The alternative approach, pursued in this study, is to compare the outcomes of specific free trade and interventionist scenarios. This involves the use of a policy simulation tool, like ECAM. While we have emphasized that this model can only serve to study the implications of specific interventions, not to derive optimal policy interventions, ECAM has the advantage of being embedded in general equilibrium theory. This makes it possible to assess proposed CAP-reforms not only in quantitative but also in qualitative, welfare theoretic terms.

The MacSharry reform served as our reference scenario. This reform is gradual, full of compromise and reveals an approach which typically belongs to what we have referred to as the *bureaucratic perspective*. Its principal aim is to reduce price support, replacing it by compensation payments per hrctare and per animal. Using ECAM, we have simulated the consequences of this reform until the year 2005, assuming that gradualism and compromise will also prevail from 1996 onwards. The simulation results suggest that the reform brings a net welfare improvement to the consumer, as the difference between a substantial gain, mainly due to lower consumer prices and to more efficient feed use, and a rather significant loss that is attributable to increased budgetary expenditures, tightened quotas and set-asides of land. By linking the compensation payments to land, the scheme maintains the market value of land and thus its value as a collateral. This avoids massive bankruptcy in agriculture but also makes the use of land for non-agricultural purposes less attractive. Through its set-asides of land and the premium quotas on cattle, the reform alleviates the frictions with competing exporters, especially regarding cereals and bovine meat. The EU's trading pattern is affected also by the rebalancing of the prices of animal feeds, which limits import demand for cereal substitutes.

The alternative, *continuation of past policies* would not have created unsurmountable budgetary problems for the EU: our calculations indicate that the indomitable rise in FEOGA expenditures that began in the eighties would have slowed down in a natural way. This conclusion is robust in the sense that it hardly depends on the specification of ECAM but follows from the simple observation that the percentage growth rate in the FEOGA budget largely depends on the growth rate of net exports, which is high around self-sufficiency but falls necessarily when the volume of exports becomes larger. However, the increase in export volume would have exacerbated the conflicts with competing exporters and would probably have made it impossible to reach a GATT agreement.

The *GATT agreement* is to a large extent compatible with the MacSharry reform but it specifies a tariffication, that constrains import tariffs in nominal terms, without indexation to compensate for ecu-inflation. If this principle is adhered to in the future, these bounds will eventually become binding, in which case the EU will have to give up the principle of Community preference and allow foreign competitors to enter its market, because it will not be in a position to raise the wedge between the internal price and the world price above the agreed tariff.

A gradual liberalisation that proceeds according to the *free trade perspective* brings larger gains to the consumer and does not cause the welfare losses due to set-asides and other quantity constraints. The decoupled MacSharry scenario illustrates this. It indicates that significant lump sum payments to farmers are needed as compensations in the medium term until 2005 but the long run scenario suggests that in the period thereafter the EU's agricultural sector will be able to survive without support and become a competitive exporter on the world market. On the EU-production side there is a potential for output growth related to the EU's natural conditions, and also to the technical progress that is still 'in the pipeline', as suggested by the difference between best practice and average current yields. Since internal demand is stagnating, because population growth is low and consumers demand is satiated, an increasing share of production becomes available for exports. Other parts of the world, notably South and East Asia offer a mirror image. Their fast economic growth boosts food demand and absorbs the most fertile lands for urbanization and manufacturing.

However, the EU could also lose more agricultural land than we assumed in the long run scenario, especially when price support and per hectare compensations will have been abolished. Then, it may even become a food importer. This is not a risky prospect for the EU itself, at least from an economic perspective, as it would have no difficulties in purchasing food and animal feed on the world market. If food supply were to break down in another part of the world, due to some environmental disaster, prolonged droughts or endless wars, other importers would probably suffer first. We have emphasized that the EU would be well advised in formulating a policy that safeguards the productive capacity of the land even when used outside agriculture, so as to protect its options for reconverting land to agricultural use.

The cartel scenario, representing the *interventionist perspective*, raises the internal prices to support farm incomes and introduces additional supply controls to limit subsidized exports. The scenario presents clear advantages: it avoids the direct payments that are needed for decoupled support and the production quota for livestock and the set-asides on land restrain exports and, together with the rebalancing in animal feeds, ease environmental pressures. There are welfare losses for EU consumers but these are only a small fraction of consumer expenditures: less than 0.7 per cent of equivalent consumer expenditures in 2005. Yet this neglects the welfare loss that is inflicted upon foreign consumers and the important income loss of the intensive livestock sector which has to face high prices for animal feeds. These problems would be aggravated further if the cartel were to be privatized, so as to become self-financing. Finally, the scenario seems unrealistic at any rate, since it shifts the policy in a direction that is almost diametrically opposed to the GATT agreement.

We conclude that free trade is the direction in which we expect the CAP to evolve. This by no means implies that all agricultural policies will be abolished, but only that the sector will be treated more like any other sector, with a government role restricted to providing a social safety net, education and promoting infrastructural and rural development. The safety net will assist farm households in difficulties, but not farmers as such and even less protect agricultural valued added. Current price policies mainly support the larger producers and even compensation payments per hectare or per animal with limits on the amount payable to a single farmer are inadequate social policy measures, as they do not take into account the income which farm households earn outside agriculture. The policies for infrastructural and rural development will have to address indivisibilities that are specific to agriculture as well as environmental issues. Farmers have a role to play as keepers of the landscape and of the productive capacity of land. Governments will have to reward them for this through payments (not by restricting imports from countries with a less stringent environmental policy).

It is questionable that agricultural policies other than trade and competition policy should be decided upon at central level in Brussels. If such policies were managed at the national level, or even at regional levels within countries, this would greatly alleviate not only the administrative tasks of the Commission but also the efforts spent in negotiations between member states. This would amount to *financial renationalization* of the CAP, whereby the Commission would only have to monitor that market unity and fair competition among producers were being respected. All other tasks could be effectuated in a decentralized manner. Financial renationalization does not have to wait for the CAP to be reformed further. We have seen that it can be implemented without any immediate impact on farm policies. It will not even impose a burden on the national budgets, as long as national governments receive compensating transfers; at the same time, these transfers would make more explicit and visible the support that consumers give to agriculture, so that an early implementation could be conducive to liberalization. Finally, and more importantly, financial renationalization would pave the way for enlargement of the EU with Central European countries. It will not be possible to maintain the present CAP if these countries join, not only because the consumers of these countries are hardly in a position to pay the food prices prevailing under the current CAP or because the FEOGA budget would rise dramatically, but primarily because the compensation payments to farmers could cause social unrest in the countries concerned. Therefore, financial renationalization of the CAP is not a step backwards. It is a reform that makes the CAP more transparent and removes important impediments to the process of European unification.

References

Adelman, I. and S. Robinson (1978) *Income distribution policy in developing countries: a case study of Korea.* Stanford, CA: Stanford University Press.

Aigner, D., C.A.K. Lovell and P. Schmidt (1977) 'Formulation and estimation of stochastic frontier production function models', *Journal of Econometrics*, 6: 21-37.

Alexandratos, N. (1990) *European Agriculture: Policy Issues and Options to 2000.* London: Belhaven Press.

Anderson, K. and R. Tyers (1993) 'Implications of EC expansion for European Agricultural policies, trade and welfare', Discussion Paper 829, Centre for Economic Policy Research, London.

Anonymous (1992) 'Legal Text of U.S.-EC Farm deal', Inside U.S. Trade-Special Report - December 25, 1992.

Arrow, K.J. and F. Hahn (1971) *General Competitive Analysis.* Edinburgh: Holden Day.

Bagwell, K. and R.W. Staiger (1990) 'A theory of managed trade', *American Economic Review*, 80: 779-795.

Behrens, R. and H. de Haen (1980) 'Aggregate factor input and productivity in agriculture: a comparison for the EC-member countries, 1963-76', *European Review of Agricultural Economics*, 7: 109-146.

Behrens, R. (1981) *Vergleichende Analyse der Entwicklung der Produktionsfactoren in der Landwirtschaft der Europäischen Gemeinschaft*, Dissertation Georg-August Universität, Göttingen.

Bender, W.H. (1994) 'An end use analysis of global food requirements', *Food Policy*, 19: 381-395.

Berkhout, P. and W.S.J.M. Buck (1994) 'EU-landbouwbeleid en de GATT', in: J. de Hoogh and H.J. Silvis, eds., *EU-landbouwpolitiek van binnen en buiten.* Wageningen: Wageningen Pers.

Binswanger, H.P. (1989) 'Brazilian policies that encourage deforestation in the Amazon', Environment Department Working Paper no. 16, The World Bank, Washington DC.

Binswanger, H.P., K. Deininger and G. Feder (1995) 'Power, distortions and reform in agricultural land markets', in: J. Behrman and T.N. Srinivasan, eds., *Handbook of Development Economics,* vol. III. Amsterdam: North-Holland.

Blanford, D., H. de Gorter, D. Harvey (1989) 'Farm income support with minimal trade distortion', *Food policy*: 14, 268-273.

Blom, J. and M. Hoogeveen (1992) 'Enkele berekeningen van de gevolgen van de MacSharry voorstellen met het graan- en mengvoedergrondstoffen model', LEI-DLO, The Hague.

Brander, J.A. and B.J. Spencer (1988) 'Export subsidies and international market share rivalry', *Journal of International Economics*, 24: 217-238.

Brooke, A., D. Kendrick and A. Meeraus (1988) *GAMS: a user's guide*. San Francisco, CA: Scientific Press.

Brown, L.R. (1989) 'Reexamining the World Food Prospect', in: *The State of the World 1989*. New York: Norton.

Brown, L. and J.E. Young (1990) 'Feeding the World in the Nineties', in: *The State of the World 1990*. New York: Norton.

CEC (1958) 'Recueil des documents de la Conférence agricole des Etats membres de la Communauté Economique Européenne à Stresa au 12 Juillet 1958', Brussels.

CEC (1969) 'Memorandum sur la réforme de l'agriculture dans la Communauté Économique Européenne' (Mansholt Plan), *Bulletin of the European Communities*, Supplement no. 1, OOPEC.

CEC (1991a) 'The development and future of the CAP: reflections paper of the Commission', COM (91) 100 final, CEC, Brussels.

CEC (1991b) 'The development and future of the Common Agricultural Policy: follow-up to the Reflections Paper', COM(91) 258 final, CEC, Brussels.

CEC (1992) 'Agriculture in the GATT negotiations and the reform of the CAP', SEC (92) 2267 final, CEC, Brussels.

CEC (1993) 'Reform of the CAP and its implementation', *CAP Working Notes*, CEC, Brussels.

CEC (1994) 'EC Agricultural Policy for the 21st century', *European Economy*, 1994: 4.

CEC (various issues) *Green Europe*.

CEC (various issues) *The Agricultural Situation in the Community*.

CEC (various issues) *Financial Report on the European Agricultural Guidance and Guarantee Fund FEOGA, Guarantee Section*.

CEC (various issues) *Official Journal of the European Communities*.

Codsi, G., K.R. Pearson and P.J. Wilcoxen (1992) *General Purpose Software for Intertemporal Economic Models*. Amsterdam: Kluwer.

Court of Auditors (various issues) *Financial Reports*.

CPB (1992) *Scanning the Future: Four Long Term Scenarios for the World Economy*. The Hague: Central Planning Bureau.

CPB (1993) 'Selected Economic Indicators', Working Paper 93-12, Central Planning Bureau, The Hague.

Critchley, W. (1991) *Looking after the Land: Soil and Water Conservation in Dryland Africa*. Oxford: Oxfam.

Crook, F.W. (1988) 'China's Grain Production to the Year 2000', in: *Agriculture and Trade Report: China*, RS-88-4, USDA, Washington DC.

Crosson, P. and J.R. Anderson (1992) 'Resources and global food prospects. Supply and demand for cereals to 2030', Technical Paper no. 184, The World Bank, Washington DC.

Crosson, P. and N.J. Rosenberg (1989) 'Strategies for Agriculture', *The Scientific American*, September 1989, pp. 78-85.

Daly, H. (1993) 'The perils of free trade', *The Scientific American*, November 1993, pp. 24-29.

Dasgupta, P. and D. Ray (1986) 'Inequality as determinant of malnutrition and unemployment: theory', *Economic Journal*, 96: 1011-34.

Deaton, A. and J. Muellbauer (1980) 'Economics and consumer behaviour'. Cambridge: Cambridge University Press.

De Gorter, H. and K.D. Meilke (1989) 'Efficiency of alternative policies for the EC's Common Agricultural Policy', *American Journal of Agricultural Economics*, 71: 592-603.

De Koning, G.H.J. and C.A. van Diepen (1992) 'Crop production potential of rural areas within the European Communities; IV Potential, water-limited and actual production', Wetenschappelijke Raad voor het Regeringsbeleid, The Hague.

Delorme, H. (1994) 'French agricultural policy objectives', in: R. Kjeldahl and M. Tracy, eds. *Renationalisation of the Common Agricultural Policy?* La Hutte, Belgium: Agricultural Policy Studies Publications.

De Melo, J. (1988) 'Computable general equilibrium models for trade policy analysis in developing countries: a survey', *Journal of Policy Modeling*, 10: 469-503.

De Wit, C.T. (1992) 'Over het efficiënte gebruik van hulpbronnen in de landbouw', *Spil*, 109-110: 40-52.

Diewert, W.E. and T.J. Wales (1987) 'Flexible functional forms and global curvature conditions', *Econometrica*, 55: 43-68.

Dijkstra, J. and C.A. Makkink (1993) 'Verkennende studie fundamenteel dierfysiologisch onderzoek: onderdeel stofwisselingsfysiologie', NLRO report 93/5, NLRO, The Hague.

Dixon, P.B., B.R. Parmenter, A.A. Powell and P.J. Wilcoxen (1992) *Notes and Problems in Applied General Equilibrium Economics*. Amsterdam: North-Holland.

Don, F.J.H. (1985) 'The use of generalized inverses in restricted maximum likelihood', *Linear Algebra and its Applications*, 70.

Dosi, S., K. Pavitt and L. Soete (1990) *The Economics of Technical Change and International Development*. New York: Harvester Wheatsheaf.

Dowler, E.A. and Y.O. Seo (1985) 'Assessment of energy intake. Estimates of food supply v. measurement of food consumption', *Food Policy*, 10: 278-288.

Eurostat (various issues) *Demographic Statistics*, theme 3, series C.

Eurostat (various issues) *Economic Accounts for Agriculture and Forestry*, theme 5, series C.

Eurostat (various issues) *Employment and Unemployment*, theme 3, series C.

Eurostat (1992) 'Total income of agricultural households', Eurostat, Luxembourg.

FAO (1992) *Supply Utilization Accounts*, Rome: Food and Agricultural Organization.

FAO (1993) *Agriculture: towards 2010*. Rome: Food and Agricultural Organization.

FAO (various issues) *Fertilizer Yearbook*, Rome: Food and Agriculture Organization.

FAO (various issues) *Production Yearbook*, Rome: Food and Agriculture Organization.

FAO (various issues) *Trade Yearbook*, Rome: Food and Agricultural Organization.

Fernandez-Cornejo, J., C.M. Gempesaw, J.G. Elterich and S.E. Stefanou (1992) 'Dynamic measures of scope and scale economies: an application to German agriculture', *American Journal of Agricultural Economics*, 74: 330-342.

Fischer, G., K. Frohberg, M.A. Keyzer and K.S. Parikh (1988) *Linked national models: a tool for international food policy analysis*. Dordrecht: Kluwer.

Folmer, C. (1989) 'Capital and investment in EC-agriculture. Part 1: the data', Internal Note IV/89/18, Central Planning Bureau, The Hague.

Folmer, C. (1991) 'Capital and investment in EC-agriculture. Part 2: model and estimation results', Internal Note IV/91/24, Central Planning Bureau, The Hague.

Folmer, C. (1992) 'ECAM data input 1983/1992', report IV/92/11 (with statistical annex), Central Planning Bureau, The Hague.

Folmer, C. (1993) 'Labour migration out of the agricultural sector in EC-9 member states', Research Memorandum 104, Central Planning Bureau, The Hague.

Folmer, C., M.A. Keyzer, M.D. Merbis, E. Phimister, H.M.E. Schweren, H.J.J. Stolwijk, and P.J.J. Veenendaal (1987) 'Budgetary consequences of changing rules for financing EC-farm support: some outcomes from the European Community Agricultural Model', paper presented at the Fifth Congress of the European Association of Agricultural Economists, Balatonszéplak, Hungary, 31 August - 4 September 1987.

Folmer, C., E. Phimister, H.M.E. Schweren, and P.J.J. Veenendaal (1988) 'Social accounting matrices for EC-1982. Documentation of the construction', Working Paper 87-12, Centre for World Food Studies, Amsterdam.

Folmer, C., M.A. Keyzer, M.D. Merbis, H.M.E. Schweren and P.J.J. Veenendaal (1989) 'Modelling alternative Common Agricultural Policies', in: S. Bauer and W. Henrichsmeyer, eds., *Agricultural Sector Modelling*. Kiel: Vauk, pp. 287-305.

Folmer, C., M.D. Merbis, H.J.J. Stolwijk and P.J.J. Veenendaal (1990) 'Modelling EC feed demand', Internal Note IV/90/36, Central Planning Bureau, The Hague.

Frohberg, K. (1994) 'Assessment of the effects of a reform of the CAP on labour income and outflow', *European Economy*, 1994: 5.

Funke, N. (1993) 'Timing and sequences of reforms: competing views and the role of credibility', *Kyklos*, 46: 337-362.

GATT (1991) 'Draft Final Act', mimeograph, GATT, Geneva.

GATT (1993) 'Final act embodying the results of the Uruguay Round of multilateral trade negotiotions', 15 December 1993, GATT, Geneva.

Ginsburgh, V. and J.L. Waelbroeck (1981) *Activity Analysis and General Equilibrium*. Amsterdam: North-Holland.

Goldin, I. and O. Knudsen, eds. (1990) *Agricultural Trade Liberalization. Implications for developing countries*. Paris: OECD.

Grabowski, R., S. Kraft, C. Pasurka and H.Y. Aly (1990) 'A ray-homothetic production frontier and efficiency: grain farms in Southern Illinois', *European Review of Agricultural Economics*, 17: 435-448.

Grilli, E.R. and M.C. Yang (1988) 'Primary commodities, manufactured goods prices, and the terms of trade of developing countries: what the long run shows', *World Bank Economic Review*, 2: 1-47.

Grilli, E.R. (1995) '"Creativity" of Europe's trade policies towards developing and Eastern European countries', in: A. Kuyvenhoven, ed., *Implications of the transformation in Central and Eastern Europe*. Boston: Kluwer.

Gunning, J.W. and M.A. Keyzer (1995) 'Applied general equilibrium models for policy analysis', in: J. Behrman and T.N. Srinivasan, eds., *Handbook of Development Economics,* vol. III. Amsterdam: North-Holland.

Guyomard, H. and L.P. Mahé (1992) 'CAP-reform and EC-US Agricultural trade relations', INRA-ENSA, Rennes.

Guyomard, H. and L.P. Mahé (1994) 'Measures of distortionary support in the context of production quotas', *European Review of Agricultural Economics*, 21: 5-30.

Hamilton, C.B. and L.A. Winters (1992) 'Trade with Eastern Europe', *Economic Policy*, 14: 77-116.

Harris, S., A. Swinbank and G. Wilkinson (1983) *The Food and Farm Policies of the European Community*. Chichester: John Wiley.

Hazell, P.B.R. and P.L. Scandizzo (1979) 'Optimal price intervention policies when production is risky', in: J.A. Roumasset, J-.M. Boussard and I. Singh, eds., *Risk, Uncertainty and Agricultural Development*. New York: Agricultural Development Council.

Hungerford, Th.L. (1991) 'GATT: a cooperative equilibrium in a noncooperative trading regime?', *Journal of International Economics*, 31: 357-369.

IPCC (1990) 'IPCC First Assessment Report' (Overview, policy-makers' summaries and reports of the Working Groups), WMO/UNEP.

Johnson, N.L. and V.W. Ruttan (1994) 'Why are farms so small?', *World Development*, 22: 691-706.

Kehoe, T.J. (1991) 'Computation and multiplicity of equilibria', in: W. Hildenbrand and H. Sonnenschein, eds., *Handbook of Mathematical Economics,* vol. IV. Amsterdam: North-Holland.

Keyzer, M.A. (1989a) 'On the specification and parameter estimation of a decomposed, mixed primal-dual model of agricultural supply', Research Memorandum 89-01, Centre for World Food Studies, Amsterdam.

Keyzer, M.A. (1989b) 'Application of continuation methods to the solution of non-linear complementarity problems', Research Memorandum 89-02, Centre for World Food Studies, Amsterdam.

Keyzer, M.A. (1989c) 'Note on the valuation of green fodder', Working Paper 89-05R2, Centre for World Food Studies, Amsterdam.

Keyzer, M.A. (1991) 'On the approximation of infinite horizon allocations', in: H. Don, Th. van de Klundert and J. van Sinderen, eds., *Applied General Equilibrium Modelling.* Amsterdam: Kluwer.

Keyzer, M.A. and W. Tims (1994) 'Voluntary transfers and the rights of the poor', in: J.W. Gunning, H. Kox, W. Tims, Y. de Wit, eds., *Trade, Aid and Development.* London: MacMillan Press.

Keyzer, M.A., C. Folmer, M.D. Merbis, H.J.J. Stolwijk and P.J.J. Veenendaal (1994) 'CAP reform and its differential impact on member states', *European Economy,* 1994: 5.

Kirman, A.P. (1992) 'Whom or what does the representative individual represent?', *Journal of Economic Perspectives,* 6: 117-136.

Kjeldahl, R. and M. Tracy, eds. (1994) *Renationalisation of the Common Agricultural Policy?* La Hutte, Belgium: Agricultural Policy Studies Publications.

Klein, L.R. (1958) 'The estimation of distributed lags', *Econometrica,* 26: 553-565.

Krugman, P.R. (1990) *Rethinking International Trade.* Cambridge, MA: MIT Press.

Kuipers, A.D. (1993) 'Agrarische huishoudens en hun inkomen', CBS, Voorburg-Heerlen.

Kydland, F. and E.C. Prescott (1982) 'Time to build and aggregative fluctuations', *Econometrica,* 50: 1345-70.

LEI-DLO (various issues) *Landbouwcijfers.*

LEI-DLO (1993) 'Farm Accountancy Data System, 1993-outcomes', LEI-DLO, The Hague.

Linnemann, H., J. de Hoogh, M.A. Keyzer and H.D.J. van Heemst (1979) *MOIRA, Model of International Relations in Agriculture.* Amsterdam: North-Holland.

Louwes, S.L. (1970) 'Proeve van een landbouwbeleid in de EEG op lange termijn', in: *Het EEG Landbouwbeleid. Pre-adviezen Vereniging voor Staatshuishoudkunde.* The Hague: Martinus Nijhoff.

Loyat, J. (1992) 'La réforme de la Politique Agricole Communautaire: une évaluation par le modèle ECAM', *Economie Rurale,* 211: 10-17.

Luiting, P. (1991) *The Value of Feed Consumption Data for Breeding in Laying Hens,* Ph.D. Thesis, Wageningen.

Manne, A.S. (1985) 'On the formulation and solution of economic equilibrium models', *Mathematical Programming Study,* 23: 1-22.

Mansholt, S. (1986) 'Prijsverlaging, contingentering en areaalbeperking gewogen als middel tot produktiebeperking', *Spil*, 55-56: 5-20.

Markish, Y. and K. Gray (1989) 'Agricultural Outlook: Inputs', in: *Agriculture and Trade Report USSR*, RS-89-1, USDA, Washington DC.

Martin, J.P., J.-M. Burniaux, F. Delorme, I. Lienert, D. van der Mensbrugghe (1989-90) 'Economy-wide effects of agricultural trade policies in OECD countries, simulation results with Walras', *OECD Economic Studies*, 13: 131-172.

Meester, G. and D. Strijker (1985) 'Het Europese landbouwbeleid voorbij de scheidslijn van zelfvoorziening', Voorstudies en achtergronden, WRR V46, Staatsuitgeverij, The Hague.

Melillo, J.M., A.D. McGuire, D.W. Kicklighter, B. Moore, C.J. Vorosmarty and A.L. Schoss (1993) 'Global climate change and terrestrial net primary production', *Nature*, 363: 234-239.

Merbis, M.D. (1994) 'Yield estimates for ECAM', Working Paper WP-94-03, Centre for World Food Studies, Amsterdam.

Merbis, M.D. (1995a) 'SOWDBF at work. Supply accounts for the European Union', Working Paper, Centre for World Food Studies, Amsterdam.

Merbis, M.D. (1995b) 'Supply documentation of the ECAM-model', Working Paper, Centre for World Food Studies, Amsterdam.

Merbis, M.D., H.M.E. Schweren and H.J.J. Stolwijk (1994) 'Data collection and processing for the feed-mix module of ECAM', Working Paper WP-94-04, Centre for World Food Studies, Amsterdam.

Messerlin, P.A. (1995) Comments on E. Grilli, '"Creativity" of Europe's trade policies towards developing and Eastern European countries', in: A. Kuyvenhoven, ed., *Implications of the Transformation in Central and Eastern Europe*. Boston: Kluwer.

Michalek, J. and M.A. Keyzer (1992) 'Estimation of a two-stage LES-AIDS consumer demand system for eight EC countries', *European Review of Agricultural Economics*, 19: 137-163.

Mueller, D.C. (1989) *Public Choice II*. Cambridge: Cambridge University Press.

Neary, J.P. (1994) 'Cost asymmetries in international subsidy games: should governments help winners or losers?', *Journal of International Economics*, 37: 197-218.

Negishi, T. (1972) *General Equilibrium Theory and International Trade*. Amsterdam: North-Holland.

OECD (1970) 'Capital and Finance in Agriculture, volume II: Country studies', Agricultural Policy Reports, OECD, Paris.

OECD (1985) 'The OECD Feed Supply Utilization Account (FSUA) A methodology to compute FSUA's at the national level', Document AGR/WP2/CF(85)3, OECD, Paris.

OECD (1986) 'The OECD Feed Supply Utilization Account (FSUA): results for the EEC-9, 1973-1981', Document AGR/WP2/CF(86)4, OECD, Paris.

OECD (1987) *National Policies and Agricultural Trade. Study on the European Community.* Paris: OECD.

OECD (1989/1990) 'Modelling the effects of agricultural policies', *OECD Economic Studies*, 13.

OECD (various issues) *Agricultural Policies, Markets and Trade: Monitoring and Outlook.*

OECD (various issues) *National Accounts, Detailed Tables.*

Oskam, A.J. (1991) 'Weather indices of agricultural production in the Netherlands 1948-1989. 1. General methodology and the arable sector', *Netherlands Journal of Agricultural Science*, 39: 149-164.

Overbosch, G.B. (1990) 'S.O.W. Data Management Program User's Guide', Working Paper 86-21R3, Centre for World Food Studies, Amsterdam.

Overbosch, G.B. (1992) 'SOW-AGE User's Guide', Working Paper 92-08, Centre for World Food Studies, Amsterdam.

Parikh, K.S., G. Fisher, K. Frohberg and O. Gulbrandsen (1988) *Towards Free Trade in Agriculture.* Dordrecht: Martinus Nijhoff.

Parry, M.L., T.R. Carter and N.T. Konijn, eds. (1988) *The Impact of Climate Variations on Agriculture,* vol. 1 and 2. Dordrecht: Kluwer.

Perrigne, I. and M. Simioni (1993) 'Kernel estimation of multi-product cost functions and scale economies', paper presented at the Seventh Congress of the European Associationof Agricultural Economists, Stresa.

Phimister, E.C. (1993) *Savings and Investment in Farm Households: Analysis using Life Cycle.* Aldershot: Avebury.

Pinstrup-Andersen, P. (1994) 'World food trends and future security', mimeograph, International Food Policy Research Institute, Washington DC.

Postel, S. (1990) 'Saving Water for Agriculture', in: *The State of the World 1990.* New York: Norton.

Produktschap voor Zuivel (1991) 'Wereldhandel in Zuivelprodukten', deel 3, Produktschap voor Zuivel, Rijswijk.

Reis, E.J and S. Margulis (1991) 'Options for slowing Amazon jungle clearing', in: R. Dornbusch and J.M. Poterba (eds.), *Global Warming: Economic Policy Responses.* Cambridge, MA: MIT Press.

RIVM (1989) *Concern for Tomorrow: a National Environmental Survey 1985-2010,* F. Langeweg (ed.). De Bilt: RIVM.

Rodrik, D. (1989) 'Credibility of trade reform; a policymaker's guide', *The World Economy*, 12: 1-16.

Roningen, V.O. (1992) 'Whither European Community Common Agricultural Policy, MacSharried or Dunkeled in the GATT?', Working Paper 92-3, IATRC, Washington DC.

Rosenzweig, C., M.L. Parry with G. Fischer, and K. Frohberg (1992) 'Climate change and world food supply', mimeograph, Environmental Change Unit, Oxford.

Ruttan, V.W. (1991) 'Challenges to agricultural research in the 21st century', in: P.G. Pardey, J. Roseboom and J.R. Anderson (eds.), *Agricultural Research Policy: International Quantitive Perspectives*. Cambridge: Cambridge University Press, pp. 399-411.

Salvatore, D., ed. (1993) *Protectionism and World Welfare*. Cambridge, UK: Cambridge University Press.

Scheele, C.W. and M.T. Frankenhuis (1989) 'Stimulation of the metabolic rate in broilers and the occurence of metabolic disorders', in: Y. van der Honing and W.H. Close, eds., *Energy Metabolism of Farm Animals*. Wageningen: Pudoc, pp. 251-254.

Schrader, J.V. (1993) 'EG-Agrarreform und GATT-Vereinbarungen: von Leistungsinkommen zur Quasi-rente', Kiel discussion paper 217, Institut für Weltwirtschaft, Kiel.

SER (1992) 'Sociaal-Economische Betrekkingen met Midden- en Oost-Europa', Sociaal-economische Raad (SER), The Hague.

Shoven, J. and J. Whalley (1992) *Applying General Equilibrium*. New York: Cambridge University Press.

Smil, V. (1994) 'How many people can the earth feed?', *Population and Development Review*, 20: 255-292.

Stiglitz, J. (1976) 'The efficiency wage hypothesis, surplus labour and the distribution of income in LDC's', *Oxford Economic Papers*, 28: 185-207.

Stiles, D. and R. Brennan (1986) The food crises and environmental conservation in Africa', *Food Policy*, 11: 298-310.

Stolwijk, H.J.J. (1991) 'De wereldvoedselvoorziening op de lange termijn: een evaluatie van mogelijkheden en knelpunten', Research Memorandum 83, Central Planning Bureau, The Hague.

Stolwijk, H.J.J (1992) 'De Nederlandse landbouw op de drempel van de 21ste eeuw', Research Memorandum 95, Central Planning Bureau, The Hague.

Swinnen, J. and F.A. van der Zee (1993) 'The political economy of agricultural policies', *European Review of Agricultural Economics,* 20: 261-290.

Tangermann, S. (1989) 'Evaluation of the current CAP reform package', *The World Economy,* 12: 175-188.

Todaro, M.P. (1976) *Internal migration in developing countries*. Geneva: ILO.

Tracy, M. (1989) *Government and Agriculture in Western Europe, 1880-1999*. Third edition. New York: Harvester Wheatsheaf.

Tutt, N. (1989) *Europe on the fiddle: the Common Market scandal.* London: Helm.

Tyers, R. and K. Anderson (1992) *Disarray in World Food Markets. A Quantitative Assessment*. Cambridge: Cambridge University Press.

Tyson, L. D'A. (1992) *Who's Bashing Whom? Trade Conflict in High-technology Industries.* Washington DC: Institute for International Economics.

UNCTAD (various issues) *Monthly Commodity Price Bulletin.*

UNDP (1992) *Human Development Report 1992.* New York: United Nations.

Upton, M. and S. Haworth (1987) 'The growth of farms', *European Review of Agricultural Economics*, 14: 351-366.

USDA (1988) 'Programs boost US farm export', *Agricultural Outlook*, May 1988, pp. 20-22.

USDA (1989) 'Hope for the Sahel?', *Agricultural Outlook*, July 1989, pp. 24-28.

USDA (1990) 'Irrigated area to grow', *Agricultural Outlook*, March 1990, pp. 15-18.

USDA (1992) 'Preliminary analysis of the economic implications of the Dunkel text for American Agriculture', USDA Office of Economics, Washington DC.

Van Amstel, A.A., E.E.M. Baars, J. Sijm and H.M. Venne (1986) 'Tapioca from Thailand for the Dutch livestock industry', Report 86-7, Institute for Environmental Studies, Amsterdam.

Van Berkum, S. (1994) 'Gevolgen van het GATT-akkoord voor de EU-landbouw', mededeling 505, LEI-DLO, The Hague.

Van Kersbergen, K. and B. Verbeek (1994) 'The politics of subsidiarity in the European Union', *Journal of Common Market Studies*, 32: 215-236.

Van Tuijl, W. (1993) 'Improving water use in agriculture: experiences in the Middle-East and North Africa', The World Bank, Washington DC.

Varian, H.R. (1992) *Microeconomic Analysis*, Third edition. New York: Norton.

Vos, M.P.M. (1989) 'The impact of energy metabolism research on feed evaluation and animal feeding in The Netherlands', in: Y. van der Honing and W.H. Close, eds., *Energy Metabolism of Farm Animals.* Wageningen: Pudoc, pp. 396-404.

Weersink A. and L.W. Tauer (1991) 'Causality between dairy farm size and productivity', *American Journal of Agricultural Economics*, 42: 1139-1145.

Wetenschappelijke Raad voor het Regeringsbeleid (WRR, 1992) 'Grond voor keuzen: Vier perspectieven voor de landelijke gebieden in de Europese Gemeenschap', WRR, The Hague.

World Bank (1992a) 'Market Outlook for Major Primary Commodities', Report 814/92, The World Bank, Washington DC.

World Bank (1992b) *World Development Report 1992.* Washington DC: World Bank.

World Bank (1993) *Global Economic Prospects and the Developing Countries.* Washington DC: World Bank.

Yunlong, C. (1990) 'Land use and management in the People's Republic of China: Problems and strategies', *Land Use Policy*, 7: 337-350.

Zachariasse, L.C. (1990) 'Trends in bedrijfsgrootte en gezinsbedrijf in verschillende sectoren van de Nederlandse land en tuinbouw', *Tijdschrift voor Sociaal Wetenschappelijk Onderzoek van de Landbouw*, 5: 183-200.

Index